The
Wine
in Ireland
1997 Edition

The Best of
Wine
in Ireland

1997 Edition

Jacinta Delahaye

A. & A. Farmar

British Library Cataloguing in Publication data
A CIP catalogue record for this book is available from the
British Library.

Cover design by Source
Cover photograph Slidefile
Proof-reading Pat Carroll
Design and typesetting A. & A. Farmar
Printed and bound by Betaprint

ISBN 1 899047 23 9

Published by
A. & A. Farmar
Beech House
78 Ranelagh Village
Dublin 6

Contents

The Wines

Acknowledgements

The author and publishers would like to thank the many people whose generosity and enthusiastic commitment made the guide possible. In particular:

• Our tasting panel, who again gave generously and voluntarily of their expertise and time.

• The wine importers, who supplied samples for tasting and patiently answered our many requests for further information about their wines.

The tasting panel

All the members hold professional qualifications in wine. Some members of our panel act as advisers to particular wine importers. These members withdrew from the panel when the wines of the firm they advise were tasted.

Jacinta Delahaye (chair of the panel) is a wine consultant, educator and writer.

Tom Franks, wine lecturer and correspondent, has spent over forty years in the wine trade. He was Chairman of the Wine Promotion Board of Ireland for five years.

Catherine Griffith is a wine educator and wine consultant to the Molloy Group.

Breda McSweeney, of Lacken House Restaurant, has won many national sommelier competitions and has represented Ireland in three world finals.

Monica Murphy of the Cheeseboard Ltd, Dublin, is a professional wine and cheese consultant, lecturer and writer who travels extensively to vineyard areas as a guide for consumer and trade wine tours.

Aideen Nolan joined the Wine Development Board of Ireland at its inception and was heavily involved in setting up educational courses for the trade and for consumers.

Dermot Nolan is an independent wine writer and consultant.

ACKNOWLEDGEMENTS

Mary O'Callaghan is a trained chef, wine educator and sommelier, and has represented Ireland in international sommelier competitions.

David Power worked in the wine trade in Ireland for over thirty years with Edward Dillon and Co. He is now an independent wine consultant and lectures for the Wine Development Board of Ireland.

David Whelehan is a wine educator who lectures for the Wine Development Board of Ireland.

Preface

For this second edition of *The Best of Wine in Ireland* over 1,600 wines, ranging in price from under £4 to over £60 a bottle, were blind tasted between March and November 1996. The wines were submitted by importers. Not all the wines submitted and tasted have been included, so you can be sure that those that are represent good quality.

Over 800 of the wines included this year are new to the book: that is, they did not appear in the first edition. Over 100 of the wines included last year were resubmitted in the same vintage and retasted. The remaining wines were resubmitted in different vintages and newly tasted. All the wines were tasted blind, and judged and scored within their style and price categories. All the wines are available in the Irish market at the time of publication.

The wines we have included all fulfilled the basic requirements of being well made at a reasonable price for their category. A number of the wines submitted for tasting were rejected, either because they did not meet our quality standards or the particular sample was in poor condition or past its peak.

Although some of the wines included will continue to improve for some years (and this is mentioned in the tasting note), we have concentrated mainly on wines that are to be drunk now rather than laid down. Indeed, many wines in today's market should be drunk young while fresh and fruity. This applies as much to red as to white wine.

Styles such as basic Beaujolais and Beaujolais Nouveau, basic Côtes du Rhône and major brands (such as Piat d'Or or Jacob's Creek) are produced to be bought quickly and drunk immediately. Other styles, such as Rioja Reserva and Gran Reserva, have done all their ageing in cask and bottle and are ready to drink when released from the winery.

What we found

The overall quality of the wines in this year's *Best of Wine in Ireland* has greatly improved. This reflects partly a great improvement in the quality of wines submitted by the importers, as they came to understand our objectives better, and partly a continued general improvement in the marketplace. Wine consumption in Ireland is growing at 8% per annum, and is now 2.24 million cases a year.

Reflecting this upward trend, this year we have removed wines scoring only 11 points from the book. The average score has gone from 13 to 15.

The £6–£10 price categories proved the most exciting. The word from the trade is that Irish consumers, unlike their British counterparts, are willing to trade up from low prices if the quality demands. However, for unforgettable wines you still have to pay from £12 upwards. This year's top-quality wines were not simply very good, they were outstanding. They were both memorable to drink and difficult to describe due to their complexity. There is much less 'bad' wine on the market than there used to be—in other words wines are technically better made. Inexpensive whites are usually fault free, but they can be very boring. The mid-price category offers more structure and flavour. Corked wine, with tainted corks irreparably damaging the aroma and flavour of the wine, is still a problem at all price levels.

Wines from France dominate the book as they do the market, but it is interesting to see New World wines (especially from Australia, New Zealand and Chile) scoring a higher proportion of stars. This reflects the extremely good value for money that these wines deliver.

The French Vin de Pays category also offers good-value white and red wines. The classic styles from Bordeaux and Burgundy hold their own, especially when it comes to matching food with wine. There are lots of tasty, fruity, Pinot Noir styles available, especially at the basic level. Complex styles cost a lot more. Delicious, vibrant styles of Beaujolais are most appealing—pity they are so expensive.

Portugal, Greece, the lesser-known areas of Spain and Provence in the South of France are producing a range of unusual wines, many in savoury, sturdy styles that offer something different from varietals. Italy is producing a wonderful diversity of styles for those prepared to trade up a little.

The Northern Rhône produces top-class savoury wines with unmistakable spice appeal. Basic Côtes du Rhône styles vary greatly—some are superb, some mediocre.

Some top-class styles from Germany were tasted this year. It's a pity they are not more widely available.

Chile is improving all the time, offering real value for money, with very little 'rough' wine and Reserva styles particularly good. Some interesting styles from Argentina are coming on stream, while California has greatly improved, with more premium wines coming on to the Irish market. The Merlots are delicious, with some top-quality red Zinfandel styles.

Australia came out top this year for sheer drinking pleasure. Whites are becoming more restrained in style, with interesting regional red styles more available. It is worth trading up to taste the difference. Vibrant fruity Sauvignon Blanc still dominates New Zealand wine production. Its reds are also impressive—they have improved enormously with more emphasis on fruit.

How to use this guide

Each wine is listed first under its country of origin (and region in the case of France), then by colour and price band, and finally in alphabetical order by the name of the wine, as indicated on the label. In interpreting the often confusing layout of labels, we have tried to present the essential information that will enable the consumer to identify particular wines on the retailer's shelf. The index of wine names presents the same information. Each country is preceded by a short fact file for easy reference to principal grape varieties, labelling guide etc. The notes on vintages should be viewed as simple guidelines.

Scores

There is no ideal way to rate a wine: wine-drinking is a pleasure, and its appreciation is an art. A numerical rating is useful, however, when trying to pick out exceptional wines, or to convey our panel's view of a straightforward, perfectly acceptable, but not outstanding wine. Each wine is given a score out of 20 and a tasting note.

The scores were averaged from those assigned by the panel. Only wines which scored 12 or above out of 20 are included in this year's guide. Wines were assessed within their price categories, so that scores reflect the panel's judgement of the wine's price/quality ratio. The average score (which of course does not include the wines we discarded) was 15. Star wines, that is those scoring 15, 16 or 17, are indicated with one, two or three stars.

The scores indicate:

	12 = acceptable quality with good flavour
	13 = good quality in its price/style category
	14 = very good quality
☆	15 = excellent quality and worthy of attention
☆☆	16 = top quality
☆☆☆	17 = superb quality and very difficult to fault

In the price bands up to £5.25 we looked for well-made wines with some flavour; from £5.25 to £6 fruity flavours. Between £6 and £10 we wanted more structure, and between £10 and £15 structure, flavour and balance. Beyond £15 we increasingly sought complexity and ageing ability.

Most wines included in the guide are available throughout the country in supermarkets, off-licences and/or wine merchants. The importer's name is given (in *italics*); if you have trouble finding a particular wine, we recommend that you contact the importer, who will be happy to advise you. A list of importers with their addresses and telephone numbers is included in this guide just before the Index.

Prices

Wine prices are not fixed. Different retailers may raise or lower the price of individual wines as they choose. On the other hand, we felt it desirable to indicate the approximate price. All the wines are therefore listed in order of price band. The following bands were chosen:

Under £4.50	£4.50–£5.25
£5.25–£6	£6–£8
£8–£10	£10–£12
£12–£15	£15–£20
£20–£30	£30–£50
Over £50	

We have made every effort to assign wines to their appropriate price bands, but please remember that these are guide prices only: prices may vary from one outlet to another, because of promotions, for example, or bulk buying; or they may change because of fluctuations in exchange rates, changes in taxes and excise, and so on.

Wine and food

When someone complained to M. Delmas, the manager of the Bordeaux first growth Château Haut Brion, that his wine had compared badly with Château Lafite in a tasting, he loftily replied: 'My wine is designed to be drunk with food, not with Château Lafite.' (The Irish lawyer and wine expert Maurice Healy used mischievously to claim—quite erroneously—that Haut Brion was named for one of the Wild Geese, and should rightly be called Château O'Brien!)

M. Delmas has a point. Wine has nearly always been produced primarily to be drunk with meals, not on its own, and certainly not in competition with other wines. In France, wine has long been called the 'second sauce'; just as robust, dark mushroom sauce is an unlikely accompaniment to a delicate fish dish, so a full-bodied red wine is similarly inappropriate.

That regional combinations of wine and food are so strikingly successful is the first clue to understanding this unpretentious matching. Wine and food can be compatible in different ways. They can form a contrast like sweet and salt with Sauternes and Roquefort, or Port and Stilton, or a harmony as in lamb and a Médoc. The choice is often influenced by the occasion and environment and by other wines and food if the dish is part of a meal.

In vine-growing areas of France, Italy, Spain and indeed much of Europe, surprising examples of perfect matches are constantly found. For instance, the strange, dry, woody white wines of Cassis in the South of France come into their own with local fish stews; olive-oil-bathed sardines are perfect with dry, woody Portuguese reds while the much maligned Lambrusco is the only accompaniment to the impossibly rich *zampone* of its North Italian home.

In traditional regions the wine blends not just with a type of food, but also with a method of cooking and with particular flavours such as garlic, herbs and olive oil. This must be remembered in matching wine and food from other areas—it is the whole dish, with its flavourings, sauces and garnishes, that combines with the wine, not just the dish's principal ingredient. For example, a pan-fried chicken breast with a lemon and parsley butter goes well with a light dry white wine such as a Frascati. If it had a sauce of wild mushrooms, wine and cream, a medium-bodied red such as Chianti would be more appropriate, while an exotic stir-fried chicken would need an equally spicy wine like Gewürztraminer of Alsace.

Nowadays, the fashionable multi-cultural cuisine, in which the dishes, cooking and seasonings of far-flung nationalities come together not just in one menu, but on one plate, presents a new challenge for wine. Consider a simple dish like fishcakes, transformed by the addition of hot, Thai spices, garlic and coriander and served with a very Mediterranean *aioli*, spiked with chilli. Or think of a long-simmered Navarin of lamb, cooked with ginger and soy and served on a bed of Japanese noodles.

When choosing the appropriate wine for a specific dish certain general principles apply. As well as individual flavours, wine and food have weight or texture, intensity of flavours and complexity. These are good starting points for matching the two.

A delicate fish like plaice served with a simple butter sauce would be overpowered by a full-bodied, oak-influenced Burgundy with its layers of taste. It needs a wine which is light, simple and with enough acidity to cut the butter and bring out the taste of the fish, for example, a Muscadet. On the other hand, a fine slice of turbot with a cream sauce would completely overwhelm the Muscadet but would be greatly enhanced by a Meursault.

In both these examples it is the weight and texture of the dish as much as the flavour which influences the choice of wine.

A dish may be mild or strong, and an important key to identifying the appropriate wine is to match its vigour with the intensity of the wine. The stronger the flavours in the dish—the more garlic and herbs, the use of a sauce or marinade and the number of different flavours it combines—the more primary flavours are needed from the wine. Primary flavours are fruit, varietal character and oak tastes. A more subtle dish, in which all the ingredients are blended together in a harmonious way, will benefit from and enhance a complex wine.

For example, a leg of lamb cooked with lots of garlic and rosemary needs a vigorous young Bordeaux redolent of black-currants and spicy oak. A rack of lamb with a simple *jus* enriched with wine would be the perfect foil for an older, more fragile, Bordeaux whose complex flavours would be brought out by the simple, refined nature of the food. Remember there is only so much the palate can take on board—great complexity in the glass and on the plate may simply overwhelm the tastebuds.

There are a number of problematical ingredients which can

Wine and Flavour Check List
Dominant flavour | *Type of wine*

Salty

Clean, refreshing or sweet, or intensely fruity wines e.g. sparkling wine, unoaked Merlot, Riesling Spätlese and Auslese

Tart, citrus or sharp (if excessive will clash with wine)

Acidity cloaked with fruit eg. New Zealand Sauvignon, Beaujolais

Hot (not suitable for wine if very hot)

Aromatic, fruity, soft tannin, Fumé Blanc Riesling Spätlese, rosé, some Côtes du Rhône, Corbières, and most Coteaux du Languedoc

Earthy

Strong, full dry whites and mature, oak-aged reds e.g. Chablis, Reserva Rioja, Riserva Chianti, Pinot Noir

Smoky

Aromatic, oaky whites, fruity, spicy reds e.g. Sauvignon Blanc, Pinot Gris, north Italian reds, Rhône, Médoc

Herbal

Aromatic whites, dry medium reds e.g. Sauvignon Blanc, Verdicchio, Languedoc, Roussillon, St Émilion, California Cabernet

Meaty

Reds with tannin and richness e.g. St Estèphe, Pomerol, Provence, some New World Shiraz and Cabernet

Sweet

Depends on degree of sweetness in food. Wine should be as sweet or sweeter than the food. For sweet food try Muscat, Sauternes, late-harvested Riesling. For sweet tastes in savoury food, Gewürztraminer, Vouvray, German Riesling, soft, fruity reds make a wine choice difficult.

Acidity in food is generally seen as a problem for wine, and something really sharp in taste is almost always damaging. However, mild acidity is fine if matched with equal acidity in the wine, along with fruit flavour. Wines with high acidity such as Soave can appear thin with sharp food flavours while sweet wines tend to lose their sweetness. The combination of acidity and fruit in Beaujolais works well with, say tomato sauce, while New Zealand Sauvignon Blanc is a good match for the milder, more aromatic acidity of prawns and lemon grass.

Egg dishes, including sauces and mayonnaise, and very rich, creamy foods have the opposite problem of being too alkaline, of simply dulling the taste of wine. The answer is a wine with body from either alcohol and extract or sweetness as well as acidity which will counteract the richness and low acidity of the food. Sauternes with *foie gras* is an obvious, somewhat extreme example.

Spices are also difficult. Very hot chillies are impossible; leave it to lager, or water. Gentler, aromatic spices can work well with flavoursome white and rosé wines while Chinese flavours go with fruity or floral wine notes. Tannic reds will positively clash with spicy foods as both are bitter flavours and together taste harsh.

Sweet tastes are generally considered to be more difficult to match than savoury ones. The basic rule is that the wine must be as sweet, or sweeter, than the food it accompanies. This can be difficult as fine dessert wine is naturally sweet, its lusciousness coming from super-ripe fruit and concentrated, natural sugars. It also has balancing acidity.

Many desserts, cakes and pastries are based on pure sugar, which, because it lacks acidity, is much more cloying. The natural sweetness of the wine simply cannot match this. Perfectly ripe fruit, simple fruit tarts or peaches and apricots, nutty cakes and certain hot soufflés are excellent foods for dessert wines.

The basic principle is to balance weight, intensity and complexity of food and wine; however, the sense of taste is perhaps the most subjective of all the senses and is influenced by mood, environment and company. As wine and food are both natural products (or at least should be), they are far from consistent; the same wine or the same dish will rarely taste the same twice.

Sandy O'Byrne

Argentina

Main wine regions

Mendoza (the largest), Rio Negro and Nequén, San Juan, Jujuy (Salta and Catamarca), La Rioja (don't confuse with Spain)

Principal grape varieties

White	*Red*
Torrontés	Malbec
Chardonnay	Merlot
Sauvignon Blanc	Cabernet Sauvignon
Moscatel	Syrah
Chenin Blanc	Pinot Noir
Riesling	Tempranillo (Tempranilla)
Pedro Giménez	Bonarda
Sémillon	Barbera

Labelling guide

Special: two years old.
Reserva: six years old.
Pago: single estate.

Varietal wines must be produced from at least 75% of the named variety. All wines undergo chemical and organoleptic tests before being released for sale.

Reserva styles with oak influence can mature for up to six years from date of vintage.

WHITE WINE

White £4.50–£5.25

Etchart Cafayate Torrontés 94   **14**
Fitzgerald
Has that distinctive 'grapey' Muscat aroma associated with the Torrontés grape. Good limey acidity adds zip to the 94 vintage.

Santa Julia Mendoza   13
Taserra
Off-dry, easy-drinking style with a hint of spritz. Fruity.
White £5.25–£6

Etchart Cafayate Chardonnay 95   14
Fitzgerald
The 95 is a much fresher, livelier vintage than the 93 tasted last
year. Delicious peaches and cream tones.

Santa Julia Mendoza Chardonnay 95   14
Taserra
The 95 is yellow-gold in colour with a weighty texture and the
same hint of tropical fruit and coconut as the 94.

Santa Julia Mendoza Torrontés Riojana 95   13
Taserra
The pleasant aromatic honey and rose-petal touches are
holding up since last tasted. Medium-long, fruity finish.
White £6–£8

Alamos Ridge Chardonnay 93   ☆
Searson
Such a balanced wine! Straw-gold in colour with delicate
balance between fruit and acidity. Note the long clean finish.

Señor del Robledal Chenin/Sémillon 95   14
Verlings
A 'zippy' wine all the way. Stony fruit aromas are followed
through on taste, ending in a tangy bite.
White £10–£12

Luigi Bosca Chardonnay 95   13
Verlings
Grapefruit and lemon appeal with a definite hint of spritz add
up to enjoyable drinking.

Luigi Bosca Sauvignon Blanc 95   14
Verlings
Apples all the way, which surprises for this style. Balanced
acidity and good alcohol.

The vineyards of the Santa Julia Winery are located in the Mendoza Valley east of the Andes, in Argentina.

They are irrigated by the melting snow of the Andes. At 2,000 feet above sea level they enjoy the purest of air— free from all pollution.

The careful handling of the grapes complemented by a high level of technology at the winery permits fermentation at low temperature and the hygienic bottling ensures that the wines produced encapsulate all the goodness and richness of the grape.

Santa Julia wines have received many international awards for excellence.

Santa Julia wines are distributed by

Taserra Wine Merchants Ltd.
Hogan House, Grand Canal St., Dublin 2
Ph. 490 0537 Fax: 490 4052

Navarro Correas Mendoza Chardonnay 94   14
Verlings
Gentle aromas of vanilla and stony fruit have emerged since
this wine was last tasted. The lemon acidity adds a fresh tone.
White £12–£15

Catena Chardonnay 94   ☆
Searson
Yellow-gold in colour. Lemon fresh appeal and oak influence
cut through the fruit, ending in a roasted nut finish.

RED WINE

Red £4.50–£5.25

Etchart Lujan de Cuyo Malbec 93   13
Fitzgerald
The wine has developed well since last tasted. The fruit is there
but also good structure from the supple tannins and good
acidity. It ends in a savoury tone.

Santa Julia Mendoza nv   13
Taserra
Bright crimson in colour. Closed on aroma, but stalky fruit
comes through on flavour. A well-structured wine.
Red £5.25–£6

Etchart Cafayate Cabernet Sauvignon 91   14
Fitzgerald
The pea-pod aromas are still obvious since last tasted, but the
fruit emerges on taste with a nice rounded texture.

Santa Julia Mendoza Cabernet Sauvignon 93   14
Taserra
Since last tasted, the wine has more than lived up to its
promise. The fruit has emerged into a classic cedar and cassis
tone with a nice velvet texture.
Red £6–£8

Alamos Ridge Cabernet Sauvignon 93   14
Searson
A decent hearty drink with bay-leaf and herbal aromas. Good

attack of fruit and lots of structure due in part to the drying tannins.

Santa Julia Mendoza Malbec Oak Reserve 93   ☆
Taserra
Matured in small oak barrels, this is a super example of its style. Cassis jelly aromas with an impressive stalky tannic structure and good length of flavour.

Señor del Robledal Malbec/Merlot 89   13
Verlings
A savoury wine, quite austere in style. The fruit is tiring, but the overall impression is of classic winemaking.

Red £10–£12

Humberto Canale Rio Negro Cabernet Sauvignon Special Reserva 90
Verlings
Estate grown and bottled, this is a big wine in every sense. The fruit shines through the gum-drying tannin. Big long finish.

Luigi Bosca Syrah 88
Verlings
The harmonious balance is still obvious, with the wine developing a more soft-centred end. Intense and spicy—buy to drink now.

Navarro Correas Collección Privada 91
Verlings
Beautifully presented in a frosted bottle with artist-designed label. The classic mix of Cabernet Sauvignon, Cabernet Franc and Merlot produces a deeply flavoured wine with classic cedar and ripe berry fruit appeal.

Navarro Correas Malbec 92   14
Verlings
Garnet in colour with a bouquet of tar and cedar. Enjoy now for its classic appeal and savoury finish.

Red £12–£15

Catena Cabernet Sauvignon 94
Searson
Deep crimson in colour and quite closed on aroma. However, it explodes on the palate with lots of wild cherry and dark chocolate flavours. A big chunky wine.

Australia

Main wine regions

South Australia

Adelaide Hills, Clare Valley, Barossa Valley, McLaren Vale, Coonawarra, Padthaway, Riverland, Eden Valley

New South Wales

Mudgee, Cowra, Lower Hunter, Upper Hunter, Riverina, Corowa/Rutherglen

Victoria

Glenrowan/Milawa, Mildura, Great Western/Avoca, Murray River, Goulburn Valley,Yarra Valley, Geelong, Mornington Peninsula, Pyrenees, Bendigo

South Eastern Australia on the label indicates a blend of wines from the three states of New South Wales, Victoria and South Australia.

Western Australia

Margaret River, Mount Barker/Frankland River, Swan Valley

Tasmania

Principal grape varieties

White	*Red*
Chardonnay	Shiraz
Semillon	Cabernet Sauvignon
Verdelho	Merlot
Rhine Riesling	Pinot Noir
Sauvignon Blanc	Grenache
Muscat	Mourvèdre
Chenin Blanc	Tarrango

Labelling guide

If a wine is varietal (named after a particular grape variety), it must contain at least 85% of the named grape

If a vintage is stated on the label, 85% or more of the wine must be from the named vintage

If a geographical area is mentioned on the label, 85% or more of the product must come from that specific area

Where two varieties are named, for example Semillon/ Chardonnay, the first one mentioned must be the predominant one in the blend

Wine styles

White

Semillon: as a variety can vary from oily and herbaceous to full-bodied and weighty with oak influence. Noted for its great bottle-ageing ability, especially in the Hunter Valley, where it assumes honeyed nuances.

Chardonnay: has regional characteristics depending on where it is produced. Examples are the lush exotic fruit tones when produced in the Hunter and the more restrained complex styles of Padthaway and Margaret River. Has a great affinity with oak. Judicious use of oak is producing more restrained and subtle styles.

Semillon/Chardonnay: the blend that helped launch Australian wines on the world market produces ripe melon-type aromas and flavours and is usually competitively priced.

Other styles include the dry, medium-dry or sweet styles of Rhine Riesling, the fresh and highly aromatic dry and dessert styles of Muscat, and the dry lemony or rich styles of Australia's most widely planted white grape, Verdelho.

Red

Shiraz: Australian name for the Syrah grape of Rhône fame, thought to have originated in Persia. Produces a vast array of styles, from easy-drinking to full-bodied to Australia's most famous and long-lived wine, Penfold's Grange, which Max Schubert first created in 1951.

Cabernet Sauvignon: always has an attractive blackcurrant fruitiness. Very complex styles are produced in Coonawarra, Victoria and the cooler wine-growing regions of the Adelaide Hills and Tasmania. Barossa is rated for its opulent minty styles.

Shiraz/Cabernet Sauvignon: these grapes are often blended to produce well-structured rich wines. Different wine-making techniques result in varying styles, but most wines have oak (American or French) influence.

Other styles include the succulent appealing styles of Merlot, fruity upfront flavoured Pinot Noirs, and the pronounced raspberry character of Australia's most widely planted red

AUSTRALIA

Wakefield Wines

Estate grown and bottled

Australia's Most Awarded Top Selling Premium Cabernet Sauvignon

Also Chardonnay, White Clare, Shiraz/Cabernet, Riesling, Pinot Noir

Available from Cheers, Pettitts, Superquinn, SuperValu and discerning independent off-licences.

grape—Grenache.

Sparkling

Every third bottle of wine drunk in Australia is a 'fizzy' produced by the traditional method.

Vintages

Very consistent in quality. In recent years drought has caused a shortfall in grapes. However, 96 is generally superb in both quality and quantity.

WHITE WINE

White £4.50–£5.25

Castle Ridge Colombard/Chardonnay 95   14
Gilbeys
A pleasant wine for the money—fresh and clean with floral appeal.

Duck's Flat Dry White nv   14
Barry & Fitzwilliam
Nice lemon and marmalade peel touches make this an easy choice for those who like fruity white wine.

Moyston Semillon/Chardonnay 95   14
Dunnes Stores
Typical example of this unique Australian style with its deep yellow colour and ripe melon fruits backed up with zesty acidity.

Penfolds Rawson's Retreat Bin 21 95   13
Findlater
Water-pale, this blend of Semillon/Chardonnay/Colombard produces a fruity style with a bite of acidity on the finish.

Tollana Chardonnay 96   14
Quinnsworth
Deep yellow in colour, with pithy fruit appeal enhanced by crisp acidity, leaving a clean fresh finish.

Tollana Semillon/Chardonnay 96 14
Quinnsworth
Offers value for money with its herbaceous tones, good fruity
development and fresh finish.
White £5.25–£6

Hardy's RR Riesling/Gewürztraminer 95 14
Allied Drinks
For those who like their wine off-dry, this is an extremely
interesting blend in a fresh New World style. It has citrus fruit
appeal with a long clean finish.

Hardy's Stamps Semillon/Chardonnay 95 14
Allied Drinks
Deep golden yellow with typical citrus and exotic fruit tones.
The 95 vintage has a good long finish.

Jacob's Creek Chardonnay 95 14
Fitzgerald
The 95 is green-gold in colour with a very pleasant smoky
bacon character. Limey acidity, good fruit tones and balanced
alcohol make this a very acceptable, good-value wine.

Jacob's Creek Dry Riesling 95 13
Fitzgerald
Pale gold with green hints, this example of Aussie Riesling is
full of grapefruit appeal with a typical oily touch. Nice
surprising crisp finish.

Jacob's Creek Semillon/Chardonnay 95 14
Fitzgerald
Green-gold in colour, the 95 vintage has an extra touch of
grassiness with a long clean finish.

Rosemount Estate Semillon/Chardonnay 95 ☆
Grants
Who can resist this wine, especially the zippy fruit and citrus
crisp acidity? Simply chill and enjoy on its own.

Salisbury Estate Dry Riesling 94　　　　　　　**14**
Gilbeys
A good buy for the money with a nice hint of attractive
pungency. Those who like fruity whites will enjoy the fresh
finish with a bite of fruit.

Stoney Vale Semillon/Chardonnay 96　　　　　**14**
Barry & Fitzwilliam
A hint of oak influence with good citrus acidity and texture add
up to a balanced easy-drinking style.
White £6–£8

Best's Victoria Colombard 94　　　　　　　　**13**
Mitchell
For drinking cool in summer with its sea-fresh chalky appeal
and just a hint of spritz.

Carlyle Estate Victoria Chardonnay 94　　　　**14**
Greenhills
Yellow-gold with pleasant aromas of peach that don't disap-
point on flavour. Good finish and follow-through.

Corella Ridge Chardonnay 94　　　　　　　　☆
Dunnes Stores
Barrel fermentation and maturation add a creamy touch to this
toasty, smoky-bacon style Chardonnay.

d'Arenberg The Dry Dam Riesling 96　　　　　**14**
Taserra
Water-pale with a delicious bite of lemon and a hint of spritz.

d'Arenberg The Other Side Chardonnay 95　　☆
Taserra
Beautifully presented, this wine smacks of creaminess from
American and French oak influence with good exotic fruit
flavours.

Deakin Estate Chardonnay 95   14
Mackenway
A modern 'cool' Chardonnay packed with delicious fruit
cocktail aromas and flavours with good length of flavour.

Hardy's Nottage Hill Chardonnay 95   13
Allied Drinks
Obviously Australian in style with its marked toasty oak
appeal. Doesn't quite live up to its promise on aroma, but judge
for yourself!

Hardy's Tintara Chardonnay 95   14
Allied Drinks
Deep yellow in colour. Full of biscuit and cream aromas with a
super attack of fruit, balanced acidity and long clean finish.

Houghton HWB Dry White 95   14
Mitchell
One of Australia's biggest-selling white wines, produced from
Chenin Blanc, Semillon and Chardonnay. Enjoy the subtle
pungency and lively finish.

Lindemans Bin 65 Chardonnay 95   ☆
Gilbeys
A big intense fat wine with fruit holding out to give an extra
long flavoursome finish.

Lindemans Cawarra Homestead Semillon/Chardonnay 95
Gilbeys   14
Vanilla and spice with a gentle limey tang.

Long Gully Riesling 93   14
Verlings
A wonderful fresh style even though it's a 93. Fruit hits back
right at the end. A nice touch of spritz adds liveliness.

Maglieri Cellar Reserve Riesling 94   12
Greenhills
Produced from 100% Riesling. A grapefruit pithy style with a
medium-long finish.

McWilliam's Mount Pleasant Chardonnay 93   ☆
Quinnsworth
Released after two years' ageing in the winery, this style is rich,
creamy and exotic and has developed well since tasted last
year. A good example of Hunter Chardonnay. Try it with
grilled salmon.

McWilliam's Mount Pleasant Elizabeth Semillon 90   14
Quinnsworth
Released from the winery after five years' bottle ageing. Since
last tasted has developed nutty, ashy and honey characteristics
typical of aged Hunter unoaked Chardonnay. Works well with
smoked salmon.

Penfolds Koonunga Hill Chardonnay 95   ☆ ☆
Findlater
This Chardonnay is all about balance with a super mouthful of
ripe exotic fruits that expand and finish with a smack of toast.
Big, rich and harmonious.

Rosemount Estate Chardonnay 95   ☆
Grants
Golden sunshine in a glass. A perfect introduction to this style
of wine, with its creamy peach tones and beautiful balance. The
95 vintage is pure opulence.

Rosemount Estate Sauvignon Blanc 95   14
Grants
Mouth-watering watermelon aromas give way to rich ripe
gooseberry flavours that hold up right through to the well-
balanced spicy finish.

Rosemount Estate Semillon 95   14
Grants
A delightful mouthful of creamy textured apple fruit veering
towards the unripe style. Supple long elegant finish.

Seppelt Terrain Chardonnay Series 96   14
Dunnes Stores
Green-gold in colour with primary fruit flavours of peach and
apricot. Delivers more on flavour than aroma.

Wakefield Clare Valley Chardonnay 93   ☆
Koala Wines
Very pale yellow with a good mouthful of fruit. A well-
structured wine with subtle toasty oak influence.

Wakefield Clare Valley Riesling 94   14
Koala Wines
Nice example of this style, with its delicious limey appeal.
Lives up to its promise on aroma. A little touch of kerosene
shouts the grape variety. Drink young and fresh and enjoy its
slightly off-dry finish.

Wakefield White Clare Crouchen/Chardonnay 92   14
Koala Wines
Peach and butter tones harmonise on the palate. Good weight
and texture with enough acidity to give a lively tangy finish.

Wolf Blass Semillon/Chardonnay 94   ☆
Dillon
Highly aromatic—shows just how good this marriage between
the two grapes is. Full of ripe exotic fruit tones.

Wolf Blass Semillon/Sauvignon Blanc 'White Label' 95   14
Dillon
The 95 has a hint of gooseberry and lanolin. Very fresh with
tingling acidity.

Yaldara Reserve Chardonnay 95   13
Barry & Fitzwilliam
Easy-drinking style, French oak fermented and matured. The
texture is quite waxy with a lemon tang on the finish.
White £8–£10

Barwang Chardonnay 94   14
Quinnsworth
Since tasted last year this wine has developed well while still
maintaining its toasty finish and lively limey appeal.

Brands Coonawarra Laira Chardonnay 94   14
Quinnsworth
The smoky bacon tones are still very obvious since last tasted.
Barrel fermentation ensures that this Chardonnay with good
citrus acidity can take bottle age.

Brown Brothers Family Selection Sauvignon Blanc 95   ☆
Molloy's
A delicious Sauvignon. The pungency is obvious, but the mid-
palate is held up with good fruit tones and an extra-long finish.

Leeuwin Estate Rhine Riesling 94   ☆☆
Searson
Deep yellow-straw in colour. The classic kerosene of Riesling
and floral chalky tones intertwine to create an interesting
aroma. Delivers on flavour with a whack of refreshing acidity.
A fine example of Riesling.

Long Gully Sauvignon Blanc/Semillon 95   14
Verlings
Water-pale with delicious tart, peachy flavours overladen with
typical nettle aromas. Flavour explodes on the palate. Offers
something different.

Long Gully Semillon 92   13
Verlings
A mature style with nuances of honey and lanolin and a
medium-long finish.

McGuigan Brothers Bin 6000 Verdelho 95   14
Kelly
A super zippy style from this grape, which has adapted so well
to Australia from its native Madeira. Ripe limey aromas come
through on flavour. Something different.

Moculta Chardonnay 95
Allied Drinks
A new arrival on Irish shores which will delight the drinker
looking for good nutty oak influence and ripe fruit appeal. Very
long succulent finish.

St Hallett Barossa Chardonnay 95
Dunnes Stores
A classic style of Chardonnay with rich nutty tones from lees
ageing. Well balanced with good alcohol and acidity.

Tim Knappstein Wines Clare Valley Riesling 95   14
Dunnes Stores
To understand dry classic Australian Riesling, start here. Note
the pungent stony fruit appeal overladen with a hint of oil.
Limey acidity adds interest.

Wolf Blass Barrel-Fermented Chardonnay 95
Dillon
The 95 vintage is a stunner with subtle vanilla tones. Weighty
on the palate with lots of fruit and a characteristic long toasty
finish.

White £10–£12

Château Reynella Chardonnay 94   14
Allied Drinks
Yellow-gold in colour with buttery tones and a hint of spicy
new oak. Wait for a minute after swirling the glass and note
how the vanilla and toasty oak jump out.

Long Gully Chardonnay 93 14
Verlings
Rich and lively at the same time. The subtle use of oak is
particularly attractive, ending on a sumptuous nutty note.

Maglieri Chardonnay 94 ☆
Greenhills
A full-flavoured wine with important but subtle oak influence.
Imposing nutty nuances add a touch of class to the long finish.

Rosemount Estate Show Reserve Chardonnay 93
Grants
Outstanding example of this rich buttery style, which manages
to achieve excellent balance between oak, fruit and acidity.
Extra roundness has emerged with some bottle age.

Wirra Wirra Vineyards Church Block 93 14
McCabes
A generous wine with pungent Sauvignon gooseberry and
rhubarb tones that don't overpower. Semillon adds weight and
texture and Chardonnay a classic core. Extra time in bottle adds
smoothness to this creamy, oak-fermented and matured style.
White £12–£15

Ebenezer Chardonnay 94 14
Allied Drinks
Primrose yellow with concentrated aromas of canteloupe melon
and peach. Packs a huge mouthful of fruit. Very weighty on the
palate—sip and note the long biscuit finish.
White £15–£20

d'Arenberg The Olive Grove Chardonnay 95 14
Taserra
Pale straw in colour. Lively fruit appeal. Very forthcoming with
a dry crisp clean finish.

Eileen Hardy Padthaway Chardonnay 93 14
Allied Drinks
Great colour, breed and balance. The wine has matured with
some bottle age and has developed obvious aromas of butterscotch. Smooth succulent finish.

Mountadam Eden Valley Chardonnay 94 ☆ ☆

Wine Vault

Stunning with its pineapple and peach fruit aromas whipped up with cream. Doesn't overpower on flavour. Epitomises balance and class.

Rosemount Estate Roxburgh 93 ☆ ☆ ☆

Grants

From the Hunter Valley this is a jewel in the crown of the Rosemount range. Deliciously fruity with tangy citrus acidity and nutty flavours that linger on. A complex wine of great depth.

White £20–£30

Leeuwin Estate Chardonnay 93 ☆ ☆

Searson

World-class Chardonnay with its delightful mango fruit, superb balance and structure and long lingering finish. A special occasion drink.

RED WINE

Red £4.50–£5.25

Castle Ridge 94 14

Gilbeys

Great value with its deep crimson colour, bite of cherry fruit and supple finish.

Duck's Flat Dry Red nv 14

Barry & Fitzwilliam

Juicy with blackberry appeal in an opulent silky style.

Penfolds Rawson's Retreat Bin 35 Cabernet Sauvignon/Shiraz 94

Findlater

Smoky minty tones which turn towards liquorice on the palate. Full flavours with a big chewy texture and a hint of herbs on the finish.

Red £5.25–£6

Hardy's Stamps Shiraz/Cabernet Sauvignon 95   14
Allied Drinks
Ribena in colour with cold tea aromas overladen with blackberry fruit. The fruit shines through with a delicious mid-palate
of flavour, good grip and supple tannins.

Jacob's Creek Dry Red 94   14
Fitzgerald
Distinct jammy aromas and flavours. Has more grip on the
palate than expected. A nice easy style both on flavour and
pocket.

Moyston Shiraz/Cabernet Sauvignon 94   ☆
Dunnes Stores
This vintage is full of pure wine-gum aromas, emerging as
blackcurrant on flavour. Long lingering finish. A satisfying
chewy chunky wine.

Rosemount Estate Shiraz/Cabernet Sauvignon 95   14
Grants
Really shows how good this blend is with its leafy blackcurrant
appeal ending in a very pleasant smack of spice.

Seppelt Gold Label Shiraz 92   ☆
Dunnes Stores
Bright ruby with a dense saturation of colour. Savoury and
appetising with good chewy fruit and a smooth silky finish.

Tollana Cabernet Sauvignon 93   14
Quinnsworth
Garnet in colour, with wine-gum aromas and a hint of mint.
Good mid-palate flavours with an extra long finish.

Tollana Shiraz 93
Quinnsworth
Everything comes together in this wine. A good example of
how delicious Shiraz can be with a sweet-sour fruit appeal and
good acidity binding the fruit and supple tannins together.

Red £6–£8

Carlyle Estate Shiraz 93   14
Greenhills
Light oak influence adds a vanilla touch to the nutmeg, spicy
tones.

Chalambar Shiraz 92
Dunnes Stores
A delicious cool-climate Shiraz with lots of spice and fruit.
Aroma and flavours harmonise with a long classic finish.

---

d'Arenberg d'Arry's Original Shiraz/Grenache 92   14
Taserra
The 92 vintage shows more structure than the 91, with cherry
fruit flavours and the same vibrant long finish.

---

d'Arenberg The High Trellis Cabernet Sauvignon 91   14
Taserra
This vintage is extremely well balanced. The minty appeal of
the 91 tasted last year is there, but this wine veers more
towards loganberry fruit. The finish is long and juicy.

---

d'Arenberg The Old Vine Shiraz 94
Taserra
This is a stunner with its delicious harmony of chewy fruit, rich
peppery tone and savoury yet silky finish.

David Wynn Red 93   14
Wine Vault
From a master winemaker, this delightful wine has liquorice
and bullseye flavours that expand and linger on the palate.

Hardy's Nottage Hill Cabernet Sauvignon/Shiraz 94   14
Allied Drinks
Garnet in colour, this vintage has meaty gravy appeal. An extra
long savoury finish makes it a good choice with food.

Hardy's Tintara Cabernet Sauvignon/Shiraz 94
Allied Drinks
Creamy, plummy jam springs to mind. Rich fruit attack cuts
through the balancing acidity, ending in a long satisfying finish.

Jamieson's Run 94
Gilbeys
This rich, well-structured wine broke away from the varietal
straitjacket with a superb blend dominated by Cabernet
Sauvignon with Shiraz, Merlot, Cabernet Franc and Malbec. It is
a modern Australian classic.

Lindemans Bin 45 Cabernet Sauvignon 94
Gilbeys
Mint and jelly rolled into one. What a whopper—not overladen
with too much ripe fruit. Restrained and classic.

Lindemans Bin 50 Shiraz 94 14
Gilbeys
Bright crimson in colour, with earthy savoury aromas that
expand and finish in a good firm style.

McWilliam's Mount Pleasant Philip Shiraz 89 14
Quinnsworth
This wine needed to be opened an hour before drinking.
Released on the market after five years' bottle maturation in the
winery, it has earthy tones with a pleasant easy finish. It throws
a natural sediment. Buy to drink now.

Penfolds Bin 2 Shiraz/Mourvèdre 94
Findlater
A classy wine in every sense, with dense ripe plum aromas and
layers of concentrated flavour. Nothing is overblown. Perfect
harmony reigns.

Penfolds Koonunga Hill Shiraz/Cabernet Sauvignon 94
Findlater ☆ ☆
Extremely appealing, with its soft ripe fruit tones that pack a
punch of succulent flavour ending with a smack of supple
tannins.

Rosemount Estate Cabernet Sauvignon 95 ☆
Grants
Wonderful cerise colour which explodes into blackberry fruit
aromas overladen with just a hint of mint. The nice bites of
acidity and tannin give grip to the long flavoursome finish.

Seppelt Gold Label Cabernet Sauvignon 93 14
Dunnes Stores
Deep and dense. Packs a superb punch of classy spicy fruitiness
with a long delicious aftertaste.

Seppelt Harpers Range Cabernet Sauvignon 93 ☆
Dunnes Stores
Full, big and round, with chunky berry fruit appeal in an
impressive complex style.

Tyrrell's Old Winery Shiraz 94 ☆
Remy
Produced from Hunter Valley fruit, this rich opulent wine has
delicious fruity appeal with a hint of spice. Extra-long smooth
finish.

Wakefield Clare Valley Cabernet Sauvignon 90 ☆
Superquinn
A big mouthful of loganberry fruit with a delicious bite of tangy
acidity. Smooth and easy-drinking.

Wakefield Clare Valley Shiraz/Cabernet 94 14
Koala Wines
Cherry red with just a hint of brick at the edge. Vibrant
raspberry fruit tones on aroma which are masked by acidity on
the mid-palate. Pleasant fresh finish.

Wolf Blass Red Label Shiraz/Cabernet 95　　　　14
Dillon
Ruby red with a smack of mint and bay leaf. Easy-drinking style with flavour holding up right through to the end.

Yaldara Reserve Shiraz 94　　　　☆
Barry & Fitzwilliam
Garnet in colour. Produced from old vines with American oak influence. This is an appealing big fruity wine with minty tones.

Red £8–£10

Ballandean Estate Cabernet Sauvignon/Malbec 93　　　　14
Parsons
Attractive label. This wine has an underlying minty tone with lingering fruity flavours.

Barwang McWilliams Shiraz 94　　　　14
Quinnsworth
A wonderful vintage with an inky black colour and fistfuls of cherry and blackberry fruits.

Brands Coonawarra Laira Shiraz 93　　　　☆
Quinnsworth
This wine has developed lots of everything since tasted last year. It still maintains its top-quality Shiraz fruit and with some bottle age has gained a star for sheer fruit flavour appeal.

Brown Brothers Merlot 94　　　　
Woodford Bourne
Deep ruby with minty overtones and rich fruit cake appeal. Restrained and elegant with soft-centred fruit attack that slips and glides over the palate.

Browns of Padthaway Shiraz 93　　　　
Bacchus
Intense savoury tones with a hint of Oxo. French and American oak influence add a toasty touch.

A perfect report card

Look who came "Top of the Class" in the
London International Wine Challenge

**1996 International Wine Magazine Wine Challenge
7 ENTRIES - 7 MEDALS**

● d'Arenberg - **GOLD** 1995 The Olive Grove Chardonnay	✓
● d'Arenberg - **SILVER** 1994 d'Arry's Original Shiraz-Grenache	✓
● d'Arenberg - **SILVER** 1994 The Old Vine Shiraz	✓
● d'Arenberg - **COMMENDED** 1994 The High Trellis Cabernet Sauvignon	✓
● d'Arenberg - **BRONZE** 1994 The Ironstone Pressings Grenache Shiraz	✓
● d'Arenberg - **GOLD** 1994 The Dead Arm Shiraz	✓
● d'Arenberg - **BRONZE** 1995 Vintage Fortified Shiraz	✓

d'Arenberg

Established 1912
McLaren Vale, South Australia

Taserra Wine Merchants Ltd.,
Hogan House, Grand Canal St., Dublin 2.
Ph: 4900537   Fax: 4904052

Cape Mentelle Cabernet/Merlot 94 ☆☆☆
Findlater
Has the 'wow' factor with its deep purple-red colour. Its
capsicum aromas and flavours flow and swirl silkily across the
palate. The Cabernet adds a classic claret structure while the
Merlot adds concentrated fruit character. Superb use of oak.

Coriole Redstone Shiraz/Cabernet 93 ☆
McCabes
Produced from 65% Shiraz and 35% Cabernet Sauvignon, this is
an opulent style with prune and mint overtones. Restrained
due to its extra bottle age, it has a hint of austerity. The finish is
impressive.

Hardy's Bankside Shiraz 93 14
Allied Drinks
Deep ruby red with a very pleasant spicy touch that continues
to the last swallow. Good depth of flavour with harmonious
tannins taking over on the well-structured finish.

Moculta Cabernet Sauvignon/Merlot 94 ☆
Allied Drinks
A big rich wine. Caraway seed aromas give way to good fruit
tones and a pleasant toast and warm red berry fruit finish.

Moculta Shiraz 94 ☆
Allied Drinks
Fruity blackberry appeal. Ripe, mouthfilling flavours that end
in a long silky finish.

Rosemount Estate Shiraz 95 ☆☆
Grants
What a stunning introduction to Australian Shiraz, with its
deep, dark colour! Full of chunky fruit that flows over the
palate. Its flavour goes on and on.

Tyrrell's Old Winery Cabernet/Merlot 95
Remy
Produced from grapes sourced in the Hunter Valley,
Coonawarra and McLaren Vale, this upfront fruity wine has
layers of flavour ranging from plum to dried prune and mint. A
big wine in every sense.

Wolf Blass Yellow Label Cabernet Sauvignon 95　　　14
Dillon
Close your eyes and think of mint! This aroma gives way to a
rich generous berry fruit flavour. Smooth supple finish.

Wynn's Coonawarra Cabernet/Shiraz 90 ☆
Findlater
An opulent sumptuous style, tight-knit yet packed with
creamy, minty chocolate tones. Super follow-through on
flavour.

Red £10–£12

Château Reynella Cabernet Sauvignon 92 ☆
Allied Drinks
Mint and tomato-stalk aromas mark this wine, with its classic
attack loaded with gum-drying tannins. Packs a punch in every
sense.

Château Reynella Shiraz 92
Allied Drinks
This wine simply oozes ripe blackcurrant appeal with aromas
spilling over into crushed fruit flavours. Big and opulent. A
must for the lover of Australian red wine who will still savour
it the day after tasting.

---

d'Arenberg The Custodian Grenache 94
Taserra
Nice to see this grape variety being taken seriously by Australian producers. This fine example has aromas of blackcurrant
jam and smooth rich fruit appeal with an attractive wholesome
finish. It wins two stars for originality.

d'Arenberg The Twenty Eight Road Mourvèdre 95   **14**
Taserra
Beginning to gain a reputation for itself in Australia, this purple crimson wine has aromas of black wine-gum. It has a lively, vibrant fruit appeal with good acidity and a whack of drying tannin.

Hardy's Coonawarra Cabernet Sauvignon 93
Allied Drinks
Don't even try to see the bottom of the glass. Dense in colour and packed with savoury rich concentrated powerful yet restrained fruit. A classic from Australia that slips down easily in a lipsmacking fashion.

Houghton Cabernet Sauvignon 92
Mitchell
Deep crimson in colour. Intriguing mint and ripe blackberry fruit held together with a bite of tangy acidity and obvious drying tannins.

Long Gully Irma's Cabernet 92
Verlings
A deeply coloured mature wine with concentrated ripe fruit appeal and a super backbone of solid structure.

Maglieri Cabernet Sauvignon 93   **14**
Greenhills
Partially barrel-fermented, this wine is much better on flavour than aroma. Juicy and savoury in a cool Aussie style. Good long finish.

Maglieri Shiraz 93
Greenhills
Displays good use of oak. Fruity flavours that fill out on mid-palate in a rich sumptuous style and end in a strong silky generous and assertive tone.

Rosemount Estate Show Reserve Cabernet Sauvignon 93

Grants ☆ ☆

An excellent year which produced intense concentrated aromas of blackcurrants followed by layers of flavour with hints of smoky oak. This classy drink from Coonawarra has been improving all the time since tasted last year.

Wirra Wirra Vineyards Church Block Cabernet/Shiraz/Merlot 94 *McCabes* ☆

This blend, dominated by Cabernet Sauvignon, with Shiraz and Merlot, makes a very interesting wine. The rich flavours are obvious but not overpowering. An extremely balanced style.

Wolf Blass President's Selection Cabernet Sauvignon 93

Dillon ☆ ☆

Ireland has the highest per capita consumption in the world of this wine! Crushed freshly picked blackberry with minty overtones. Classic structure. A rich flavoursome finish.

Wolf Blass President's Selection Shiraz 93 ☆

Dillon

Has the huge appeal of blackberry fruit—warm and generous from start to finish.

Yarra Ridge Cabernet Sauvignon 94 **14**

Fine Wines

Lots of spicy oak appeal with very pleasant treacle toffee aromas. Flavour carries through to the finish, ending in a hint of mint.

Red £12–£15

Best's Great Western Pinot Noir 94 ☆ ☆

Mitchell

A big Australian style of Pinot Noir. Very seductive with masses of ripe strawberry/raspberry flavours, velvet smooth tannins and a long tangy finish.

Best's Great Western Shiraz 93 ☆☆
Mitchell
An appetising wine—the white pepper aromas jump out of the glass followed by wild aromas of cassis. Extremely meaty and savoury. Two stars for individuality.

d'Arenberg Ironstone Pressings Grenache/Shiraz 93   14
Taserra
Deep purple-crimson. Packs a punch of flavour with a smoky savoury tone. Robust long finish. Offers something different.

Dorrien Vineyard Cabernet Sauvignon 91 ☆☆
Dunnes Stores
Deep saturation of crimson. Newly made red berry jelly aromas. Good attack of fruit. Better on flavour as fruit expands and develops. Lively acidity adds freshness to the long finish.

Ebenezer Cabernet Sauvignon/Merlot/Cabernet Franc 93
Allied Drinks ☆☆
Incredible aromas of sweet ripe cassis rise from the glass with a hint of mint. Has the 'wow' factor with its wonderful fruit character and velvet tannins.

Lindemans Limestone Ridge Shiraz Cabernet 91 ☆☆
Gilbeys
This style leans towards the attractive stalky tomato appeal of Coonawarra. Appealing intense flavours end in a rich heart-warming finish.

Seppelt Great Western Vineyards Shiraz 91 ☆☆
Dunnes Stores
Deep saturation of garnet. Wonderful wine-gum and plum aromas. Mouthfilling flavours expand and fan out with very supple tannins. A smooth generous wine with an opulent finish.

St Hallett Old Block Barossa Shiraz 93
Dunnes Stores
This blockbuster of a wine, produced from 80–100-year-old vines and aged in American oak, has superb structure. At this level the fruit should kick back through the assertive tannins and it does!

Tyrrell's Wines Vat 9 Shiraz 90
Remy
From one of Australia's oldest wineries steeped in tradition, this sumptuous wine is a top example of Hunter Valley Shiraz.
Red £15–£20

d'Arenberg The Dead Arm Cabernet/Shiraz 93
Taserra
Rich in colour, with deep ripe red berry fruit appeal overladen with an earthy touch. Good flavour attack, with fruit fanning out to leave a long smooth succulent finish.

Hardy's Eileen Hardy Shiraz 93
Allied Drinks
A black pearl of colour with aromas that waft across the room. Savoury Shiraz-like scraping the juices from the roasting tin. Rich and concentrated.

Hardy's Thomas Hardy Coonawarra Cabernet Sauvignon 92
Allied Drinks
Brambly and stalky. Just close your eyes and you're picking ripe blackberries in a fine Irish autumn! Fruit swirls around the palate with enough tannin and acidity to add structure.
Red £20–£30

Ravenswood Hollick Wines Coonawarra Cabernet Sauvignon 91 *Parsons*
This wine has developed extremely well since last tasted. The rich blackcurrant flavours have assumed a hint of spice. The finish is still extra long and complex.

Austria

Main wine regions

Niederösterreich, Styria, Burgenland, Vienna

Principal grape varieties and styles

White

Grüner Veltliner (native): produces lively fresh whites.
Welschriesling: light apple-type wines and superb sweet wines.
Riesling: lively, peachy acidic wines.
Weissburgunder (Pinot Blanc): fresh nutty styles.
Chardonnay (Morillon): a veritable artist's palette of flavours.
Gewürztraminer: aromatic spicy styles.
Rotgipfler: full-bodied whites.
Müller-Thurgau: light easy-drinking wine.
Muskat Öttonel: good aperitif wines.

Red

Blaufränkisch (native): light fruity red styles.
Zweigelt: dark-skinned; produces light and full-bodied styles.
Blauer Burgunder (Pinot Noir): capable of producing top quality.
Blauer Portugieser: easy-drinking fruity styles.
Cabernet Sauvignon: full-bodied tannic styles.

Labelling guide

Quality is classified by the ripeness of the grapes at harvest. Exported wines carry an official certificate. Varietal wines must be produced from 85% of the stated grape and, if a region is stated, 100% from grapes grown in that region.
Tafelwein: table wine. *Landwein:* higher-quality table wine.
Qualitätswein: quality wine.
Prädikatswein: wine with a special distinction.
Spätlese: wines produced from fully ripe grapes.
Auslese: as above with a higher sugar content.
Beerenauslese: wines produced from overripe grapes, usually affected by noble rot.
Ausbruch: unique to Austria, this is a sweet high alcohol wine rich in texture produced from grapes affected by *Botrytis cinerea*.
Trockenbeerenauslese: naturally shrivelled grapes affected by noble

rot.

Eiswein: grapes harvested and pressed when frozen.

Strohwein: grapes stored and air dried for at least three months.

Bergwein: wine produced from grapes grown on a certain gradient (26%) slope.

Trocken: dry. *Extra Trocken:* extra dry. *Halbtrocken:* medium dry. *Lieblich:* sweet. *Süss:* extra sweet.

WHITE WINE

White £4.50–£5.25

Servús Burgenland Trocken Q 94   12
Barry & Fitzwilliam
Modern style with a touch of pithy grapefruit. The 94 has a fresh touch of lemon peel on the finish.

White £8–£10

Joahanneshof Reinisch Weissburgunder 94   14
Terroirs
Good depth of fruit with pleasant citrus appeal and fresh finish.

White £10–£12

Johanneshof Reinisch Riesling 94   ☆
Terroirs
Attractive lemon and lime tangy aromas and flavours, with a good bite of acidity that still allows fruit to show through.

RED WINE

Red £4.50–£5.25

Servús Burgenland Trocken nv   14
Barry & Fitzwilliam
A definite food wine for pizza and meat-based pasta dishes. Has lots of cinnamon and pepper tones that continue right through to the finish.

Red £12–£15

Johanneshof Reinisch Pinot Noir Reserve 92   ☆
Terroirs
Deep crimson in colour with fine raspberry aromas. Extremely pleasant sweet-sour finish in a long chewy chunky style.

Bulgaria

Principal grape varieties

White	Red
White	*Red*
Rkatsiteli	Cabernet Sauvignon
Chardonnay	Merlot
Dimiat	Melnik
Riesling	Gamza
Misket	Mavrud
	Pinot Noir
	Pamid

Labelling guide

Country Wines: declared geographical region stated on the label, usually showing the name of the grape and the region (there are over forty). Can also be a blend of two grape varieties.

Controliran Wines: established in 1985, a top-quality category indicating wines coming from one of 27 strictly controlled areas.

Reserve/Special Reserve: terms indicating oak-aged wines that have been matured for longer than other categories; usually varietal wines.

Wine styles

White

Most should be drunk young and fresh. Interesting wines include: Misket (a crossing of Dimiat and Riesling); oak-aged Chardonnays, which are improving all the time and can be matured for several years in bottle; Novi Pazar, Schumen and Khan Krum are good sources of white wines on the Irish market.

Red

Varietal wines such as Cabernet Sauvignon, Merlot and Pinot Noir are produced in attractive supple styles.

Gamza and Melnik offer spicy everyday wines of fresh appeal.

Reserve wines offer classic tastes at everyday prices and are released for sale from the winery when ready for drinking.

Suhindol, Svishtov and Russe are good sources of Cabernet Sauvignon and Merlot on the Irish market.

WHITE WINE

White £4.50–£5.25

Bulgarian Vintners Reserve Chardonnay 92
Fitzgerald
Top quality for the price with ripe melon appeal. A super fresh fruit attack and lively finish.

RED WINE

Red £4.50–£5.25

Bulgarian Vintners Reserve Cabernet Sauvignon 90
Quinnsworth
Summer fruit compote aromas and flavours with a pleasant touch of caramel from American and Bulgarian oak influence. The juicy fruity appeal has a long follow-through on flavour. Buy to drink.

Bulgarian Vintners Reserve Merlot 90   13
Fitzgerald
Ruby red. Stalky fruit character. Medium-bodied with high acidity and medium finish.

Chile

Main wine regions

Grape-growing is concentrated in the Central Valley. Within this vast area are smaller valleys familiar from wine labels, including: Aconcagua (of which the most famous sub-region is Casablanca) and Maule (of which the most famous sub-region is Curicó), Rapel, Maipo, Bío-Bío.

Principal grape varieties

White	Red
Sauvignon Blanc	Cabernet Sauvignon
Sauvignon Vert Merlot	
Chardonnay	Carignan
Muscat	Pinot Noir (Pinot Negro)
Sémillon	Syrah
Riesling	Cabernet Franc
Gewürztraminer	

Labelling guide

Wines are usually called after the name of the grape variety or varieties. Knowing the producer is also a vital clue to quality. Reserva wines indicate wines with extra maturity and oak influence. Wineries usually name their most prized wine after a family ancestor. Since 1995 a new appellation system has singled out specific regions.

Wine styles

Quality Chilean wines are based on classic French wine-making techniques. Varietal whites are fresh, crisp and lively for early drinking. Oak-influenced whites can mature for several years. Varietal reds are juicy and plummy and are also for early drinking, but some have enough structure to mature in bottle for a few years.

Reserva styles, usually with oak influence, have good mid-term ageing ability. Whites are noted for their creaminess and reds for their attractive capsicum (pepper) aromas.

WHITE WINE

White £4.50–£5.25

Caliterra Chardonnay/Semillon 95   14
Quinnsworth
Pale bright with floral tones. Fruity and fresh with good length.

Caliterra Sauvignon Blanc 95   13
Quinnsworth
The 95 vintage has a touch of exotic fruit flavours. Easy-drinking, uncomplicated style.

Carta Vieja Chardonnay 95   13
Barry & Fitzwilliam
An easy-drinking style with broad flavours of ripe apple.

Carta Vieja Sauvignon Blanc 95   14
Barry & Fitzwilliam
This vintage is much more typical in style than the 94, with the herbaceous attractiveness of Sauvignon coming through.

Concha y Toro Chardonnay/Sauvignon Blanc 96   14
Findlater
Good straw colour with clean very fresh fruity appeal and medium weight on the palate.

San Pedro Sauvignon Blanc 95   14
Dunnes Stores
Interesting ripe fruit tones, lively acidity and long crisp finish.

Santa Carolina White 95   14
TDL
Golden-toned with creamy peach fruit attack balanced with lively acidity. Good fresh finish with nice length of flavour.

Santa Helena Sauvignon Blanc 95   14
Taserra
The 95 offers the same zesty pleasure as the 94 with more

Aurelio Montes: 1995 Chilean Wine Maker Of The Year.

MONTES
THE NAME ON CHILE'S FINEST WINES

emphasis on fruity aromas and flavours.

Valdezaro Sauvignon Blanc nv 13
Barry & Fitzwilliam
Easy-drinking style. Clean and fresh with a hint of gooseberry.

Villa Montes Sauvignon Blanc 96 14
Grants
A crisp lively style. The 95 has far more pungent appeal than
the 94. Perfect seafood wine.

White £5.25–£6

Carmen Chardonnay 95 14
Dillon
Appealing in colour, with creamy melon and pear fruit aromas
and flavours. Tart and weighty with an extra-long succulent
finish.

Carmen Sauvignon Blanc 95 13
Dillon
Very pleasant floral and sherbet aromas carry through on
flavour. An ideal fruity wine with a medium-long finish.

Errázuriz Sauvignon Blanc 95 14
Allied Drinks
This vintage has fruity aromas reminiscent of rhubarb, which
fan out and finish in gooseberry tones. Long crisp finish.

Miguel Torres Santa Digna Sauvignon Blanc 95 14
Woodford Bourne
This vintage is pungent with good fruit tones. Crisp fresh attack
with a slight touch of elderflower.

San Pedro Chardonnay 95 14
Dunnes Stores
Deep golden yellow with a touch of tropical fruit and good
lively attack. The finish has a nice creamy tone.

Santa Carolina Chardonnay 95   14
TDL
Deep yellow with coconut aromas. Good weight and texture on
the palate. Melon-type fruits round out the lengthy finish.

Santa Carolina Sauvignon Blanc 95   14
TDL
This vintage is golden with hints of green. Zippy fresh citrus
fruit attack continues through to the end, leaving a fresh feeling
on the palate.

Santa Monica Chardonnay 95   13
Kelly
Pale gold in colour, with pleasant creamy melon fruit appeal.

Sergio Traverso La Parra Sauvignon Blanc 95   14
Terroirs
Pure lemon zest appeal with a clean fresh tingling finish.

Villa Montes Chardonnay 95
Grants
Deep golden in colour, this wine has huge ripe fruit salad
appeal. Fruit sings its way from start to finish. Long and
flavoursome.
White £6–£8

Caliterra Reserva Chardonnay 95
Quinnsworth
The 95 vintage is lime gold in colour with hints of pineapple
fruit. Good use of French oak adds weight and a pleasant
toastiness.

Carmen Reserva Chardonnay 95
Dillon
Youthful with lots of spicy oak appeal. Nutty nuances with
smooth exotic fruit.

Carmen Reserva Sauvignon Blanc 94   14
Dillon
Pale in colour, with herbaceous grassy tones ending in a crisp
dry finish.

Casa Porta Chardonnay 95   14
Fine Wines
Very pleasant delicate 'bon-bon' aromas with more fruit
influence on the palate. Flavour holds up to the last sip.

Concha y Toro Casillero del Diablo Chardonnay 95   14
Findlater
Yellow-gold in colour, with creamy nutty tones that spill over
on the palate, supported by a tang of lemon acidity.

Concha y Toro Marqués Chardonnay 95   ☆
Findlater
Barrel fermentation in small French oak barrels imparts rich
creamy buttery nuances. The acidity binds everything together.
A long succulent finish impresses.

Cousiño-Macul Chardonnay 95   14
Ecock
Mouthfilling flavours with plenty of creamy exotic fruit tones
mark this vintage. Appealing long flavoursome finish.

Errázuriz Barrel-fermented Reserve Sauvignon Blanc 92
Allied Drinks   ☆
A hint of smoky bacon suggests oak. Creamy and toasty with an
extra-long fine elegant finish.

Errázuriz Chardonnay 93   13
Allied Drinks
This wine has developed ice cream and wafer tones since last
tasted. The attack is fresh and crisp, but fruit stops short on its
promise of long length.

San Juan de Pirque Chardonnay 94
Febvre
Barrel-fermented, this interesting Chardonnay from William
Fèvre, the famous Burgundian winemaker, has excellent texture
with good melon-type fruits overlain with toastiness.

San Pedro Reserve Chardonnay 95
Dunnes Stores
Toasty and appealing, with limey appeal and a big fresh finish.

Santa Carolina Reserva Chardonnay 94   14
TDL
Bright golden yellow. Nutty creamy vanilla tones with stewed
apple flavours. Subtle but recognisable oak influence adds
weight and length to the finish.

Santa Carolina Special Reserve Sauvignon Blanc 93   14
TDL
For those who like tropical fruit flavours cut through with the
zest of limes. Weighty mouth feel with good length.

Santa Ines Legado de Armida Chardonnay 93
Mackenway
Produced by the de Martino family, this oak-fermented wine
has delicious overtones of hazelnuts with a long creamy toasty
finish. Oak and Chardonnay in perfect harmony.

Santa Ines Sauvignon Blanc 96
Mackenway
Very appealing. Crisp, lively and fresh, with upfront goose-
berry fruit appeal. A top example of a Chilean white.

Santa Rita Medalla Real Chardonnay 95
Gilbeys
A rich ripe style. The 95 vintage is a must for those who like oak
influence. It has a refreshing bite of lemon shining through the
polished oak character.

Viña Porta Chardonnay 95   13
Greenhills
Deep yellow in colour, with surprising pea-pod aromas. Good
attack, follow-through and finish.
White £8–£10

Errázuriz Barrel-fermented Reserve Chardonnay 94
Allied Drinks
This vintage is better than ever. Hints of ripe melon develop
into a delicious explosion of flavours whipped together with
creamy vanilla tones and a long satisfying finish.

Peteroa Barrel-fermented Chardonnay 94
Mitchell
Delicious oaky nuances of coconut and exotic fruit in a well-
balanced harmonious style that is smooth and toasty on the
finish.

Santa Carolina Gran Reserva Chardonnay 93
TDL
Hints of smoky bacon give way to a weighty wine with super
balance between fruit, acidity and oak. Long waxy satisfying
finish.

RED WINE

Red under £4.50

Miraflores 94
McCabes
Extremely bright and clear in appearance, the stalky fruit
appeal of this wine overladen with a creamy mid-palate is hard
to beat at the price. A definite food wine.
Red £4.50–£5.25

Caliterra Cabernet Sauvignon 94   ☆
Quinnsworth
The vibrant 95 vintage maintains the star quality of the 93
tasted last year, offering great drinking pleasure. The very ripe
fruit character is overlain with a spicy youthful touch.

Caliterra Cabernet/Merlot 94   14
Quinnsworth
Deep crimson in colour, with intriguing woodland aromas
typical of Merlot. A top-quality Chilean at the price. American
oak ageing adds a creamy touch to the stalky Cabernet fruit.

Carta Vieja Cabernet Sauvignon 94   14
Barry & Fitzwilliam
The 94 vintage has youthful purple tones with cherry fruit
overlain with a hint of style. Good drinking.

Carta Vieja Merlot 96   14
Barry & Fitzwilliam
Leafy with a touch of woodland aromas. Well made in an easy-
drinking style.

Concha y Toro Merlot 95   ☆
Findlater
The label attracts first, the colour of deep ruby second, and
above all the pleasant damson and plum aromas and flavours.
Velvety smooth.

San Pedro Cabernet Sauvignon 94   14
Dunnes Stores
Pungent vegetal aromas. Juicy red berry fruit flavours. Plenty of
grip and bite make this a good choice with food.

Santa Carolina Red 94   14
TDL
Cherries all the way, both in colour and taste. Uncomplicated
drinking with a hint of liquorice. Good food wine.

Santa Helena Cabernet Sauvignon 95   14
Taserra
A 'friendly' wine, this vintage is fruity with crushed red berry
appeal. An easy-drinking style.

Undurraga Cabernet Sauvignon 95
Superquinn
A sturdy wine with a deep saturation of inky purple. Aromas
are reminiscent of baked red berry fruit. The tannins are very
assertive but with a little more bottle age this well-structured
wine will prove its potential.

Valdezaro Cabernet Sauvignon 96 13
Barry & Fitzwilliam
A juicy fruity style with a pleasant hint of spice.
Red £5.25–£6

Carmen Cabernet Sauvignon 94 14
Dillon
Never disappoints with its minty smoky aromas. Harmonious
and balanced in flavour with a long concentrated finish.

Carmen Merlot 95
Dillon
Deep crimson, the 95 vintage is deliciously smooth and creamy.
Those who like fruity reds will enjoy its voluptuous long finish.

Cono Sur Pinot Noir 95 14
McCabes
A delicious easy-drinking style with good raspberry fruit
flavours.

Errázuriz Cabernet Sauvignon 94 14
Allied Drinks
Still 'closed' on aroma, with hints of herbs and mint. The fruit
emerges on the palate backed up with balanced acidity and
mouth-drying tannins, indicating the wine has time to develop.

Miguel Torres Santa Digna Cabernet Sauvignon 94 14
Woodford Bourne
Deep ruby in colour, this vintage has aromas of red berry fruits.
Very pleasant with smoky tones. Soft-centred with easy-
drinking appeal.

San Pedro Merlot 94
Dunnes Stores
Deep crimson in colour, with very pleasant leafy blackcurrant
and pea-pod aromas. Good attack of fruit with a nice bite of
tannin adding structure. Good food wine.

Santa Carolina Cabernet Sauvignon 94
TDL
Another star, with its leafy tomato tone giving way to a hint of
liquorice. The big whack of drying tannin still allows the
creamy finish to linger.

Santa Carolina Merlot 93
TDL
This purple-crimson wine is packed with plum and chocolate
flavours. Soft supple tannins add a touch of opulence to the
texture.

Santa Carolina Merlot/Cabernet Sauvignon 94   14
TDL
Deep cherry in colour, with a mineral tarry tone. The fruit
expands on the palate with a nice bite of acidity breaking
through the soft tannins. Good food wine.

Santa Monica Cabernet Sauvignon 93   14
Kelly
A flavoursome wine, good at the price with capsicum aromas
giving way to riper fruit on the palate.

Santa Monica Merlot 93   13
Kelly
Easy drinking with soft plum appeal and smooth round finish.

Santa Rita 120 Merlot 94   14
Gilbeys
The 94 vintage has lots of plummy fruit attraction with a smoky
touch.

Sergio Traverso La Parra Cabernet Sauvignon 94
Terroirs
Deep crimson with delightful chocolate plummy flavours,
smooth texture and a long finish.
Red £6–£8

Caliterra Reserva Cabernet Sauvignon 94
Quinnsworth
A real stunner, with cassis and mint flavours that sing their
way to a rich opulent weighty finish.

Carmen Reserve Cabernet Sauvignon 94
Dillon
Deep crimson. Very attractive wine that displays fresh youthful
red berry fruit appeal. Flavours fan out on the palate with
smooth supple tannins. A seductive wine with a nice bite of
acidity on the finish to add freshness.

Concha y Toro Casillero del Diablo Cabernet Sauvignon 94
Findlater
Deep blackberry in colour and simply bursting with fruit and
minty aromas. Very attractive finish with fruit kicking back
through the lively acidity.

Concho y Toro Marqués Cabernet Sauvignon 93   **14**
Findlater
Baked fruit appeal with very pleasant mint and spice tones. The
flavour holds up with a slight austerity at the end. Good food
wine.

Errázuriz Merlot 95
Allied Drinks
This vintage wins, as did the 94. Deep blackberry colour. Plenty
of spice and herbs fan out and end in a peppery bite. Terrific
food wine with its savoury aspect.

Miramonte Cabernet Sauvignon 95

Febvre

Young and delicious. Deep cerise in colour, with hints of cold tea aromas. Damson fruit emerges on the palate and is shot through with good acidity. Everything is held together with drying tannins denoting its youth.

San Pedro Reserve 94

Dunnes Stores

Dark and deep with whirlpools of complex flavours. Has a big weighty structure with supple red berry fruit appeal and surprising tannic structure.

Santa Carolina Reserva Cabernet Sauvignon 92

TDL

A fine example of what Chile has to offer. Hints of capsicum with a touch of cedar trail off on the palate to damson-type fruits. Delicious easy drinking, yet the wine has lots of structure.

Red £8–£10

Carmen Reserve Grande Vidure 94

Dillon

Brilliant crimson in colour. Shy on aroma, the wine has a delicious ripe fruit character. Tannins complement the fruit style. Well balanced, with an enticing vanilla touch on the end.

Cousiño-Macul Antiguas Reservas Cabernet Sauvignon 92

Ecock

Deep garnet, with more fruit showing in this vintage overlain with a touch of herbs. Classic structure with very ripe fruit flavours and supple tannins.

Peteroa Private Reserve Cabernet Sauvignon 91

Mitchell

Full and rich with succulent mature cassis fruit. Very classic in style, with a slight smoky touch on the concentrated finish.

Santa Carolina Gran Reserva Cabernet Sauvignon 90
TDL
A big wine in every sense. Blackberry jelly and lots of minty tones roll around the palate and are cut through with zesty acidity.

Santa Rita Medalla Real Cabernet Sauvignon 93
Gilbeys
Pure ripe blackcurrant fruit appeal overlain with a hint of chocolate. Has the New World upfront fruit appeal. Ten months' oak ageing adds polish and structure.

Viña Porta Reserva Cabernet Sauvignon 94
Greenhills
Deep garnet in colour, with concentrated aromas that spill over into capsicum. Big and rich with a powerful opulent finish.
Red £10–£12

Villa Montes Alpha 91
Grants
Since last tasted the wine has continued to develop well in bottle. Classic in style, the opulent blackberry appeal has developed a more cedar tone. Long flavoursome finish.
Red £15–£20

Santa Rita Casa Real Cabernet Sauvignon 93
Gilbeys
Deep crimson. The initial pure ripe blackcurrant fruit appeal gives way to hints of liquorice and mint. Amazing persistence of flavour with a silky texture and big opulent finish.

ROSÉ WINE

Rosé £5.25–£6

Miguel Torres Santa Digna Cabernet Sauvignon Rosé 96
Woodford Bourne
Extremely appealing with its delightful bright raspberry colour. Wonderful flavours of stalky brambly fruit in a big mouthfilling style. Tingling fresh acidity adds interest to the very fruity finish.

OVER THE YEARS, OUR KNOWLEDGE OF FINE WINES HAS MATURED CONSIDERABLY.

Baron Philippe de Rothschild (France), Marques de Riscal (Spain), Penfolds (Australia), Veuve Clicquot (Champagne) and Lupe Cholet (France) are just some of the famous wine names in the Findlater list. Our knowledge of fine wines has been growing steadily since 1823 and every day our expert buyers make new discoveries on your behalf. These fine wines and many more from the Findlater cellars are available in good wine shops nationwide.

FINDLATER

The Harcourt Street Vaults,
10 Upper Hatch Street, Dublin 2.
Tel: (01) 4751699. Fax: (01) 4752530.

IRELAND'S
BEST RANGE
OF CHILEAN WINES,

FROM IRELAND'S
BEST WINE SHOPS.

THE VINTAGE

**Blackrock,
Rathmines & City
Centre
Tel. 283 1664**

Peter A. Dalton
Food & Wine

Importers of fine wines from France (Costière de Nîmes, Rasteau, Rocbere, L. Lurton), Portugal (Bonifacio) and the Award winning Geyser Peak from California

Tel: (01) 295 4945, 087 639665

France—Alsace

Main wine regions

The region extends over two departments, Haut-Rhin and Bas-Rhin. Haut-Rhin is the most important in terms of quality wine production, with the majority of large producers located there. Over 95% of production is white.

Principal grape varieties

White Riesling, Gewürztraminer, Pinot Gris, Muscat, Pinot Blanc, Sylvaner, Auxerrois. *Red* Pinot Noir.

Wine styles

Riesling: this noble grape is rated for its floral aroma and lively
   acidity, assuming great complexity with age.
Gewürztraminer: highly aromatic with high alcohol and medium
   acidity with a distinct hint of spice. Fruity yet dry on the finish.
Pinot Gris: marked by stony fruit appeal, it can be very fine and
   complex with good ageing capacity.
Muscat: characterised by a distinct grape or orange blossom aroma.
Pinot Blanc: dry crisp style. Less aromatic than the grape varieties
   already mentioned.
Sylvaner: drink young and fresh.
Pinot Noir: produces red and rosé wines. Reds are rated for their
   light colour with vibrant red berry fruit appeal. Some producers
   are experimenting with oak ageing with good results.

Labelling guide

Long before Californians termed the phrase 'varietal', Alsace producers were naming their wine by the grape variety.

Edelwicker or Vin d'Alsace on the label indicates a blended wine from several varieties.

Some producers indicate their better wines by using the terms Cuvée Spéciale or Réserve Personnelle on the label.

Alsace Grand Cru, established in 1983, indicates a wine produced from one of four permitted varieties — Riesling, Gewürztraminer, Pinot Gris or Muscat from one of over fifty individual vineyard sites.

General guidelines

Sweet styles

Vendange tardive (late harvested): wines must be made from late-picked berries that have attained above-average ripeness.

Sélection de grains nobles: wines produced from grapes with a very high sugar content due to extended ripening. In most cases they have been affected by 'noble rot' (a beneficial fungus that concentrates the sugar levels) and can be labelled with this term. The wines are rich and very complex with great ageing ability. Riesling, Muscat, Gewürztraminer and Pinot Gris are the only grapes permitted for these styles.

Crémant d'Alsace: quality sparkling wine produced in the traditional way (champagne method). Mostly produced from the Pinot Blanc and Auxerrois grape varieties.

Vintages

95 Variable. Top Riesling and late harvested wines (dessert).
94 Good to very good. Sweet wines superb from top growers.
93 Average for early drinking.
92 Very good.
91 Good to very good for table wines.
90 Superb, especially Riesling and sweet styles.
89 Superb sweet styles. Good table wines.
88 Good to superb, especially Riesling and Pinot Gris.
87 Average. Top growers best.
86 Good. Drink now.
85 Superb. Drink now or keep.
84 Variable.
83 Superb, especially top growers. For keeping.

WHITE WINE

White £6–£8

Domaine Paul Blanck Pinot d'Alsace AC Alsace 95
Foley
One of the best tasted in its style. Very impressive floral and exotic fruit touches. The dry crisp finish makes it ideal with fish or white meats. Enjoy young and chilled.

Hunawihr Pinot Blanc AC Alsace 93   13
Searson
Stony/chalky aroma and slight citrus pithy touch. Good wine for fish.

White £8–£10

Cave de Turckheim Gewürztraminer AC Alsace 95
Brangan
Turkish Delight and mangoes all the way! The wine is fat and weighty but not overblown. The acidity is well balanced with a long succulent finish—superb drinking.

Cave de Turckheim Tokay Pinot Gris Réserve AC Alsace 95
Brangan   14
Lime-tinged with aromas of lemon balm. A fruity style that fills out well on the mid-palate.

Domaine Paul Blanck Gewürtzraminer AC Alsace 95
Foley
Delicate rose-petal aromas mark this as a classic example of its style. More subtle than others with a spicy, crisp finish.

Domaine Paul Blanck Pinot Auxerrois AC Alsace 95   14
Foley
Lovely refreshing drinking. An interesting style with a steely backbone of acidity still allowing the floral tones to emerge.

Domaine Paul Blanck Riesling AC Alsace 95
Foley
A magical combination of ripe grapefruit aromas and flavours
with steely acidity, super weight and texture. A benchmark
style.

Domaine Paul Blanck Sylvaner Vieilles Vignes AC Alsace 95
Foley 14
Fresh and youthful with delicate floral aromas. Well made.

Domaine Paul Blanck Tokay Pinot Gris AC Alsace 95 14
Foley
Green-tinged with delicate ripe pear touches overlain with a
hint of smoke. Clean as a whistle.

Hugel Riesling AC Alsace 91 ☆☆
Grants
Classic mature Riesling full of typical oily aromas and a rich
mid-palate that ends with a bite of lemon acidity. Benchmark
example of just how well Riesling can age.

Kientzheim-Kayserberg Gewürztraminer AC Alsace 94
Febvre
Deep yellow in colour. Extremely balanced and elegant. Has all
the wonderful aromatic qualities of its grape without being
overblown.

Kientzheim-Kayserberg Pinot Gris Réserve AC Alsace 94
Febvre 14
Round and rich with hints of newly baked bread. Long smooth
off-dry finish.

Trimbach Gewürztraminer AC Alsace 92
Gilbeys
Drinking well since last tasted. Bigger on aroma with a
delightful smack of Turkish Delight. Good follow-through on
flavour ending in a long succulent finish.

Trimbach Riesling AC Alsace 94
Gilbeys
This younger vintage is a super example of zesty, lively
Riesling. Note how the elegant fruit flavours battle and win
over the high acidity.

Willm Gewürztraminer AC Alsace 93
Allied Drinks
Exactly what to expect from this style. Turkish Delight and
rose-petal aromas. Shows some bottle development and has an
attractive pungent finish.

Willm Pinot Blanc AC Alsace 94   13
Allied Drinks
Stony fruits with a slightly austere quality typical of the grape
variety. A refreshing drink that holds its crispness right to the
finish.

Willm Riesling AC Alsace 93
Allied Drinks
A very good example of Alsace Riesling, showing plenty of
grapefruit and citrus tones with a characteristic touch of oil on
the long finish.
White £10–£12

Domaine Paul Blanck Muscat d'Alsace AC Alsace 95
Foley
Rich in every sense—aroma, taste and finish. The fruity, slightly
honeyed aromas fan out on the palate with a powerful smooth
texture and long, elegant flavoursome finish.

Gewürztraminer Réserve Personnelle AC Alsace 93
Wine Vault
Delicious perfumed rose-petal nose with a hint of Turkish
Delight. Waxy mouth feel with dense acidity, ending in a fat
opulent finish.

Hugel Gewürztraminer AC Alsace 93 ☆☆
Grants
Pure Turkish Delight! Top class with its distinctive aroma,
unctuous but dry fruit, and medium acidity.

Kientzheim-Kayserberg Kaefferkopf Riesling AC Alsace 92
Febvre ☆
Very classic Riesling with a floral and definite oily tone. It has a
backbone of tingling acidity with a long, tasty finish.
White £12–£15

**Schoenenbourg de Riquewihr Riesling AC Alsace Grand Cru
93** *Mitchell* ☆☆☆
Well-balanced green-tinged Riesling with its obvious varietal
character, rose-petal appeal and long seductive finish.

**Sporen de Riquewihr Gewürztraminer AC Alsace Grand Cru
92** *Mitchell* ☆☆
Elegant obvious floral aromas that fan out in a smooth velvet
palate appeal, finishing in a soft, luscious finish.
White £15–£20

**Domaine Weinbach Riesling Cuvée Ste Catherine AC Alsace
94** *Terroirs* ☆
Star-bright with hints of green-gold. Good citrus aromas with a
characteristic fresh bite of acidity and marked length. Wonderful balance.

RED WINE

Red £8–£10

Domaine Paul Blanck Pinot Noir AC Alsace 95 14
Foley
Ruby pink in colour, with lots of squashed raspberry fruit tones.
Easy-drinking style displaying the light fresh appeal of young
Pinot.

France—Beaujolais

Labelling guide

AC Beaujolais (basic).

Beaujolais Nouveau or Primeur is released each year on the third Thursday in November at only six weeks old.

Beaujolais Villages: wines from blends of 39 specific villages.

Beaujolais Supérieur: wines containing a slightly higher degree of alcohol.

Beaujolais Crus: produced in ten specific villages, namely Brouilly, Chénas, Chiroubles, Côte de Brouilly, Fleurie, Juliénas, Morgon, Moulin-à-Vent, Régnié and Saint Amour.

Some white and rosé wine is produced.

Wine styles and ageing potential

Beaujolais Nouveau or Primeur: drink within six to eight months of the vintage.

Beaujolais Villages: drink within one to three years. The wines are fruity and vibrant. Drink cool.

Beaujolais Crus: from two to eight years depending on the vintage and style. Each Cru is marked with its own particular style.

Vintages (Crus)

95	Superb for keeping.
94	Variable.
93	Good. Can keep.
92	Average to good. Choose Crus carefully.
91	Superb, with good tannic structure.
90	Very good to superb, with lots of fruit.
89	Superb, with deep colour and extract.
88	Superb, one of the best ever. Drink now.

RED WINE

Red £5.25–£6

Pierre Ponnelle AC Beaujolais 94   13
Dunnes Stores
Warm strawberries and raspberries, juicy, soft and supple.
Serve cool.

Red £6–£8

Alexis Lichine **AC Fleurie 94** 12
Greenhills
Easy-drinking fruity style with some strawberry appeal that
carries through on flavour ending in a medium finish.

André Depardon **AC Beaujolais-Villages 95** ☆
Dunnes Stores
Youthful in appearance with lots of banana and strawberry
fruit. A whack of acidity adds liveliness to the smooth fresh
finish.

Barton & Guestier **St Louis AC Beaujolais 95** 13
Dillon
Jellybaby aromas in an easy, fruity, everyday drinking style.

Bouchard Père et Fils **AC Beaujolais-Villages 94** ☆
Dillon
Plummy in colour with very appealing vibrant raspberry fruit
aromas and flavours. A real thirst-quencher with good length of
flavour.

Domaine M. Pelletier **'Les Envaux' AC Juliénas 95** 14
Dunnes Stores
Bright crimson in colour. Fresh zippy fruit in a nicely balanced
style.

Georges Duboeuf **AC Beaujolais 95** ☆
Superquinn
From the uncrowned King of Beaujolais, this is a quaffing wine
full of juicy fruit typical of the best of the AC at this level.

Labouré-Roi **AC Juliénas 95**
Quinnsworth
Brick with orange tinges. Difficult to find words to describe its
leafy undergrowth tones and delicious fruity attack.

***Labouré-Roi* AC Brouilly 95**   **14**
Quinnsworth
Dense concentrated summer fruit, with flavours fanning out
and ending on a delicious note.

***Labouré-Roi* AC Fleurie 95**   ☆ ☆
Quinnsworth
Extremely appealing, with an earthy touch and good kickback
of fruit on the well-structured finish.

***Lionel J. Bruck* AC Brouilly 95**   **13**
Fine Wines
Light crimson in colour, with cherry and jam aromas. A cool
red in a very approachable style that gives more in flavour than
aroma.

***Louis Tête* 'Domaine de Joye' AC Beaujolais-Villages 94**
Allied Drinks   **12**
Ruby red with hints of brick. Sweet fruit attack reminiscent of
strawberries. Silky textured with a medium fruity finish.

***Robert Sarrau* AC Beaujolais 94**   **13**
Taserra
Garnet in colour, with pleasant jammy aromas. Soft attack of
fruit with good acidity kicking in behind. Drinking well now.

Red £8–£10

Château de Raousset AC Morgon 94   ☆
Findlater
Matured for 10 months before release for sale. Big and bold
with great fruit extract, needing time to open up.

Gilles Perroud Château du Basty AC Régnié 95   **14**
Foley
Ruby in colour. Aromas reminiscent of spice, especially white
pepper. Enough of everything—fruit, spice, acidity—to make it
approachable and easy to drink.

Domaine de Montgenas AC Fleurie 95　　　　　☆
Dunnes Stores
So pleasant and supple, with red berry fruit that gives a tasty
mouthful of ripeness persisting into a long finish.

Domaine des Pierres Bleues AC Brouilly 94　　　☆
Searson
Delicate and elegant, with light creamy cherry aromas. Very
balanced wine, with initial fruit flavour cut with pleasant
acidity and supple tannins.

Jaffelin **AC Morgon 94**　　　　　　　　　　　13
Cassidy
Youthful ruby colour with lean, red berry fruit appeal. Well
balanced but still young.

Joseph Drouhin **AC Fleurie 95**　　　　　　　　14
Gilbeys
Smooth and drinkable, with jelly jammy aromas in a soft supple
style. Appealing long finish.

Michel Brugne 'Le Vivier' AC Moulin à Vent 95　　14
Dunnes Stores
Lots of redcurrant fruit supporting a juicy bite of tangy acidity.
Has class and structure.

Mommesin **AC Moulin à Vent 94**　　　　　　　14
Mitchell
Ruby red with lots of red berry fruit appeal in an easy-drinking
style. Medium long finish

Pierre Ponnelle **AC Fleurie 94**　　　　　　　　14
Dunnes Stores
Deep garnet in colour. Gives more on flavour than aroma.
Tight-knit structure with raspberry fruits waiting to emerge
through the mouth-drying tannins.

Wines
from the
Worlds Best Cellars

The proud traditions which emanate from Gilbeys date back to 1857 when Walter and Alfred Gilbey first sought to provide the very finest of wines to the gentry of the last century.

Now in 1996, Gilbeys reputation as an importer of fine wines from around the world is unsurpassed. Gilbeys has a long and proud tradition of delivering a wide variety of premium wines to the Irish consumer.

Come and explore the world of Gilbeys wines:

- Hunters, New Zealand
- Faustino, Spain
- Santa Rita, Chile
- Jaboulet, Rhone
- De Ladoucette, Loire
- Drouhin, Burgundy
- Louis Latour, Burgundy
- Trimbach, Alsace
- Laurent Perrier, Champagne

Robert Sarrau **'Domaine de la Chapelle de Vatre' AC Beau-jolais-Villages 95** *Taserra* **13**
Zippy, fresh, fruity wine with a nice tang of acidity in an easy-drinking style.

Robert Sarrau **'Domaine de la Poyebade' AC Côte de Brouilly 94**
Taserra **14**
Cool summer-drinking red that has the fruit, acidity and tannin to keep one's interest.

Robert Sarrau **Château de Raousset AC Chiroubles 94** **14**
Taserra
Ruby red with hints of raspberry. Well balanced. Fruit shines through and rounds out with a good finish.

Robert Sarrau **Château des Capitans AC Juliénas 95** **13**
Taserra
Savoury flavours in a lively easy-drinking style with enough structure to add interest.

Robert Sarrau **Château Gaillard AC Morgon 94** **14**
Taserra
Wonderful sherbet, jammy aromas which fan out and develop, leaving a creamy tone to the finish.

Simone & Olivier Ravier **'Domaine de la Pierre Bleue' AC Côte de Brouilly 95** *Foley* **13**
A lively well-made wine with upfront fruity appeal and a smack of smoky tones on the finish.
Red £10–£12

Bouchard Père et Fils **AC Fleurie 95** **14**
Dillon
Attractive red berry fruit appeal with a hint of coffee and cream. Supple texture and silky finish with a lively bite of acidity.

Domaine des Pillets **AC Morgon 92** **14**
Moore's Wines
Deep ruby, showing signs of maturity. Has the immediate

attack of ripe fruits associated with Gamay. Smooth and elegant with a long, concentrated finish.

Louis Jadot 'Domaine de Poncereau' AC Fleurie 95   14
Grants
Deep purple-cerise colour with fruit-cake aromas topped with a creamy touch. Good balance of acidity and supple tannins add structure.

Louis Tête AC Moulin à Vent 93   13
Allied Drinks
Fruit and chocolate galore. Drinking well now. Good length.

Louis Tête AC Fleurie 95   13
Allied Drinks
Deep purple in colour with lots of jammy fruit. Decent mouthfilling fruit flavours with just a hint of tannin.

Olivier Ravier La Madone AC Fleurie 95   14
Foley
Immediate appeal in a juicy fruity style, with a vibrant persistent finish.

Robert Sarrau 'Grand Pré' AC Fleurie 95   14
Taserra
Very young, but promises to be excellent, with jammy fruits, crisp acidity and smooth tannins.

Robert Sarrau Château de St Amour AC St Amour 95   13
Taserra
Deep ruby with smoky aromas. Acidity cuts through the fruit with obvious but supple tannins.

Robert Sarrau Domaine de la Tour du Bief AC Moulin à Vent 94
Taserra   14
Harmonious wine with baked fruits ending in a twist of spice. Good example of its style, if a little expensive.

France—Bordeaux

Main wine regions

Médoc (red): Médoc and Haut-Médoc (includes St Estèphe,
   Pauillac, St Julien, Listrac, Moulis, Margaux)
Graves, (Pessac-Léognan) (red and dry white)
Sauternes, (Barsac) (sweet white)
Blaye (red)
Bourg (red and white)
Pomerol, (Lalande de Pomerol) (red)
St Émilion (red)
Entre-Deux-Mers (dry white)
Première Côtes de Bordeaux (white and red)
Fronsac (red)
Côtes de Francs (red and white)
Côtes de Castillon (red)

Principal grape varieties

White	Red
Sauvignon Blanc	Cabernet Sauvignon
Sémillon	Merlot
Muscadelle	Cabernet Franc
	Malbec
	Petit Verdot

Labelling guide

Bordeaux produces only AC wines. The basic appellation of AC
Bordeaux covers the whole area and applies to red and white
wines. Bordeaux Supérieur indicates a wine with a slightly higher
degree of alcohol and can be white, rosé or red. Bordeaux Clairet
is a style that falls between red and rosé. Sixty-three wines were
classified in the Médoc classification of 1855 and are divided as
described below.

First Growths: Château Latour, Château Lafite, Château
Margaux, Château Haut-Brion (Pessac-Léognan) and Château
Mouton Rothschild.

The rest of these great growths were divided into Second, Third,
Fourth and Fifth growths and are known collectively as Crus
Classés. At this quality vintage variation takes on special
importance. Sauternes was also classified in 1855 with Château

d'Yquem classified as the only Grand Premier Cru. Eleven wines were classified as Premier Crus and fourteen Deuxième Crus.

Other quality categories include the Cru Bourgeois wines of the Médoc. Production, which is centred on red, accounts for over 40% of the total output. St Émilion, a classification for red wines, is revised every ten years. Merlot dominates production. Two châteaux, Ausone and Cheval Blanc, are Class A Premier Grand Cru Classé. There are nine Class B Premier Grand Cru Classé and sixty-three Grand Cru Classé. St Émilion is the basic appellation covering the whole area and may include one of six outer areas, for example Montagne, St Georges, Puisseguin or Lussac St Émilion.

Wine styles

Basic generic styles, i.e. Bordeaux blanc or rouge, are at their best from one to three years. Petit châteaux rarely improve after five years from the date of vintage.

Top Cru Bourgeois and classed growths: Depending on the vintage, these wines require time to mature. In top vintages they are approachable at about eight years and can peak in drinkability at about fifteen to twenty. In lighter vintages they drink at between five and twelve years.

Sweet wines: lesser-known appellations are at their best drunk young unless affected by noble rot. Top quality can be approached at five years and can keep, depending on vintage, for up to thirty years.

Vintages

Red

95   Good to classic. Best since 90.
94   Good to very good, especially Pomerol. Graves—good.
93   Choose carefully. Average, early drinking.
92   Choose carefully, patchy, early drinking.
91   Average to poor. Dilute, choose carefully.
90   Classic, especially top Châteaux. Best are well structured.
89   Classic, especially top Châteaux. Rich and structured.
88   Very classic, rich, concentrated and long lived.
87   Average. Early drinking.
86   Very classic and intense especially Médoc (Cabernet-dominated) and St Émilion.
85   Classic, consistent quality. Enjoy now or keep.

84 Average. Choose carefully. Drink now.
83 Very classic, good fruit and tannic structure, especially Margaux.
82 Rich opulent vintage. Drink now or keep.
81 Good, a light vintage. Drink now.
80 Average, a light vintage. Drink now.

Top older vintages: 79 (drink now) 78 (drink now or keep) 75 (drink now or keep for another few years) 71 (drink now) 70 (top Châteaux will continue to mature, lesser drink now) 66 (peaking in quality drink now) 61 (top Châteaux still superb).

White

White Bordeaux produced mainly from Sauvignon Blanc such as Bordeaux Blanc and Bordeaux Blanc Supérieur and Entre-Deux-Mers should be drunk while young and fresh, so look for the youngest vintage. More full-bodied whites from Graves/Pessac-Léognan can age from 3 to 10 years. Top quality wines depending on vintage variation, can age for up to 20 years.

Sauternes

95 Promising classic vintage.
94 Average.
93 Poor.
92 Poor.
91 Poor.
90 Excellent. Best since 1893.
89 Classic, very rich.
88 Classic, rich and concentrated.
87 Light vintage.
86 Classic, intense.
85 Average to good.
84 Wet year, poor to average.
83 Classic, powerful wines.

WHITE WINE

White £4.50–£5.25

Calvet Sauvignon AC Bordeaux 94   13
Grants
Water-pale. Better on flavour than aroma, with a slight limey
sorbet touch and good crisp fresh finish.

Château Lézardière AC Entre-Deux-Mers 95   ☆
Quinnsworth
An interesting style with pleasant herbaceous aromas and
flavours of stony fruit. Fresh, whistle-clean finish.

White £5.25–£6

Château Haut Pougnan AC Entre-Deux-Mers 95   14
McCabes
'Zesty' is the word that best describes this water-pale modern
style. Perfect fish wine.

Château la Rocheraie AC Entre-Deux-Mers 95   14
Dunnes Stores
Definite Sauvignon character with zesty fresh apple attack and
good clean finish.

Château le Bouscat AC Bordeaux 95   ☆
Dunnes Stores
A super example of just how good well-made Bordeaux Blanc
can be. Ripe, pungent and earthy, with a very lively crisp finish.

Château Plessis AC Entre-Deux-Mers 95   13
Quinnsworth
Better on taste than aroma. An easy-drinking style that wins on
the clean, lively finish.

White £6–£8

Barton & Guestier AC Graves 95   13
Dillon
Water-pale with damp earth aromas. Better on flavour than
nose, with more fruit appeal and medium long finish. Good
with fish.

Barton & Guestier Fondation 1725 AC Bordeaux 95   14
Dillon
In this appealing vintage nettles give way to a fruity taste.

Calvet Réserve AC Bordeaux 94   14
Grants
Subtle grassy pungency with fruit aromas that fan out on the
palate and end in a delicate elegant finish.

Chai de Bordes-Quancard AC Bordeaux 94   ☆
Brangan
Delicious creamy-smooth gooseberry appeal that carries
through on flavour. The finish is clean and fresh with a long
fruity touch.

Château Bertinerie AC Premières Côtes de Blaye 95   ☆
Wines Direct
Ripe red apple flavours define the taste of this pale gold wine.
Ageing on lees for three months adds complexity.

Château d'Archambeau AC Graves 92   ☆
Wines Direct
Melon-yellow in colour. Six months' ageing in oak adds creamy
tones to the greengage fruit. Fresh, full-flavoured finish.

Château de Gravaillas AC Graves 92   13
TDL
Bone dry with a strong citrus fruit influence. Reasonable length
of flavour on the finish.

Château La Freynelle AC Bordeaux 95   14
Searson
Zippy acidity backed up with floral hints and good texture and
weight of flavour.

Château Thieuley AC Bordeaux 94   13
TDL
Very balanced with alcohol, acidity and fruit all harmonised.

Long elegant finish with a hint of gooseberry.

Château Tour de Mirambeau AC Bordeaux 95 ☆
Wines Direct
Lime green in colour. Flavours of green fruits with lively
acidity and a delicious lingering finish.

Château Turcaud AC Entre-Deux-Mers 94 13
Wines Direct
Deep yellow. Delivers more on flavour than aroma, with
gooseberry fruit and balancing acidity. Five months' lees ageing
adds a touch of creaminess.

Cuvée Clemence AC Entre-Deux-Mers 94 14
Brangan
Green-tinged with hints of celery on aroma. An individual style
showing better on the palate, with a hint of spice that maturation in oak imports. All in all, a teasing wine.

Gamage AC Entre-Deux-Mers 95 14
Wine Barrel
Lots of lemon and lime appeal with a smack of greengage fruit.
Upfront, lively and whistle-clean on the finish.

Les Douelles AC Bordeaux 94 12
Allied Drinks
Light and pleasant to drink, with fresh acidity and a hint of
nettles on aroma.

Malesan Bordeaux Blanc Sec AC Bordeaux 94 12
Taserra
Closed on aroma, but better on the palate. Lemon-like acidity
adds freshness to the finish.

Michel Lynch AC Bordeaux 95 14
Barry & Fitzwilliam
This vintage has a pleasant lemon tang, crisp acidity and
mouthfilling flavours.

Mouton Cadet AC Bordeaux 94 14
Findlater
Produced from the classic mix of Sémillon, Sauvignon Blanc
and Muscadelle, the 94 vintage is well balanced with touches of
apple fruit and a good bite of acidity.

White £8–£10

Château de Sours AC Bordeaux 94
Mitchell
Extremely appealing, with its deep yellow colour and big
combination of spicy oak and citrus tangy appeal. Fruit
flavours of peach are apparent on the palate—a big Bordeaux
with extra-long finish.

Château Haut-Nochet AC Pessac-Léognan 93
Dalton
Yellow-tinged with seductive creamy tones. Good use of oak
from a top winemaker (Lucien Lurton) ensures a classic elegant
style.

Château Thieuley Cuvée Francis Courselle AC Bordeaux 94
Wines Direct ☆
Attractive vanilla aromas and flavours from fermentation in
oak add huge appeal to the luscious greengage fruit. Well
balanced with an abundance of toastiness on the long finish.

White £10–£12

Château Fort de Roquetaillade AC Graves 94 13
Brangan
Pleasant nuances of butterscotch with a good attack of ripe fruit
character. Easy to drink with a very pleasant long finish.

RED WINE

Red under £4.50

Château Les Murailles AC Bordeaux 94 14
Fine Wines
Interesting ripe berry and aniseed aromas. Good balanced
acidity and a touch of tannin add structure.

Red £4.50–£5.25

Château Pied d'Argent AC Bordeaux 93   13
Dunnes Stores
Cinnamon and spice aromas with stalky fruit behind. Offers a
touch of claret at a good price.

Dulong AC Médoc 95   13
Quinnsworth
Young in style and still hiding its fruit. However, the balancing
bite of tannin and acidity adds interest to its easy-drinking
appeal.

Red £5.25–£6

Château Fayau AC Bordeaux 94   13
Remy
Easy-drinking style with good attack of fruit backed up with
lively acidity. Medium long finish.

Château Grand Bourgeois AC Bordeaux 94   13
Quinnsworth
Pleasant vanilla tones soften the stalky fruit. Appealing style,
good with food.

Château Haut Bignon AC Bordeaux 93   13
Greenhills
The 93 has more ripe fruit than the 92 tasted last year. Drink
young.

Château L'Heyrisson AC Bordeaux 94   13
Dunnes Stores
Bright crimson in colour, with good acid/tannin balance and
attractive earthy fruit appeal.

Château la Garenne AC Bordeaux 94   12
Dunnes Stores
Crimson in colour, with red jelly aromas. Has an austere finish.
Needs food.

Château le Bouscat AC Bordeaux 94   14
Dunnes Stores
Closed on aroma, the fruit emerges on flavour. Supple tannins,
high acidity and tight-knit fruit appeal add up to a typical
example of this AC.

Château Mayne-Cabanot AC Bordeaux 94   14
Dunnes Stores
Has the herb-like tones associated with this style. The tannins
are supple and the finish easy and medium long.

Château Picon AC Bordeaux Supérieur 94   13
Quinnsworth
Reasonable fruity aromas and flavours that fan out on the
palate. Easy to drink and easy to enjoy.

Château Taris AC Bordeaux 94   13
Dunnes Stores
Tea leaf aromas! Typical herbaceous Bordeaux style with a
medium long finish.

Domaine du Moulin de Mendoce AC Côtes de Bourg 94
Quinnsworth   ☆
This chewy wine, made principally from Merlot, has lots of
balance and a hint of liquorice.

Yvecourt AC Bordeaux 95   13
Superquinn
Ruby red in colour, with closed aromas denoting its youth. The
earthy tone is appealing. Tannins still mask the fruit—needs a
little time for more fruit to emerge.
Red £6–£8

Alexis Lichine AC St Émilion 94   14
Greenhills
Ripe in style, with brambly fruit appeal and a slightly austere
finish.

Baron Philippe de Rothschild Mouton Cadet AC Bordeaux 92

Findlater ☆

Shows what top-class winemaking can produce in a poor
vintage. Classic in character, with tobacco and liquorice tones.

Barton & Guestier Fondation 1725 AC Bordeaux 93   13

Dillon

Always dependable. Pleasant liquorice touches which convert
to a typical stalky fruit tone on the palate.

Calvet Réserve AC Bordeaux 94   14

Grants

Crimson in colour, with distinctive stalky fruit. A wine that
works better with food than on its own. The 94 vintage has
more fruit than the 93.

Chai de Bordes-Quancard AC Bordeaux 93   14

Brangan

This wine has developed well since last tasted. It delivers much
more on flavour, with gripping tannins and a pleasant herbaceous bite. Enjoy with food.

Château Bellevue [Cru Bourgeois] AC Médoc 94   ☆

Quinnsworth

At the price, a top example of the 94 vintage. Well-structured,
with charred toasty appeal masking the tight-knit fruit.

Château de Monrecueil AC Côtes de Castillon 94   ☆

Quinnsworth

From east of St Émilion, this is a very balanced, well-structured
wine with rich subtle red berry aromas, mouth-watering
tannins and a pleasant, slightly bittersweet finish.

Château de Rabouchet AC Bordeaux 94   14

Jenkinson Wines

Deep garnet in colour. Attractive leafy blackcurrant aromas
overlain with hints of vanilla.

Château de Tabuteau AC Lussac St Émilion 94   14
Foley
Ruby red in colour. Tarry woodland aromas are followed by
mouth-watering tannins. Still young, with fruit hidden behind.
An austere style, good of its type and needing food.

Château Haut Maco AC Côtes de Bourg 93
Wines Direct
Well structured, with pepper aromas overlain with hints of
liquorice. Drinking well now.

Château Haut Pougnan AC Bordeaux Supérieur 94
McCabes
Stalky in tone, but without the leanness associated with a lot of
wines of this style. Obvious tannic structure and enough fruit to
hold up the flavour to the last drop.

Château Holden AC Haut-Médoc 93   14
Quinnsworth
Since last tasted the wine has developed interesting smoky/
bramble fruit appeal. A classic style, easy to drink, yet well
structured.

Château la Bigarette AC Bordeaux Supérieur 94
Fitzgerald
Crimson with pleasant ripe berry aromas overlain with touches
of cedar. A nicely balanced claret style with fruit, acidity and
tannin combining well to give good structure.

Château La Croix de Millorit AC Côtes de Bourg 93
Quinnsworth
Classic cedar and pencil shavings aromas. Much more stylish
than many Bordeaux of the same vintage. A good buy and
perfect with roast meats.

Château Lataste AC Bordeaux Supérieur 94   14
Taserra
Leafy and brambly with good fruit appeal. Finishes on a high

note of tannin and acidity which at present masks the fruit.

Château Le Boscq [Cru Bourgeois] AC Médoc 93   14
Quinnsworth
Since tasted last year the slight astringent finish has softened,
giving a long fruity tone with a touch of earthiness.

Château Méaume AC Bordeaux Supérieur 93   13
Findlater
A lean style of claret with good balance and reasonable length
of fruit. Good food wine.

Château Pontus AC Fronsac 93   ☆
TDL
Offers great drinking at a decent price. Classic in style, with
developed aromas of ripe plummy fruits.

Château Rimbaud AC St Émilion 94
Quinnsworth
Very deep, almost opaque in colour. Top-quality St Émilion at
the price, with its smoky herbaceous touch followed by
plummy fruits.

Château Tanesse AC Premières Côtes de Bordeaux 92   14
United Beverages
92 is an unreliable vintage, but this is a very good wine with
classic cedar and tar tones backed up with plummy flavours,
balanced acidity and supple tannins. Enjoy now.

Château Thieuley AC Bordeaux 94   14
TDL
Deep ruby in colour. Packed tight with red berry fruits overlain
with a hint of spice. Merlot dominates, giving a soft supple
touch.

Château Tour de Mirambeau AC Bordeaux 93   13
Wines Direct
Good mix of aromas, from green pepper to stalky blackberry

MOËT & CHANDON

Fondé en 1743

Nederburg

Barton & Guestier
La passion du vin depuis 1725

Depuis 1731
BOUCHARD PÈRE & FILS

I.L. RUFFINO

CONTI SERRISTORI

BLUE NUN®

PAUL MASSON
SINCE 1852

AD VINUM
BOLLA

SANDEMAN
EST 1790

MATEUS®
PRODUCED AND BOTTLED IN PORTUGAL

FOUNDED IN 1850
CARMEN

FONTANA CANDIDA

MONTECILLO

EDWARD DILLON
& COMPANY LIMITED

Fine wines from Edward Dillon.

fruit. Fruit emerges on the palate, but tannin leaves a slightly
bitter taste. Still young, but a good example of this AC.

Club des Sommeliers AC St Émilion 95 13
Superquinn
Has enough fruit and structure to make it a good partner with
food.

Cordier AC Bordeaux nv 14
United Beverages
Garnet in colour, with delightful liquorice tones overlain with
chocolate. Stalky in flavour.

La Cour Pavillon AC Bordeaux nv 13
Gilbeys
Ruby red. The slight red and green pepper tone of this Cabernet
Sauvignon is very attractive. It delivers on taste in an easy-
drinking but well-made style.

Les Douelles AC Bordeaux 93 13
Allied Drinks
Deep crimson in colour. Good stalky leafy fruit tones in a
medium-bodied style. Good generic style of claret.

Malesan AC Bordeaux 94 13
Taserra
Offers hints of classic claret, with brambly fruit overlain with
hints of green pepper. Still young.

Michel Lynch AC Bordeaux 94 ☆
Barry & Fitzwilliam
Ruby red in colour, the 94 vintage has good coffee, cream and
spicy aromas. Easy drinking with a pleasant firm finish. Good
food wine.
Red £8–£10

Barton & Guestier AC St Émilion 94 13
Dillon
Still young and slightly austere in style, with a deep crimson
colour and good structure.

Château Canada AC Bordeaux Supérieur 91
Ecock
A super example of this appellation, with woodland and
plummy fruit aromas. Lives up to its promise on flavour. One
of the better vintages tasted.

Château Canon-Moueix AC Canon Fronsac 92   14
Searson
Well structured with lots of appealing cassis fruit. Drinking
well now.

Château Côte Montpezat AC Côtes de Castillon 93 ☆☆
Quinnsworth
This AC shows better in the 93 vintage than many generic
Bordeaux. Enjoy its savoury, meaty aromas. Drying tannins
support the savoury aspect and all combine to finish on a high
note of classic structure.

Château Dillon Cru Bourgeois AC Haut-Médoc 93
Quinnsworth
Another example of how an extra year in bottle can help
develop a wine. Since tasted last year, this 93 has smoothed out
its herbaceous tone, leaving a harmonious style big on fruit and
flavour.

Château du Taillan [Cru Bourgeois] AC Haut-Médoc 92
Fitzgerald   13
Good stalky Cabernet wine with brambly fruit flavours. Not
bad for a 92 vintage.

Château Faizeau AC Montagne St Émilion 92   14
Wines Direct
A good example of this AC, with its deep garnet colour and
woodland aromas. Vinification in oak adds complexity and
interest.

Château Grand Monteil AC Bordeaux Supérieur 93   14
Wine Vault
Pleasant plummy aromas expand on flavour, with an interest-

ing stalky bite to the finish.

Château Haut-Nouchet AC Pessac-Léognan 93   14
Dalton
Has good structure for the vintage with elegant, light leafy and
cassis touches in a classic style. Top class.

Château La Dame Blanche Cru Bourgeois AC Haut-Médoc 94
Greenhills   14
Garnet in colour, with typical stalky aromas and flavours. Still
young, the wine has good structure.

Château Lagrange AC Lussac St Émilion 93   ☆
Taserra
A good example of the quality that can be achieved in the
surrounding satellite towns of St Émilion. The wine exhibits
bottle development, adding interesting cedar and liquorice
tones to the woodland fruits.

Château Landon Cru Bourgeois AC Médoc 94   ☆
Quinnsworth
A chewy, chunky style, with dense colour and interesting
aromas of undergrowth finishing in a well-rounded style of
immense appeal.

Château le Logis de Sipian [Cru Bourgeois] AC Médoc 93
Taserra   12
Brick-toned with dusty, stalky red fruit aromas. Riper fruit
opens up on the palate with a bite of acidity on the finish.
Drinking well now.

Château le Maine Martin AC Bordeaux Supérieur 91   14
Hugan
There aren't too many 91s worth drinking, but this is definitely
one of them! It has assumed mature aromas of tar and cedar
and has a sturdy finish.

Château Loudenne Cru Bourgeois AC Médoc 93
Gilbeys
A good example of the vintage, with chocolate and mint tones.
A solid opulent wine with good balance and potential.

Château Lousteauneuf Cru Bourgeois AC Médoc 94
Dunnes Stores
Oak-aged with a deep Ribena colour and tomato stalk aromas.
Still very young. A robust tannic style with fruit just beginning
to emerge. Classic.

Château Moulin Haut Villars AC Fronsac 93 14
Quinnsworth
Deep crimson in colour. Classic Bordeaux in aroma, with a
mineral backbone, good tannic structure and fruit. A good
choice for 93.

Château Patache d'Aux Cru Bourgeois AC Médoc 93
Quinnsworth
This has developed extremely well since tasted last year. The
earthy style is still apparent, but with extra bottle age the fruit
has really emerged. Enjoy its classic structure and good length.

Château Pichon AC Lussac St Émilion 93 14
Taserra
Classic cigar and cedar aromas have developed with the extra
year's maturation in bottle since last tasted. Drink now, as the
good attack of fruit dies off a little too quickly.

Château St Christophe Cru Bourgeois AC Médoc 94 14
Dunnes Stores
A stalky, brambly wine overlain with a hint of smoke. Delivers
on flavour, with a long, rich, tannic finish.

Red £10–£12

Château Chatain AC Lalande de Pomerol 92 14
Cassidy
Good example from the unreliable 92 vintage. Tomato stalk
aromas give way to savoury flavours on the palate.

Château des Annereaux AC Lalande de Pomerol 90
Wines Direct
Dense in colour, with a tawny hint indicating maturity. The
bouquet is complex, with tar, liquorice and cedar touches. On
the palate flavours mingle and jostle for supremacy. Drinking
well now.

Château du Paradis AC St Émilion Grand Cru 89 14
Fitzgerald
Tawny with brick tones at the edge. A real classic with very
definite liquorice and tobacco aromas. Showing its age, so enjoy
it now.

Château Guadet-Plaissance AC Montagne St Émilion 90

Brangan
A true classic. Tawny-brick in colour, with very typical
mushroom woodland aromas. The fruit has powerful impact
with a complex tight-knit structure.

Château La Vieille Cure AC Fronsac 93
Quinnsworth
The old-fashioned label seems to suit this inky purple, robust,
earthy wine that has lots of fruit hidden behind the chewy
tannins. A mineral backbone gives a sturdy finish.

Château Le Bonnat AC Graves 94
Quinnsworth
The 94 vintage shows more fruit appeal than the 93 tasted last
year. Beware of the tannins, which still dominate the fruit.
Needs more bottle age, but is a top example of its appellation.
Red £12–£15

Bernard Taillan AC St Julien nv 14
Bacchus
Enjoy the brambly cassis fruit character of this claret, with its
crimson colour, good fruit appeal and long finish.

Bernard Taillan AC Margaux nv ☆
Bacchus
This generic Margaux has a delicate bouquet of secondary

aromas such as tobacco and spice. An interesting wine with good structure and long clean finish.

Château Belles Graves AC Lalande de Pomerol 93   14
Wine Vault
Garnet in colour, with marvellous undergrowth and woodland appeal. At its best now.

Château de Cantin AC St Émilion Grand Cru 89   ☆
Parsons
Brick in colour. Big, bold and delicious and a good example of the opulent ripe 89 vintage. Has developed well since tasted in 1995. Raw mushroom aromas give way to concentrated cherry liqueur flavours. Delicious drinking.

Château de France AC Pessac-Léognan 90   ☆
Jenkinson Wines
A big mouthful of opulent fruit flavours with lots of chocolate and hints of liquorice adding even more appeal. Super wine from a super vintage. Rich and satisfying.

Château de Lamarque Cru Bourgeois AC Haut-Médoc 91
Mitchell   ☆☆
Deep blood-red in colour, with upfront vegetal aromas combining with strawberry fruit. Rich and complex on the palate with flavours fanning out. Tannins are harmonious. Top example of a poor vintage.

Château Haut-Bages Libéral AC Pauillac Grand Cru Classé 91
Searson   ☆
Deep purple in colour, with a super cassis and mint aroma. The opulent attack of fruit expands and is reinforced by rich tannic structure. A good example in a poor vintage.

Château Laroque AC St Émilion Grand Cru 88
Greenhills
A multi-layered wine typical of its style, with rich fruit-cake aromas. With bottle age it has assumed a bouquet. This is

classic St Émilion which should be enjoyed now.

Château Panet AC St Émilion Grand Cru 90 ☆☆☆
Searson
Showing some hint of age, with secondary aromas of woodland
and mushroom. The big attack of flavour that continues right
through to the end makes it a top example of its AC.

Château Roc de Cambes AC Côtes de Bourg 93 ☆
Wines Direct
A super example of this AC. Packed with intense aromas of
chocolate and liquorice, the wine is big and bold, yet harmonious. Very classic.

Château Teyssier AC St Émilion Grand Cru 93 14
Findlater
Garnet with a delightful ripe red and green pepper aroma.
Brambly fruit emerges on the palate with supple tannin
supporting the fruit all the way, ending in a classic touch.

Château Tour du Haut-Moulin [Cru Bourgeois] AC Haut-Médoc 90 *Wines Direct* ☆
Extremely appealing, with the wonderful fruit-cake aromas and
flavours of Merlot supported by the cassis of Cabernet
Sauvignon. Maturation in oak adds complexity. Very attractive
style.

Lady Langoa AC St Julien 93 14
Brangan
Deep crimson, with cinnamon and nutmeg combining with
delicious ripe fruit tones. Still young, as fruit has not had time
to emerge through the supple tannins.

Ségla AC Margaux 91 ☆
Mitchell
An assertive classic style with lots of depth. White pepper and
forest undergrowth on aroma. More fruit on the palate, with
integrated tannins and good concentrated finish.

Red £15–£20

Château la Croix St Vincent AC Pomerol 94

Brangan

Crimson in colour. Closed on aroma, but much more open in flavour. A nice chewy chunky style with plenty of fruit, good yet supple tannins and a long finish.

Château Rocher Bellevue Figeac AC St Émilion Grand Cru 93

United Beverages

Deep ruby, with smoky tones and aromas of fruit-cake mix. Immediate stalky attack which softens out in the centre and knits beautifully with the tannin and acidity. Something special. Super flavour and aromas. Still young.

Connétable du Château Talbot AC St Julien 89

United Beverages

Has it all: woodland aromas with a powerful succulent attack of ripe red berry fruits and definite hints of dark chocolate at the end. Deliciously rich and concentrated. Enjoy now.

Red £20–£30

Château Bourgneuf AC Pomerol 90

Febvre

Deep cassis in colour and aroma. Very complex concentrated wine, with aromas of coffee, cream and cedar that go on and on. Ripe and rich in flavour, with assertive tannins kicking back on the long classic finish.

Château Lascombes Grand Cru Classé AC Margaux 88

Greenhills

Showing a little more brick in colour since last tasted. The wine continues to develop in bottle. Spice is emerging on aroma with rich cassis flavours breaking through. Still smooth and silky, with a satisfying finish.

Château Tertre Roteboeuf AC St Émilion Grand Cru 93

Wines Direct ☆☆☆

A whirlpool of richness, with aromas of spice, vanilla and stony red fruits from 80% Merlot and 20% Cabernet Franc. Shows great class, with excellent structure and length of flavour.

Red £30–£50

Château Clarke [Cru Bourgeois] Listrac-Médoc AC Médoc
Listrac 90   *Brangan*   ☆☆
Deep crimson in colour with a bouquet of spice, liquorice and
cedar. Acidity dominates fruit but the classic structure is
obvious as the wine develops and expands in flavour.

Château Léoville-Barton [2ème Cru Classé] AC St Julien 83
Brangan   ☆☆☆
Garnet with a tawny edge showing maturity. Woodland aromas
with liquorice tones coming through on flavour. Rich and
concentrated, with harmonious tannins and a long spicy
elegant finish. A wine you'll still taste long after the last
swallow!

ROSÉ WINE

Rosé £6–£8

Chai de Bordes-Quancard AC Bordeaux Rosé 95   14
Brangan
Pale salmon in colour. Very pleasant in both aroma and flavour.
Hints of raspberry are supported by zesty acidity. Perfect
summer drinking.

Château Thieuley AC Bordeaux Clairet 95   ☆
Wines Direct
Maceration on skins for a few hours adds extra colour and
flavour to this top-class rosé. Brambly fruit with vibrant acidity
end in a long dry finish.

Rosé £8–£10

Château de Sours AC Bordeaux Rosé 95   ☆☆
Mitchell
A wonderful example of its style. Enjoy its raspberry red
colour, fresh red berry fruit appeal, dry finish and tangy
acidity.

France—Burgundy

Main wine regions

Chablis, Côte de Nuits, Côte de Beaune (the two côtes are collectively known as the Côte d'Or), Côte Chalonnaise, Mâconnais.

Principal grape varieties

White	Red
Chardonnay	Pinot Noir
Aligoté	Gamay
Pinot Beurot (Pinot Gris)	
Pinot Blanc	

Labelling guide

The quality status in ascending order is:

Basic appellations: Bourgogne Rouge, Bourgogne Blanc, Bourgogne Aligoté.

District appellations: for example Beaujolais, Côte de Beaune, Côte de Nuits and Chablis.

Communal appellations: for example Meursault or Pommard.

Premier Cru indicates a wine bearing a commune name but followed by the name of a highly rated vineyard within the commune, for example Chambolle-Musigny Les Amoureuses, Pommard Les Epenots, Gevrey-Chambertin Les Gémeaux.

Grand Cru is the highest-quality Burgundian wine. Here the vineyard or plot of land itself is classified, for example Le Chambertin, Le Montrachet, Le Corton, Le Musigny. The majority of Grand Cru reds are located in the Côte de Nuits and the majority of whites in the Côte de Beaune.

Hospice de Beaune: established in the town of the same name in 1443 to take care of the aged, infirm and poor of Beaune. The Hospice owns over 55 hectares of Premier and Grand Cru Beaune vineyards. Each year, on the third Sunday in November, these wines are sold by auction and usually set the price for other Burgundian wines of the year.

Négociant or négociant-éleveur: négociant houses in Burgundy have existed for hundreds of years. They handle much of the wine trade, buying in wine and grapes from growers and maturing, bottling and marketing it. Many also own vineyards.

Wine styles

Chablis: white wines. Basic Chablis should be drunk young and fresh. There are seventeen Premier Cru vineyards, including Fourchaume, Montmains, Vaillons and Montée de Tonnerre. These wines can be enjoyed from one to five years. Chablis Grands Crus are the most complex, with an ability to age, and can be drunk from two to ten years. Worth remembering, there are only seven—Blanchots, Bougros, Les Clos, Grenouilles, Preuses, Valmur and Vaudésir.

Côte de Nuits: the Pinot Noir produces its bigger styles here. Can be drunk young or, depending on vintage, can age up to ten or fifteen years. Mainly red wines are produced with some white. Commune red wine appellations include Fixin, Gevrey-Chambertin, Morey-St-Denis, Chambolle-Musigny, Vougeot, Flagey-Echézeaux, Vosne-Romanée and Nuits-St-Georges.

Côte de Beaune: the best white wines of Burgundy come from this southern location of the Côte d'Or, and top-quality reds are also produced. Vintage variation does matter. The best whites can be drunk from three years up to ten, but are usually at their best at about five to eight years. Commune appellations include Savigny-lès-Beaune, Pernand-Vergelesses, Ladoix-Serrigny, Aloxe-Corton, Chorey-lès-Beaune, Pommard, Volnay, Monthélie, Meursault, Puligny-Montrachet, Chassagne-Montrachet, Auxey-Duresses, St Romain, St Aubin and Santenay.

Côte Chalonnaise: appellations include Givry, Mercurey (red wine dominates), Rully (attractive red and white) and Montagny (white). At their best from two to four years.

Maconnais: most white wine production centres on Chardonnay without oak influence. Fruity easy-drinking reds are produced from the Gamay of Beaujolais fame. Wines are meant for early consumption. Appellations include Mâcon, Mâcon-Villages (43 can affix their name, for example Viré, Lugny and Vinzelles), Macôn Supérieur and St Véran. The most famous white wine of the region is Pouilly-Fuissé.

Vintages

The golden rule is that most red Burgundy is drunk younger than Bordeaux. Lighter communal wines from southern Burgundy drink earlier than their northern cousins.

Red

95 Promises to be very good to good.
94 Light and fruity.
93 Good to very good, especially from top domaines.
92 Light. Choose top domaines for keeping.
91 Uneven quality.
90 Classic and great.
89 Superb. Fruity and balanced.
88 Superb. Rich and tannic.
87 Choose carefully. Some ready for drinking now.
86 Variable to good. Aromatic. Drink now.
85 Superb. Concentrated wines.
84 Poor. Thin and dilute.
83 Very good but inconsistent. Choose carefully.
82 Good but drink up.

White

95 Promises to be very good to superb.
94 Variable. Choose carefully.
93 Average to good.
92 Very good. Balanced and elegant.
91 Good.
90 Very good to superb, especially top quality.
89 Superb. Rich and opulent.
88 Very good, concentrated.
87 Good to average. Drink up.
86 Superb. Drink soon.
85 Superb. Drink now except for top domaines.

WHITE WINE

White £5.25–£6

***Charles Viénot* Sauvignon de St Bris Réserve VDQS nv**   **14**
Superquinn
Pale white-gold in colour. Very crisp and fresh in style, with a
lively bite of green fruits on the finish.

***Pierre Ponnelle* Chardonnay AC Bourgogne 94**   **13**
Dunnes Stores
Stony fruit appeal with good weight and texture on the palate.
Crisp clean finish.

White £6–£8

Bouchard Père et Fils AC Mâcon-Villages 94   14
Dillon
Take the oak away from Chardonnay and this is the result—
stony fruit with a good clean finish for drinking young. Good
weight and texture.

Charles Viénot AC Rully 93   14
Superquinn
Developing well in bottle since last tasted, the wine has
assumed a nice biscuit/ashy aroma. Delivers more on flavour,
with good balancing acidity and length.

Charles Viénot AC Pouilly-Vinzelles 92   14
Superquinn
A better vintage for white Burgundy than for red this Chardonnay offers an interesting alternative to Pouilly-Fuissé. Slightly
earthy in character, it has a lingering clean finish. Drink now.

Labouré-Roi AC Rully 94   14
Quinnsworth
Yellow-gold in colour. A modern international whistle-clean
style that is hard to fault. Delivers more on flavour than aroma.

Labouré-Roi AC Montagny 94   13
Quinnsworth
Gold in colour, with pleasant hints of pineapple fruit. Waxy
texture with medium acidity on the finish.

Labouré-Roi AC Mâcon-Villages Blanc 95   13
Quinnsworth
Chalky aromas give way to a hint of stony fruit such as apricot.
High acidity masks the fruit, but the wine has a reasonable
finish.

Labouré-Roi Chardonnay AC Bourgogne 95   13
Quinnsworth
The 95 vintage is livelier than the 94, with the same easy-

drinking appeal but in this case with more pronounced crisp green fruit.

Laroche AC Mâcon-Villages 94   12
Allied Drinks
Delicate floral and peach aromas carry through on flavour, but finish short.

Lionel Bruck Sauvignon de St Bris VDQS 93   13
Fine Wines
Straw-yellow in colour, this style has a round ripe character in an overripe apple style.

Pierre Ponnelle AC Mâcon-Villages 94   14
Dunnes Stores
This Chardonnay has developed well, with a slight hint of apple and attractive crisp finish.
White £8–£10

Antonin Rodet Chardonnay de Vieilles Vignes AC Bourgogne 94   *Febvre*   14
Full-flavoured and weighty on the palate, with lots of oak influence adding a creamy touch to the long finish.

Blanchard de Cordambles AC Macon-Lugny 95   14
Fine Wines
A well-made wine with a good impact of apple fruit and nice follow-through to the long weighty finish.

Bouchard Ainé et Fils AC Mâcon-Villages 95   12
Cassidy
A hint of dried fruit with balanced acidity and a streak of steely acidity. Good straightforward drinking.

Bouchard Père et Fils AC Bourgogne Aligoté 94   14
Dillon
This is the wine mixed with a little Crème de Cassis that makes Kir, the classic aperitif. On its own the style is very dry, cut through with crisp acidity.

Charles Viénot **AC Chablis 94**   **14**
Superquinn
Walnut aromas give way to an apple fruit character on the
palate. Good finish and weighty texture. A nice example of the
patchy 94 vintage.

Domaine Corsin **AC St Véran 94**   **13**
Burgundy Direct
Primrose yellow in colour. Fruit aromas are faint, but emerge
on the palate. Limey acidity cuts through the peachy tones to
leave a crisp clean finish.

Domaine Daniel Séguinot **AC Chablis 95**   **14**
Quinnsworth
This has the typical wet wood aromas associated with Chablis
with harmonious fruit and crisp acidity that gives a gentle kick
of crispness to the finish.

Domaine du Chardonnay **'Moulin du Pâtis' AC Petit Chablis 94**
Taserra   **14**
Deep yellow-gold with ripe lemon aromas. Good attack of tart
green apple fruit that continues right through to the finish.
Perfect with fish.

Domaine Manciat-Poncet **Mâcon-Charnay AC Mâcon-Villages**
95   *McCabes*   ☆
Good example of its style. Green nuances in colour. Forget the
aroma and concentrate on the classic style of this wine with its
hints of melon and apricot supported by tangy crisp acidity on
the finish.

Domaine René Michel **AC Mâcon-Clessé 93**   ☆
Searson
Deep yellow-gold. Apricot and lime mingle gently with a good
attack of crisp acidity following behind. Easy to drink with a
touch of class.

Dominique Piron **Chardonnay AC Mâcon-Villages 94**   14
Jenkinson Wines
Yellow-gold in colour, with touches of sherbet and lime in
aroma that carry through on flavour.

Edouard Delaunay et Ses Fils **AC Mâcon-Lugny 95**   14
Brangan
A fine flinty style, extremely fresh with a hint of freshly baked
bread on the finish.

Honoré Lavigne **AC Chablis 95**   12
Greenhills
An easy-drinking style with good fruit and alcohol balance and
medium length.

Jaffelin **Bourgogne du Chapitre AC Bourgogne 94**   14
Cassidy
Deep gold in colour, with creamy, peachy tones. Good weight
on the palate with a nice smack of creaminess at the end.

Labouré-Roi **AC Pouilly-Fuissé 94**   13
Quinnsworth
Hasn't lost its easy-drinking appeal since last tasted. The crisp
finish is still present with good length of flavour on the end.

Labouré-Roi **AC Chablis 95**   13
Quinnsworth
Lemon-green in colour, with lively green fruit appeal and
mouth-watering acidity.

Laroche **AC Mâcon-Lugny 94**   13
Allied Drinks
Well balanced, with hints of tangy kiwi fruit breaking through
the balanced acidity and medium long finish.

Les Vignerons d'Igé AC St Véran 94   12
Febvre
Nicely developed aromas of apricot. Medium finish with good
fruit flavours.

Louis Jadot Chardonnay AC Bourgogne 95   14
Grants
Great seafood wine, with its restrained aromas of unoaked
Chardonnay. Like tasting fresh sea air. Weighty on the palate
and smooth on the finish.

Louis Latour AC Chablis 95   ☆
Gilbeys
Bright with a hint of yellow. A classy young style. Refreshing
and elegant, with green fruit flavours fanning out on the palate.

Louis Latour 'Les Genièvres' Mâcon-Lugny AC Mâcon-Villages 95   *Gilbeys*   14
Steely in style, with zippy apple appeal and good weight and
structure. Easy to drink and easy to understand.

Louis Latour 'La Grande Roche' AC Montagny 1er Cru 94
Gilbeys   ☆☆
Apple-peel aromas and flavours. Expertly handled, it demonstrates the quality of Burgundian Chardonnay. The fruit
continues right through to the long harmonious finish.

Lupé-Cholet Château de Viviers AC Chablis 95   14
Findlater
An elegant smooth style with interesting creamy nutty touches.
Very balanced with good length of flavour.

Michel Goubard 'Mont Avril' AC Bourgogne 93   13
Ecock
Balanced and crisp with good weight and texture. Enjoy its
fruity appeal. Drinking well now.

Pierre Ponnelle **Chablis AC Chablis 94**   **14**
Dunnes Stores
Pale green-gold with good structure and a nutty finish which
adds interest to the last swallow.

Thévenin **Château de la Saule AC Montagny 1er Cru 94**   **14**
Findlater
A classy wine all the way, with good fruit attack in a citrus
style and a long, refined finish.

White £10–£12

Alain Geoffroy **Domaine le Verger AC Chablis 94**   ☆
Febvre
Apple-peel flavours wrapped around steely acidity. The finish
is long and crisp yet full flavoured. A top example of this style.

Antonin Rodet **'Les Chagnots' AC Montagny 1er Cru 93**   ☆
Febvre
Classic in style, with subtle oak tones. Has developed well since
last tasted. The fruit sings its way through to the last swallow.
Delightful drinking.

Bouchard Ainé et Fils **AC Chablis 95**   **13**
Cassidy
Stony fruit appeal with that chalky element characteristic of
Chablis. Note how the fruit and acidity hit the palate together,
with acidity winning out on the end.

Chevalier **AC Chablis 94**   **14**
TDL
Smoky and toasty with pleasant hazelnut aromas. Good attack
of acidity is followed by nice fruit development on the palate,
ending in a long crisp finish.

Domaine André Bonhomme **Cuvée Spéciale AC Mâcon-Viré 93**
Searson   **14**
Hints of primrose in colour. Fresh subtle creamy notes with
good fruit development cutting through the initial attack of
acidity.

Domaine du Chardonnay **'Moulin du Pâtis' AC Chablis 94**
Taserra **14**
Yellow-toned nutty Burgundy with plenty of zest and medium
long finish.

Domaine J-P Grossot **Chablis AC Chablis 94** **13**
Burgundy Direct
Gives more on taste than aroma, but baked apple flavours with
fresh lemony acidity add up to a pleasant lively drink.

Domaine Roger Luquet **'Les Grandes Bruyères' AC St Véran 94**
Febvre **14**
Savoury and herbal. Elegant with just the right balance between
fruit, acidity and alcohol.

Georges Pico **Domaine de Bois d'Yver AC Chablis 95** ☆
Hugan
A lively Chablis with mouthfilling flavours of greengage fruit.
Very balanced with a pleasant creamy touch. Delicious
drinking.

Jean Durup **Château de Maligny AC Chablis 94** **13**
Karwig
Straightforward style with a hint of marzipan. Well balanced
with good acidity and fruit.

Jean-Marc Brocard **Domaine Ste Claire AC Chablis 94** **14**
Moore's Wines
Since last tasted (95), the wine has developed delicious
hazelnut aromas and flavours. Hints of spice add character.
Subtle elegant long finish.

Labouré-Roi **AC Chablis 1er Cru 94** ☆
Quinnsworth
Rhubarb and custard aroma develops into green fruit flavours.
A big fresh fruity Chablis with lots of punch.

Laroche **AC Chablis 93**   **14**
Allied Drinks
Crisp, spicy wine. Balanced and elegant with a clean finish.

Laroche **St Martin AC Chablis 93**   **14**
Allied Drinks
Smoky and crisp with a bone dry finish and lots of grapefruit
tones. A delicious dry wine.

Victor Bérard **AC Pouilly-Fuissé 95**   **14**
Greenhills
Good weight and texture. A crisp steely style, particularly good
with fish.

White £12–£15

Alain Geoffroy **Beauroy AC Chablis 1er Cru 94**   **13**
Febvre
Has green fruit appeal with crisp acidity, but needs more time
to balance all elements. Nice hint of spice on the finish.

Antonin Rodet **Domaine Comtes C. de Ternay Château de Rully**
AC Rully 93   *Febvre*   ☆ ☆ ☆
This has it all! Lemon and lime aromas and flavours sing their
way through to the long classic finish, which ends in a smack of
toast. Top quality which makes one reach for more.

Domaine Corsin **AC Pouilly-Fuissé 92**   ☆
Burgundy Direct
Has all the elegance associated with this style of wine. Appeal-
ing citrus fruit with balanced alcohol and tingling fresh acidity.

Domaine des Malandes **Montmains AC Chablis 1er Cru 94**
Searson   **13**
Grated apple aromas with tingling fresh acidity add up to
pleasant drinking.

Domaine J-P Grossot 'Mont de Milieu' AC Chablis 1er Cru 94
Burgundy Direct ☆

Joyce said, 'White wine is electricity.' He could have been
discussing this Premier Cru with its intense lively acidity,
restrained apple fruit and well-balanced long finish.

Domaine Laroche 'Les Vaudevey' AC Chablis 1er Cru 93
Allied Drinks **14**

Lemon and limes all the way. Has length and elegance with a
touch of creaminess on the finish.

Domaine Manciat-Poncet AC Pouilly-Fuissé 93 **14**
Searson

Golden in colour, with just a whisper of peach. Rich succulent
creamy finish.

Domaine Roger Luquet Clos du Bourg AC Pouilly-Fuissé 94
Febvre ☆

Memorable drinking. Deep golden in colour, with hazelnuts
and spice fanning out on the palate and lingering long after the
last swallow.

Edouard Delaunay et Ses Fils AC Pouilly-Fuissé 95 ☆ ☆
Brangan

Green-tinged in colour with sea-fresh appeal. Extremely well
made with superb balance and length.

Guy Moreau Cuvée Prestige Vaillons AC Chablis 1er Cru 92
Grants ☆

Tasted again this year, this classic elegant wine is developing
extremely well with fruit and acidity harmonising all the way
to a long complex finish.

Jean Durup Château de Maligny Fourchaume AC Chablis 1er Cru 94
Karwig **14**

Subtle and elegant, with good fruit tones continuing right
through from first sip to last swallow. Acidity trails off on the
finish with hints of melon coming through.

Labouré-Roi AC Puligny-Montrachet 94   13
Quinnsworth
The good depth of colour is followed by subtle flavours.
Harmonious use of oak adds a touch of spice to the nutty finish.

Labouré-Roi 'Le Poruzot' AC Meursault 1er Cru 94   13
Quinnsworth
Rich straw-gold colour, with rounded fruit appeal reminiscent
of nuts and apples. Good long finish.

Laroche AC Pouilly-Fuissé 94   13
Allied Drinks
Fresh and fruity, with acidity a little tart. Nice long flavour-
some finish.

Louis Latour AC Chablis 1er Cru 95
Gilbeys
Green-yellow in colour. Lean and subtle with a strong mineral
tone that impresses. Very classic in style.

Louis Michel 'Montée de Tonnerre' AC Chablis 1er Cru 93
Findlater   14
Delightful apple-peel nuances—ripe yet lean with a fresh, crisp
finish. Offers great drinking pleasure.

Pierre Ponnelle AC Puligny-Montrachet 92   14
Dunnes Stores
It's got the subtle nutty tone of this appellation overladen with
just a whisper of honey. It comes together in flavour, finishing
in a fan of creamy subtle flavours.

Pierre Ponnelle Montmains AC Chablis 1er Cru 95
Dunnes Stores
A top example of an intense stony fruit style overladen with the
vigour and vim that tingling acidity adds. Still young.

René Michel **Mâcon-Clessé AC Mâcon-Villages 92**   14
Searson
Delightful nutty nuances with quite an opulent texture and
high fruity extract.

William Fèvre **Champs Royaux AC Chablis 94**   ☆
Febvre
For the Chablis lover who likes oak influence this is a must.
Butter and cream with a hint of spice add up to delicious
drinking.

William Fèvre **Fourchaume AC Chablis 1er Cru 94**   ☆ ☆
Febvre
Great balance and breed! The big attack of appealing greengage
fruit develops and finishes on a toasty nutty tone, giving extra
richness to the long finish.

White £15–£20

Alain Geoffroy **Fourchaume AC Chablis 1er Cru 94**   14
Febvre
Top class—flinty and earthy in style with good weight on the
palate. Still young.

Labouré-Roi **AC Meursault 93**   13
Quinnsworth
Yellow-gold in colour, with pleasant ripe peachy tones.
Harmonious acidity with good structure and length.

Labouré-Roi **'Les Clos' AC Chablis Grand Cru 94**   14
Quinnsworth
Touches of butterscotch, good attack of ripe fruit with a bite of
acidity. A long, steely finish.

Pierre Ponnelle **'Champ Gain' AC Puligny-Montrachet 1er Cru
93**   *Dunnes Stores*   13
Straw-gold in colour. Pleasant ripe fruit aroma with just a hint
of honey. Medium long finish.

White £20–£30

Antonin Rodet 'Les Perrières' AC Puligny-Montrachet 1er Cru

93 *Febvre* ☆☆

Rich and opulent, with creamy fruit that whistles and sings its way right through to the buttery concentrated finish.

Château Grenouille AC Chablis Grand Cru 92 ☆

Dunnes Stores

Rich gold colour. Complex aromas with a very pleasant nutty character. Biscuits and butter come to mind on the well rounded palate. Clean long finish.

M. Chenu Domaine de la Perrière AC Meursault 93 **13**

Callaghan

A very pleasant subtle example of this AC, with nutty nuances and hints of butterscotch. Needs more bottle maturation to show its promise.

William Fèvre Vaudésir AC Chablis Grand Cru 92 ☆☆

Febvre

Concentrated nutty aromas with generous apple-fruit flavours that fan out and are cut through with a backbone of pungent acidity. Delicious!

RED WINE

Red £5.25–£6

Charles Viénot AC Mâcon Supérieur 93 **14**

Superquinn

The plummy fruit tones have held up since last tasted. A well-made wine with instant fruity appeal.

Charles Viénot Bourgogne Pinot Noir AC Bourgogne 94 **14**

Superquinn

A touch of spiciness and tangy acidity add interest to this very appealing easy to drink fruity wine.

Pierre Ponnelle **AC Mâcon Supérieur 94**   **13**
Dunnes Stores
Summer fruit appeal with a soft attack. Well balanced.
Red £6–£8

Blanchard de Cordambles **Bourgogne Pinot Noir AC Bourgogne**
94   *Fine Wines*   ☆
Elusive evocative Pinot aromas all the way. Young and vibrant,
with plummy fruit appeal and a supple kick of tannin at the
back. Big warm spicy finish.

Bouchard Père et Fils **AC Mâcon Supérieur 95**   **14**
Dillon
White pepper aromas nearly make you sneeze! Good fruity
attack with fresh acidity. A nice, everyday style.

Labouré-Roi **AC Mâcon Supérieur 95**   ☆ ☆
Quinnsworth
Elegance, class and finesse are all found here! Great length on
the finish.

Labouré-Roi **AC Bourgogne Hautes-Côtes de Beaune 94**
Quinnsworth   **13**
Offers plenty of ripe sweet red berry fruit appeal with a
lingering finish. Perfect for cool summer drinking.

Labouré-Roi **AC Bourgogne Passe-Tout-Grains 93**   **14**
Quinnsworth
Produced from two-thirds Gamay and one-third Pinot Noir,
this wine is showing maturity. Smooth fruity appeal with a bite
of spice.

Labouré-Roi **Pinot Noir AC Bourgogne 93**   **13**
Quinnsworth
Since last tasted the young Pinot fruit has held up, with the
subtle tannins and good bite of acidity giving some length.

Louis Latour **Cuvée Latour AC Bourgogne 94** 14
Gilbeys
A light saturation of ruby tones with a delicious whiff of
elusive mature Pinot fruit.

Pierre Ponnelle **AC Bourgogne Hautes-Côtes de Beaune 93** 13
Dunnes Stores
Bright ruby in colour, with light refreshing fruity tones. Good
flavour evolution on the palate with supple fruity appeal.

Pierre Ponnelle **Pinot Noir AC Bourgogne 94** 14
Dunnes Stores
Typical light saturation of colour with raspberry and strawberry fruit appeal. Delicious summer drinking when served
cool.

Red £8–£10

Antonin Rodet **Château de Mercey AC Hautes-Côtes de Beaune**
92 *Febvre* 14
Savoury Pinot fruit with a hint of smoke. Well-spread cherry
flavours continue to the end with integrated tannin. Medium to
long finish.

Antonin Rodet **Pinot Noir Vieilles Vignes AC Bourgogne 94**
Febvre 14
Bright ruby with just a hint of pink at the edge. Jammy raspberry fruits with a smack of tannin coming through on the
finish. Well-structured wine.

Bouchard Père et Fils **AC Côte de Beaune-Villages 92** 14
Dillon
Ruby red with a tawny hint. The enticing aromas spill over into
a delicious attack of raspberry with tannin fighting back.
Overall a delicate silky Pinot.

Charles Viénot **AC Rully 93** 14
Superquinn
Deep raspberry red in colour, with juicy brambly fruit appeal,
lively acidity and good lengthy finish.

Charles Viénot **'Les Lavières' AC Savigny-lès-Beaune 1er Cru**
92   *Superquinn*   ☆ ☆
This has gained from an extra year in bottle. Wonderful mature
Pinot characteristics with the same hint of nutmeg combining
with the rich fig and woodland undergrowth appeal. A classic
seductive style.

Domaine Daniel Rion et Fils **AC Bourgogne Passe-Tout-Grains**
92   *Brangan*   **14**
Medium ruby red with fleshy raspberry fruit flavours. A lively
example from a top Burgundian producer.

Edouard Delaunay et Ses Fils **AC Bourgogne 94**   **14**
Brangan
Light ruby in colour, with creamy strawberry aromas and
flavours. Easy on the palate, with good fruity appeal from start
to finish.

Jaffelin **Bourgogne du Chapitre AC Bourgogne 93**   **14**
Cassidy
Pinot farmyard aromas are followed by a sweet fruit attack.
Acidity and tannin cut through the fruit, leaving good grip and
length.

Louis Jadot **Pinot Noir AC Bourgogne 94**   **13**
Grants
Light young Pinot characteristics such as raspberry fruit with a
slight vegetal overtone on aroma, serve as a good introduction
to this style.

M. Chenu **Domaine de la Perrière Pinot Noir AC Bourgogne 94**
Callaghan   **14**
Pale garnet in colour, with a tasty mouthful of ripe raspberry
fruits. Smooth finish with a delicious bite of lively acidity and
mouth-drying tannins.

Michel Goubard (Mont Avril) **Côte Chalonnaise Rouge AC**
Bourgogne 93   *Ecock*   **13**
Bright ruby in colour with cerise reflections. Closed on aroma.
Opens up on the palate in waves of ripe fruit tones and
harmonious tannins.

Pierre Ponnelle **AC Côte de Nuits-Villages 93**   ☆
Dunnes Stores
Stylish wine with the whiff of farmyard so typical of Pinot Noir
fruit. This doesn't mask the delicate fruity flavours and long
supple elegant finish.

Red £10–£12

Bouchard Ainé et Fils **AC Mercurey 90**   **12**
Cassidy
Brick-toned in colour, with an inky touch that gives way to
vegginess. Lean style with more fruit on the palate. Good with
red meat.

Bouchard Père et Fils **AC Mercurey 93**   **14**
Dillon
Earthy fruit appeal, a dart of crisp acidity and long elegant
finish.

Bouchard Père et Fils **AC Bourgogne Hautes-Côtes de Beaune**
93   *Dillon*   **14**
Bright crimson in colour. Typical of a young Pinot style with
vibrant fruit and a pleasant bite of acidity. Austere finish
would work very well with cold meats.

Edouard Delaunay et Ses Fils **AC Côte de Beaune-Villages 94**
Brangan   **12**
Pale ruby in colour with closed aromas. The fruit is hidden by
assertive tannins and acidity.

Jaffelin **AC Bourgogne Hautes-Côtes de Beaune 93**   **14**
Cassidy
Elegantly structured wine with concentrated plum and
liquorice tones. Supple tannins add interest to the long juicy
finish.

Jules Belin AC Côte de Beaune-Villages 92 14
Febvre
Light colour saturation. Mushroom and raspberry mingle
together. Quite rustic in style with good length.

Labouré-Roi AC Volnay 93 14
Quinnsworth
A wine with potential! Closed and tight on aroma, it has a
smooth classy texture with hints of spice bursting through the
fruit. Long lively finish.

Labouré-Roi AC Pommard 93 14
Quinnsworth
The 93 vintage is brick in colour with a light saturation. It
exhibits good squashed red berry fruit flavours that carry
through to the finish. A light example of the appellation.

Labouré-Roi AC Beaune 92 14
Quinnsworth
Difficult to ignore the bite of ripe red berry fruit supported and
eventually dominated by zesty acidity. An assertive style.

Labouré-Roi AC Nuits-St-Georges 93 ☆
Quinnsworth
The 93 vintage is still closed on aroma, but the Pinot fruit is
beginning to emerge. Better on flavour, with a silky texture.
Mouth-puckering tannins indicate it still has time to mature.

Labouré-Roi AC Gevrey-Chambertin 93 13
Quinnsworth
Has the tantalising vegetal aromas of Pinot, but doesn't quite
live up to its promise on taste. The fruit is masked by too much
acidity.

Laroche AC Côte de Beaune-Villages 90 13
Allied Drinks
Vegetal aromas, but good sweet ripe fruit attack. Overtaken by
acidity on the long finish.

Red £12–£15

***Antonin Guyon* AC Savigny-lès-Beaune 93** ☆ ☆
Febvre
A rich style of Pinot with a big sweet ripe fruit attack, velvet
tannins and a nice bite of acidity on the long flavoursome
finish. An extremely seductive Pinot.

***Antonin Rodet* Comtes C. de Ternay Château de Rully AC**
Rully 92 *Febvre* ☆
Big and beefy with nutmeg spice. Very well balanced with solid
structure. A natural choice for pheasant.

***Bouchard Père et Fils* AC Savigny-lès-Beaune 93** 14
Dillon
Full of plummy raspberry fruit appeal, this is a lighter style
than the 90 tasted last year. The Pinot appeal is still obvious.

***Edouard Delaunay et Ses Fils* 'Clos L'Évêque' AC Mercurey 1er**
Cru 94 *Brangan* 14
Crimson in colour. Fruity flavour with a medium long finish.
Vibrant and plummy in style.

***Jean-Marc Boillot* AC Bourgogne 93** ☆
Terroirs
Deep crimson in colour. Concentrated savoury aromas give
way to ripe succulent fruit backed up with zippy acidity. Long
flavoursome finish.

***Jules Belin* AC Chassagne-Montrachet 93** 14
Febvre
Cherry aromas and flavours. Interesting wine that promises
more with bottle age. The tannins are concentrated, the acidity
is high and the fruit still hidden.

***Jules Belin* AC Santenay 93** 13
Febvre
Cooked red berry fruit aromas which die off very quickly. A

little thin on the mid-palate, but should balance out better with
a little more bottle age.

Jules Belin **AC Côte de Nuits-Villages 92**   13
Febvre
Pale in colour, showing a hint of brick. Some strawberry fruit
tones, but acidity masks fruit.

Labouré-Roi **AC Chambolle-Musigny 93**   ☆
Quinnsworth
Very pleasant seductive perfumed aromas. A well-structured
wine, needing a little more time for the fruit to show its
tantalising promise.

Lupé-Cholet '**Clos Bellefond' AC Santenay 92**   14
Findlater
What one expects from fine Pinot fruit. Delicate and elegant
with good follow-through on flavour, ending in a pleasant bite
of acidity and tannin.

Pierre Ponnelle **AC Nuits-St-Georges 93**   14
Dunnes Stores
Attractive red berry fruits. Gum-drying tannins mask the fruit,
but a hint of spice fights back, leaving a nice chewy finish.

Pierre Ponnelle **AC Gevrey-Chambertin 94**   14
Dunnes Stores
Ruby crimson in colour. Subtle aromas of Pinot with a smoky
touch. Raspberry fruit dominates flavour. Still young.

Pierre Ponnelle **AC Gevrey-Chambertin 92**   14
Dunnes Stores
Medium ruby in colour. Silky and supple in texture, with a very
balanced fruity finish.

Tollot-Beaut et Fils **AC Chorey-lès-Beaune 93**   ☆
Findlater
A super Pinot with its vibrant chunky fruit appeal and zesty
acidity. An extremely appealing finish with fruit flavours
lingering on and on.

Red £15–£20

Antonin Rodet AC Gevrey-Chambertin 93 ☆☆
Febvre
A vibrant succulent Pinot with layers of ripe fruit reminiscent of strawberry and cherry that echo on after the last seductive swallow.

Cécile Chenu Domaine de la Créa 'Les Montrevenots' AC Beaune 1er Cru 93 *Callaghan* ☆☆
Mature brick colour. Everything combines in this wine to catch attention—perfumed aromas, attractive fruity flavours and silky texture finish in a high note of classic Pinot taste.

Domaine Besancenot-Mathouillet AC Aloxe-Corton 90 ☆☆
Burgundy Direct
A dream to drink! Well balanced and structured with flavours of aniseed, plum and spice ending in a supple long finish.

Domaine Besancenot-Mathouillet 'Bressandes' AC Beaune 1er Cru 90 *Burgundy Direct* ☆
Brick in colour. Packed with layers of flavours, from cherry to strawberry. Supple and luscious, with a good backbone of acidity and velvet smooth tannins.

Domaine de l'Arlot 'Clos du Chapeau' AC Côte de Nuits-Villages 92 *Febvre* ☆☆
For the true Pinot fan this wine has the 'wow' factor. The essence of classic Burgundy, with its pale brick colour followed by layers of sweet fruit and clean fresh acidity. Smooth supple tannins and a long concentrated finish.

Domaine Denis Mortet AC Gevrey-Chambertin 93 ☆☆
Burgundy Direct
Top-class Pinot. Note the amazing purple colour of this usually garnet-coloured grape. The sweet ripe fruit flavours of damson

and raspberry show great depth. High acidity denotes its
youth. Mouth-drying tannins indicate good ageing potential.

***Domaine des Beaumont* AC Morey-St-Denis 91**   ☆ ☆ ☆
Callaghan
What a stunner! Ripe fruit tones lead to an explosion of chunky,
chewy red fruits. Excellent structure and balance with enor-
mous length.

***Domaine Thomas-Moillard* Pinot Noir AC Beaune-Grèves 1er
Cru 92**   *Moore's Wines*   ☆
Ruby red with strawberry aromas and the characteristic vegetal
tone of good Pinot Noir. Big attack of ripe fruits followed by
high acidity. Well balanced with a very pleasant lingering
finish.

***Edouard Delaunay et Ses Fils* AC Gevrey-Chambertin 93**
Brangan   **14**
Deep strawberry in colour. Pleasant wine-gum aromas. Juicy
and fruity with refreshing yet balanced acidity and harmonious
tannins.

***Jean Boillot et Fils* Caillerets AC Volnay 1er Cru 93**   ☆
Findlater
Garnet in colour, with complex pleasant smoky ashy aromas
behind the red berry fruit tones. Good fruit attack followed by
lively acidity, ending in a medium long multi-layered finish.

***Louis Jadot* AC Nuits-St-Georges 89**   **14**
Grants
From a top vintage and drinking well now, has evolved into a
spicy, plummy wine with a distinct brick colour and that
wonderful Pinot farmyard aroma.

Moillard-Grivot 'Monts Luisants' AC Morey-St Denis 1er Cru
92   *Moore's Wines*   ☆☆
Superb example of this AC. Ripe raspberry fruits cut through
the whole wine from first taste to last swallow. An opulent
style, very balanced with extra-long flavour.

Pierre Ponnelle 'Les Damodes' AC Nuits-St-Georges 1er Cru 93
Dunnes Stores   **14**
Deep ruby red with lots of fruit-of-the-forest aromas. Lighter
fruit style on the palate with supple tannins and medium long
finish.

Red £20–£30

Antonin Guyon 'Clos des Chênes' AC Volnay 1er Cru 92
Febvre   ☆☆
Excellent balance between fruit and acidity. Much better on the
palate than aroma, promising even greater drinking pleasure to
come. A serious wine with complex fruit and savoury tones.
Smoky and dense with lots of character.

Antonin Guyon 'Les Fournières' AC Aloxe-Corton 1er Cru 93
Febvre   ☆☆☆
All about spice and bite! So young and full of promise. Note the
structure of this wine, with intense cherry earthy flavours cut
through with a backbone of high acidity held together with
mouth-drying tannins.

Antonin Guyon Clos du Village AC Chambolle-Musigny 92
Febvre   ☆☆
Savoury Pinot—reminiscent of the 'jus' from the Sunday joint.
Layers of intense fruit with tannin and spice cutting through
the acidity. Fruit shouts back on the end leaving a lasting
impression.

Antonin Rodet 'Les Epenots' AC Pommard 1er Cru 93   ☆☆
Febvre
A seductive wine—sweet and ripe with delicious raspberry and

earthy tones. Supple and smooth with a nice bite of acidity.

Clos de l'Arlot AC Nuits-St-Georges 1er Cru 89 ☆
Febvre

This classic wine rolls around the palate in gentle waves of spice and fruit. Smooth tannins and assertive acidity combine to make a complex, concentrated wine.

Domaine de l'Arlot AC Nuits-St-Georges 92 ☆☆☆
Febvre

Classic Pinot. Aromas begin with strawberry, but are quickly overtaken by woodland earthy tones. A pleasant touch of spice with mouth-drying tannins leaves a lasting impression.

Pierre Ponnelle 'Clos du Roi' AC Corton Grand Cru 93 14
Dunnes Stores

Deep ruby in colour, with gentle fruity and cold tea aromas. Very fresh in flavour, with vibrant fruit appeal, zesty acidity and a long supple finish.

Red £30–£50

Domaine Daniel Rion Clos des Argillières AC Nuits-St-Georges
1er Cru 89 *Brangan* ☆☆☆

Tawny in colour, with delicious seductive elusive aromas. Has the definite 'wow' factor for Pinot fans. Smooth silky finish full of class and breed.

France—Loire

Main wine regions

Nantais, Anjou-Saumur, Touraine, Upper Loire.
The above are all subdivided into smaller wine areas.

Principal grape varieties

White	Red
White	*Red*
Melon de Bourgogne (Muscadet)	Cabernet Franc (le
Chenin Blanc	Breton)
Sauvignon Blanc	Pinot Noir
Folle Blanche	Malbec (Côt)
Chardonnay	Grolleau
plus a diversity of other grapes	Gamay

Labelling guide

Nantais: the most famous white wine is Muscadet, which is named
after the grape from which it is produced. There are several
distinct appellations, one that mentions 'Muscadet' only, and
a second, which adds 'Sèvre-et-Maine', indicating that the wine
was produced within the areas of these two tributaries of the
Loire. A new appellation, established in 1994, is Muscadet Côtes
de Grand Lieu. The words 'sur lie' on the label indicate that the
young wine was left on its own lees or sediment up to the time
of bottling.

Gros Plant: white. Not often seen here, this VDQS is bone dry and
once again named after the grape variety.

Anjou: famed for its rosé wines.

Anjou Gamay: red wine produced from the Gamay grape of
Beaujolais fame.

Rosé d'Anjou: medium-sweet rosé wine.

Cabernet d'Anjou: sweet or dry.

Saumur: red and white wines.

Saumur-Champigny: fashionable red wine.

Sparkling Saumur: large production of quality wine.

Savennières: this tiny area in the Anjou region produces some of
the longest lived of all French white wines from the Chenin
Blanc grape. Two sub-appellations, Coulée de Serrant and
Roche aux Moines, can mature for decades.

Sweet wines: Bonnezeaux and Quarts de Chaume. Usually affected

A small excerpt from our cellars, stocked with the benefit of years of experience in satisfying the discerning Irish palate.

by noble rot, these are some of the most prized dessert wines of France, with great ageing ability.

Coteaux du Layon: a large area also producing sweet but much less complex wines from Chenin Blanc.

Touraine: the red grape variety Cabernet Franc (known locally as 'le Breton') comes into its own here. Particularly suited to this cooler climate, there are three major appellations covering red wines. Named after individual towns, they are Chinon, Bourgueil and St Nicolas de Bourgueil. Although produced from the same grape variety, styles differ according to soil and vineyard location. Some of the best examples are from vines grown in the chalk-based soil known as tufa.

Vouvray: produced entirely from the Chenin Blanc grape (known locally as 'Pineau de la Loire'), this white wine can be dry, off-dry, sweet or sparkling. Not always indicated on the label, the degree of sweetness is described as sec, demi-sec and molleux.

Sancerre: these vineyards produce the finest examples of zesty aromatic Sauvignon Blanc in France. The villages of Sancerre and Pouilly sur Loire carry their own appellations. Pinot Noir is used to make red and rosé Sancerre. Menetou-Salon: white, red and rosé styles. Whites are produced from Sauvignon Blanc, reds and rosés from Pinot Noir. Other appellations not often seen in Ireland include St Pourçain, Côtes du Forez, Quincy and Reuilly.

Wine styles

Crémant de Loire: top-quality sparkling wines, often produced by the traditional method.

Whites to look out for are Sancerre, which should be drunk young and fresh (1–2 years), Pouilly Fumé (1–4 years), and Muscadet (1–2 years).

Red wines such as Bourgueil, Chinon and St Nicolas de Bourgueil are produced principally from Cabernet Franc: drink cool. Bourgueil in good vintage years can age. Chinon is fresh and fruity when young yet can, depending on the vintage, improve for 20 years or more. St Nicolas de Bourgueil has a little less weight than Bourgueil and can be enjoyed at 2–3 years and in good vintages mature for up to 10.

Vintages

95   Promises to be superb.
94   Average whites. Reds light, sweet best.
93   Good all round.

92   Average. Light white and red.
91   Very average. Light whites (no Muscadet was
      produced). Light reds.
90   Superb, especially sweet wines. Top quality reds.
89   Superb, especially sweet wines.

WHITE WINE

White under £4.50

Labouré-Roi Chenin/Sauvignon Blanc VdP Jardin de la France
95   *Quinnsworth*   **13**
A 'cool' Loire with stony fruit appeal and medium long finish.

Le Haut de Sève AC Muscadet de Sèvre et Maine 95   **12**
Dunnes Stores
Easy drinking with lively acidity and medium long finish.

White £5.25–£6

Barton & Guestier AC Muscadet de Sèvre et Maine 95   **14**
Dillon
Fresh in a clean dry style with surprising length on the finish.
Enjoy young and chilled.

Domaine du Petit Val Chardonnay VdP Jardin de la France 95
Terroirs   **14**
Well-made wine. Chalky, with good acidity and a balanced
finish.

Domaine Souchais AC Muscadet de Sèvre et Maine 95   **13**
Dunnes Stores
Fresh and youthful with pleasant fresh bread nuances and
refreshing finish.

Vouvray AC Vouvray 93   ☆
Superquinn
The balance of fruit and acidity is terrific. Zesty, crisp fruity off-
dry style made from the Chenin Blanc grape.

White £6–£8

Butte de la Roche AC Sancerre 95 ☆
Dunnes Stores
All the tanginess one expects with pungent grassy tones,
delicious gooseberry fruit and a crisp lively finish.

Château de l'Hyvernière AC Muscadet de Sèvre et Maine 94
Allied Drinks 12
Typical green apple scents with a medium long finish and a
hint of spritz. Produced 'sur lie'.

**Château de Rochefort AC Muscadet de Sèvre et Maine sur lie
94** *Cassidy* 13
Good example of Muscadet with its sea air aroma, hint of spritz
and crisp fruit.

Château la Berrière AC Muscadet de Sèvre et Maine 94 14
Foley
Very impressive with its stony fruit appeal, fresh lemon tang
and crisp finish.

Domaine de Salvard AC Cheverny 95 14
Brangan
From Touraine in the Loire, this is an interesting wine in a
modern style. Lean and green. Top-quality winemaking.

**Domaine Les Grands Houx AC Muscadet de Sèvre et Maine
sur lie 95** *Wines Direct* 14
Green-hued, pungent and herbaceous with just a slight hint of
spritz. Refreshing, clean, dry drinking.

La Chenaye AC Sancerre 95 14
Quinnsworth
Grassy aromas mark this Sauvignon Blanc with good lemon
zest appeal ending in a fresh finish.

Le Soleil AC Muscadet de Sèvre et Maine sur lie 95 13
Searson
This Muscadet goes particularly well with seafood. Note the

mineral steely edge with a clean fresh finish.

Les Roches Blanches AC Pouilly-Fumé 94 ☆
Dunnes Stores
Herbaceous aroma reminiscent of Sancerre. A more subdued
fruity flavour emerges in taste, finishing with a nice bite of
acidity.

**Marquis de Goulaine AC Muscadet de Sèvre et Maine sur lie
95** *Gilbeys* ☆
Whistle clean with good fruity extract and an extremely
pleasant nutty tone.
White £8–£10

**Château de la Ragotière 1er Cru du Château AC Muscadet de
Sèvre et Maine sur lie 95** 14
Brangan
Granny Smith apple appeal. Bone dry with a whistle-clean
finish.

Clos St Fiacre Orléanais VDQS 93 ☆
Brangan
Pale white-gold in colour with subtle vanilla and floral tones. A
big wine on flavour, with good weighty texture and a very
classy long finish.

Domaine de L'Échalier Sauvignon VdP Jardin de la France 95
Brangan 14
Most appealing, with its cool climate herbaceous tone spilling
over into grated raw apple flavours. A great wine with fish.

Domaine du Closel AC Savennières 91 ☆
Superquinn
The combination of fruit ripeness, which gives an impression of
sweetness, with refreshing acidity leaves the palate tingling
fresh.

Domaine du Petit Val AC Coteaux du Layon 93 13
Terroirs
Deep succulent honeyed nose with a good smack of *Botrytis*

cinerea (the noble rot that adds such richness to sweet wines).
Doesn't quite live up to its promise on the palate.

Domaine du Vieux Prêche AC Sancerre 95 ☆
Moore's Wines
Bright lemon in colour, with the typical earthy nettle aromas
associated with Sauvignon Blanc. Fruit emerges on the palate
and the steely core of acidity adds a fresh bite to the finish.

Thauvenay AC Sancerre 94 14
Wines Direct
Unusually for Sancerre, this example has been vinified in oak,
which adds a touch of cream to the fruit. Still has the crisp
lively acidity associated with this AC.

Villa Paulus AC Pouilly-Fumé 94 13
Wines Direct
Lime-tinged in colour, with lots of citrus fruits such as grape-
fruit coming through on flavour. Well-balanced, lively finish.

White £10–£12

Alphonse Mellot AC Pouilly-Fumé 95 14
Kelly
Lean and lively, with a hint of gooseberry appeal followed by
an attractive lemon touch. Good seafood wine. Enjoy young.

Cuvée du Troncsec AC Pouilly-Fumé 93 14
Allied Drinks
Concentrated floral aromas with pleasant nutty nuances. Big
attack of ripe fruit followed by zesty acidity. Rich and ripe.

Domaine des Berthiers AC Pouilly-Fumé 94 14
Allied Drinks
Herbaceous aroma with grapefruit coming through on flavour.
Good balance between fruit and acidity adds interest to the
medium long finish.

Domaine Jean-Paul Balland AC Sancerre 94 ☆
Taserra/Reynolds
Packs a punch of green apple flavours and pungent nettle-leaf

aromas backed up with tangy citrus acidity. Wonderful chalky element cuts through everything.

Domaine La Croix Canat 'Les Blancs Gateaux' AC Sancerre Blanc 94   *Searson*   ☆ ☆
Lemon-tinged with excellent, yet not screeching, pungency. A top example of Sancerre. Enjoy it while it's young.

Domaine La Moussière AC Sancerre 95   14
Kelly
Water-pale with a hint of citrus over the crunchy grassy tone. Lean and lively with a zesty finish.

La Chatellenie AC Sancerre 94   14
Allied Drinks
Mouthfilling flavours of pungent greengage fruit with an arrow of crisp acidity.

La Coulée d'Or AC Vouvray 93   13
Callaghan
Bone dry, with tingling acidity and hints of melon.
White £12–£15

Chatelain AC Pouilly-Fumé 95   ☆
Findlater
A serious wine showing real strength in flavour. Alpine freshness and hazelnut tones. A smoky touch adds elegance. Top-class winemaking.

Clos de la Bergerie AC Savennières 92   ☆ ☆
Gilbeys
Produced from Chenin Blanc, this wine is bone dry with hints of asparagus aromas. The high acidity content, rich fruit and classic structure make it the hidden gem of the Loire.

Clos Joanne D'Orion AC Pouilly-Fumé 94   14
Karwig
Stylish, with a hint of smokiness and subtle grassy tones.

Comte Lafond AC Sancerre 94 14
Gilbeys
Dry hay aromas with a touch of exotic and citrus fruits mark
this well-made wine, which has a whistle-clean finish.

De Ladoucette AC Pouilly-Fumé 93
Gilbeys
Smoky leafy tones with fresh citrus-type fruit appeal, bound
together with tangy acidity. Classic style.

Domaine des Baumard AC Savennières 93 14
Brangan
Savennières, with the fruit quality and nervy acidity of the
Chenin Blanc grape, can go through a dumb phase, to re-
emerge to a glorious old age. Try this interesting example.

Domaine Jacques Bailly AC Sancerre 95
Ecock
An interesting pungent Sancerre with a floral touch.
Mouthfilling flavours are cut through with crisp acidity. A
classy style to savour and sip.

Pascal Jolivet AC Pouilly-Fumé 95
Brangan
Water-pale with creamy vanilla ice cream aromas. The 95 has
excellent balance with a touch of citrus fruit which continues
from the first sip to the last swallow.
White £15–£20

Prestige du Colombier AC Sancerre 94
Brangan
Delicious gooseberry aromas with an earthy touch. A top
example of this style, with flavours fanning out on the end.

RED WINE

Red £8–£10

Réserve des Vignerons AC Saumur-Champigny 94   ☆
Hugan
This top example of Cabernet Franc has wonderful aromas of chocolate and brambly fruits. Lively fruit finish.

Red £10–£12

Clos de Danzay AC Chinon 93
Brangan
Another majestic Cabernet Franc wine produced from a vintage with ageing potential. Note the brambly fruit appeal with a hint of pea-pod. Mouth-watering fruity appeal.

Red £12–£15

Cuvée Beauvais AC Bourgeuil 93
Brangan
From top Touraine producer Pierre-Jacques Druet, this is a wine that needs more bottle ageing to show its true potential. Very classic in style, with stalky fruit appeal and good structure.

Red £15–£20

Clos de la Dioterie Vieilles Vignes AC Chinon 93   13
Brangan
Garnet colour, pepper and spice touch and herb-like flavour.

ROSÉ WINE

Rosé £4.50–£5.25

Louis de Bruc AC Rosé d'Anjou 95   12
Dunnes Stores
Orangey-pink in colour, with strawberry fruit tones. Offers
simple easy drinking.

Rosé £5.25–£6

Barton & Guestier AC Rosé d'Anjou 94   13
Dillon
For those who like lots of fruit and a medium-sweet style.

Drouet Frères AC Rosé d'Anjou 94   13
Cassidy
Onion skin in colour. Better on flavour than aroma, with fresh
attack. Off-dry finish with pleasant acidity and medium long
finish.

Rosé £6–£8

Domaine des Baumard AC Cabernet d'Anjou 95   13
Brangan
Very pale onion skin in colour. Neutral aromas open out into a
medium sweet fruity style backed up with refreshing acidity.

France—Rhône

Principal grape varieties

White	Red
Viognier	Syrah
Marsanne	Cinsaut
Roussanne	Carignan
	Mourvèdre
	Grenache

Labelling guide and wine styles

Northern Rhône

Côte Rôtie: the 'roasted slope' produces only red wines. Syrah is king, but a little Viognier can be used in the blend. Full-bodied wines with an ageing ability of up to twenty years.

Cornas: produced from 100% Syrah. Full-bodied, needing time to mature.

St Joseph: supple silky reds and fruity whites at their best drunk young.

Hermitage: powerful full-bodied red wines produced from the Syrah grape which can mature for up to thirty years. White Hermitage is produced from Marsanne and Roussanne grape varieties.

Crozes-Hermitage: lighter in style than Hermitage, this appellation covers a larger area surrounding Hermitage. Red and white wines are produced.

Condrieu: white wines produced from 100% Viognier, at its best drunk young.

St Péray: still and sparkling wines are produced.

Southern Rhône

Côtes du Rhône: fruity, easy-to-drink red and white wines.

Côtes du Rhône-Villages: blended from seventeen villages, these wines are fuller-bodied. If produced from one village, the name of the village can appear on the label.

Vacqueyras: awarded its appellation in 1990.

Gigondas: full-bodied red wines with good ageing ability of up to ten years.

Châteauneuf-du-Pape: red wine dominates production and can be produced from up to thirteen grape varieties. Traditional styles are rich and full-bodied, with an ageing ability of up to twenty years. More modern styles are fruitier and can be drunk young. White wine represents a tiny percentage of overall production. Domaine wines have the papal coat of arms embossed on the bottle.

Tavel: high-alcohol dry rosé wines.

Lirac: red and rosé wines.

Vin Doux Naturel: naturally sweet wine whose fermentation has been stopped by the addition of grape spirit. Muscat de Beaumes de Venise is the most famous.

Rasteau: based on Grenache. There are several styles, from dry to sweet to port-like. Rancio indicates a style of wine that has been matured in cask, usually in the open air, for some years.

Vintages

95	Promises to be superb.
94	Very good. Northern Rhône superb.
93	Average. Light wines.
92	Poor to average. Early drinking.
91	Very good, especially northern Rhône.
90	Superb, especially north.
89	Superb, especially southern Rhône.
88	Superb, north and south.
87	Average to good, north and south.
86	Very good.
85	Superb all round.
84	Very good, north and south.
83	Very good to superb, north and south.
82	Very good to superb, especially north.

WHITE WINE

White £8–£10

Coudoulet de Beaucastel AC Côtes du Rhône 94　　　　**13**
Allied Drinks
A fat juicy wine with perfumed floral tones.

Domaine des Remizières AC Crozes-Hermitage 94　　　　**14**
Wines Direct
Low acidity and high alcohol give a weighty, waxy mouth feel. Ripe fruit flavours add interest to the finish. A good example of this style.

Domaine du Vieux Chêne AC Côtes du Rhône-Villages 95   **14**
Brangan
A pleasant perfumed aroma of floral and ripe peachy tones.
Medium acidity adds weight. Good length of flavour. Nice
example of its style.
White £15–£20

Domaine Ste Anne Le Viognier AC Côtes du Rhône 95   **13**
Brangan
Lemon tangy appeal with good zippy fruit character. A
pleasant drink with a long refreshing finish.
White £20–£30

Delas Cuvée 'Marquise de la Tourette' AC Hermitage 94   **13**
Febvre
Deep yellow in colour. Interesting subtle aromas of honey,
spice and caramel. Rich and full with a smooth finish and tasty
subtle hazelnut tone. Medium acidity.

RED WINE

Red £5.25–£6

Côtes du Rhône AC Côtes du Rhône 95   **13**
Dillon
Bright crimson with red jelly appeal. Nice spicy touches in an
easy-drinking, fruity style.

Paul Jaboulet AC Côtes du Ventoux 93   **14**
Gilbeys
Bright crimson. Vibrant style with good spicy appeal and
medium long finish.
Red £6–£8

Bouchard Père et Fils AC Côtes du Rhône-Villages 95   **13**
Dillon
Ruby red. Gives more on flavour than aroma, with touches of
cherry and chocolate. A good bite of acidity and supple tannins
add structure.

Cave de Tain l'Hermitage AC Crozes-Hermitage 94   ☆
Dunnes Stores
A vibrant fruity style with wine-gum aromas and flavours.
Plenty of zip and zap with good length.

Château du Grand Moulas AC Côtes du Rhône 95 ☆
Findlater
Crimson-purple in colour, with wonderful aromas of wild
berries and pepper. What one expects from this style, elegant
yet savoury with a nice bite of tannin and acidity. Great value.

Châteauneuf-du-Pape AC Châteauneuf-du-Pape 94 14
Quinnsworth
The 94 drinks better than the 93, with herby savoury aromas
turning to sweet fruit on the palate with mouthfilling flavours.

Domaine Richaud Cairanne AC Côtes du Rhône-Villages 94
Wines Direct 14
A wine that holds promise on aroma and delivers on taste.
Plummy fruits are held in check with mouth-gripping tannins
and high alcohol (13%).

Domaine Santa Duc AC Côtes du Rhône 94 13
Searson
Pleasant easy-drinking style; better in flavour than aroma.

La Vieille Ferme 'Le Mont' AC Côtes du Ventoux 93 14
Allied Drinks
Wonderful cerise-purple colour. Concentrated herb and spice
aromas carry through on flavour, ending in a slightly bitter
twist.

Parallèle '45' AC Côtes du Rhône 95 14
Gilbeys
The 95 vintage is bright crimson in colour, with classy tobacco
and cherry fruit appeal. Long, very drinkable finish.

Rasteau Carte Blanche AC Côtes du Rhône 95 13
Dalton
Jammy style with easy appeal and medium long finish.

Red £8–£10

Coudoulet de Beaucastel AC Côtes du Rhône 93   14
Allied Drinks
Wonderful deep purple tones with concentrated spice and
jammy flavours. Ends with a smack of tangy acidity.

Cuvée Sommelongue AC Côtes du Rhône 94   14
Karwig
Deep blackberry in colour. Offers a big mouthful of spice and
tannin. Robust and solid with fruit fighting the tannin.

Delas 'Les Launes' AC Crozes-Hermitage 94
Febvre
The white pepper of this AC is so easy to identify. Its savoury
appeal really gets the gastric juices going. Don't be put off by
the light saturation of colour—it has a very concentrated palate.

Domaine Brusset Cairanne AC Côtes du Rhône-Villages 94
Mitchell   ☆
Some wines are recognisable by their individual style—this is
one of them. The prune and fig aromas with mouth-drying
tannins, good weight and structure in a traditional style offer
serious red drinking pleasure.

Domaine St Gayan AC Côtes du Rhône 94   14
Callaghan
Well-structured Rhône style with plenty of strawberry fruit
flavours backed up with spice. Good length of flavour on the
finish.

Laudun Hauts Terroirs AC Côtes du Rhône-Villages 90   14
Wine Vault
Hints of brick show through the crimson colour. Pleasant
vegetal aromas with touches of spice and tannin add up to a
harmonious wine with an extra-long finish.

Laurent Charles Brotte AC Vacqueyras 93
Cassidy
Lots of spice followed by rich berry fruits. Full bodied with a

good whack of acidity and tannin. Interesting drinking.

Les Nobles Rives AC St Joseph 93　　　　　　　14
Dunnes Stores
Blood-red in colour. Peppery and savoury with a big spicy
finish. Good food wine.

Paul Jaboulet Aîné 'Les Jalets' AC Crozes-Hermitage 94　☆
Gilbeys
Rich deep purple tint with lots of savoury herbal and white
pepper tones, a backbone of acidity, and firm tannic finish.

Paul Jaboulet Aîné Pierre Aiguille AC Gigondas 93　　☆
Gilbeys
A super wine with a deep crimson colour. Packed tight with
spice and red berry fruit appeal. A delicious big, fruity
assertive style.

Pierre Ponnelle AC Châteauneuf-du-Pape 93　　　　14
Dunnes Stores
Deep crimson in colour, with savoury meaty tones and the
typical black pepper of the AC. Falls between the modern and
traditional styles.

Pierre Ponnelle AC Côtes du Rhône-Villages 94　　　12
Dunnes Stores
Ruby red in colour, with ripe red berry fruits and a burst of
black pepper.

Victor Bérard AC Châteauneuf-du-Pape 95　　　　14
Greenhills
Pleasant modern style. Wine-gum aromas with a nice bite of
acidity and tannin.

Red £10–£12

Barton & Guestier AC Châteauneuf-du-Pape 93　　　14
Dillon
A little maturity adds interest to this easy-drinking style, which
has a hint of cedar and spice with just a touch of Mocha.

Cave de Tain l'Hermitage AC Hermitage 92
Dunnes Stores
Meaty and beefy, this is an example of top-class Syrah from the
Rhône. Winter warming and perfect with strong-flavoured
meat dishes.

Delas 'Les Challeys' AC St Joseph 94 14
Febvre
Distinctive white pepper aromas. Smooth on the palate. Very
savoury with an extra-long finish.

**Domaine de la Mordorée Cuvée de la Reine des Bois AC Lirac
93** *Brangan* ☆ ☆
Rich and concentrated, with layers of interesting fruit, savoury
and spicy flavours. A top example of the Lirac southern Rhône
appellation.

Domaine Ste Anne 'St Gervais' AC Côtes du Rhône-Villages 94
Brangan 14
Bright ruby in colour, with enticing peppery appeal and smooth
tasty finish.

Laurent Charles Brotte AC Gigondas 92 ☆
Cassidy
Ignore the light saturation of colour, instead concentrate on the
amazing white pepper spice that cuts through all the elements.
Finishes on a high note.
Red £12–£15

Carte Or AC Châteauneuf-du-Pape 89 13
Allied Drinks
Rich, warm and spicy, with a slight bittersweet twist to the
extra-long finish.

Cuvée de la Reine Jeanne AC Châteauneuf-du-Pape 90 14
Remy
Ripe and rich, with noted subdued spicy tones. Good follow-
through on flavour with a medium long finish.

Domaine du Vieux Télégraphe AC Châteauneuf-du-Pape 93
Findlater ☆☆
The 93 is rich, complex and robust, with layers of savoury
tones, spice and herbs. A wine for strong meats such as venison.

Les Cailloux AC Châteauneuf-du-Pape 93 **14**
Karwig
Baked red berry aromas like fruit crumble cut right through this
wine. It ends in a good smack of acidity.

Red £15–£20

Château de Beaucastel AC Châteauneuf-du-Pape 93 ☆
Allied Drinks
A real stunner—cedar, chocolate, liquorice all spring to mind.
Powerful fruit attack and wonderful rich finish.

Château La Nerthe AC Châteauneuf-du-Pape 91 ☆
Ecock
Ripe berry fruit appeal with very balanced acidity, high alcohol
and a whack of tannin from a very good Rhône vintage.
Concentrated and long on the spicy blackcurrant finish.

Delas 'Chante-Perdrix' AC Cornas 91 ☆
Febvre
Deep crimson with earthy savoury tones. Great fruit and
assertive tannins which add structure. Classic style.

Domaine de la Mordorée AC Châteauneuf-du-Pape 93 ☆
Brangan
Purple-crimson in colour. Gamey savoury tones. A big wine in
every sense, with mouth-drying tannins and rich concentrated
flavours ending in a long robust finish.

Domaine Ste Anne Syrah AC Côtes du Rhône 92 ☆☆☆
Brangan
Deep, purple-black colour. Extremely rich and concentrated,
with a heart of raisiny fruit overladen with herbs. Superb!

Laurent Charles Brotte AC Châteauneuf-du-Pape 89   **14**
Cassidy
Inky in colour, with savoury meaty aromas and flavours and a
good bite of spice on the finish. Well structured with a slightly
austere finish.

Les Hauts de Montmirail AC Gigondas 93
Mitchell
If you want to understand this AC, start right here! The lovely
presentation is matched by the strong robust savoury tone of
the wine. With its spice, fruit and herbs it has everything.

Paul Jaboulet Ainé 'La Chapelle' AC Hermitage 94
Gilbeys
A powerful majestic example of Syrah at its best. Deeply
concentrated, with cedar and spice and a complex mineral
touch. Needs time to demonstrate its richness.
Red £20–£30

Delas 'Seigneur de Maugiron' AC Côte-Rôtie 90
Febvre
Deep purple-black in colour. Amazing aromas, rich and
concentrated, ranging from deep ripe fruit to black olive juice.
A savoury multi-layered wine, with a long, robust and meaty
finish. Needs more time to show its greatness.

Delas 'Les Bessards' AC Hermitage 91
Febvre
Deep crimson. Baked and spicy. Austere due to its youth but
promises a lot, with fruit trying to emerge behind the drying
tannins. More bottle age will ensure that a beauty is born.

Robert Jasmin AC Côte-Rôtie 88   ☆☆☆
Searson
Gloriously deep in colour. Complex aromas of spice, meaty
'jus', pepper and cinnamon. On taste, the herbs and spices are
noticed first, then the fruit and tannins, which are rich and
obvious. Wonderful.

France—South

Principal grape varieties

Languedoc

White	Red
Rolle	Carignan
Marsanne	Aramon
Viognier	Mourvèdre (Mataro)
Chardonnay	Cinsaut
Picpoul	Grenache
Clairette	Syrah
Bourboulenc	Cabernet Sauvignon
Sauvignon Blanc	Merlot

Roussillon

White	Red
Maccabeo	Grenache
Malvoisie	Cinsaut
Roussanne	Syrah
Marsanne	Mourvèdre
Grenache Blanc	
Vermentino	
Muscat	

Provence

White	Red
Grenache Blanc	Tibouren
Rolle (Vermentino)	Mourvèdre
Ugni Blanc	Grenache
Clairette	Carignan
	Calitor
	Cinsaut

Labelling guide

Languedoc Roussillon: All styles and wine categories are produced.
Vin de Pays on the label also indicates the name of the
production area e.g. VdP d'Oc, VdP l'Herault, VdP du Gard.
Many also indicate the name of the grape variety. AC wines
include Côteaux du Languedoc, a large AC area with smaller
sub-regions of higher-quality such as Faugères and St Chinian.

Coteaux du Roussillon: Produces soft silky reds with AC Collioure producing full bodied reds.

Coteaux du Roussillon-Villages: Covers only red wine.

Fitou: For red wines only. The best should be big and spicy.

Minervois: Red wine production dominates with some white and rosé also being produced.

Corbières: Mostly red wine with a little red and rosé also.

Vin Doux Naturel: This is a naturally sweet fortified wine. Whites are produced from the Muscat grape, reds from the Grenache. Muscat de Rivesaltes, Muscat de Frontignan and Banyuls are available in Ireland. Banyuls is one of the rare wines to go with chocolate.

Provence: White, red and rosé are produced. Dry rosé dominates production, whites need to be drunk very young and fresh. Reds are exciting with a remarkable cerise colour and lots of herb and spice aromas and flavours. AC wines include:

Côtes de Provence: 60% of production is devoted to rosé wine, with some red and white. Other appellations include Bellet, Palette and Cassis, three tiny areas rarely seen outside their region.

Côteaux d'Aix-en-Provence: Production is centred on red with some white and rosé. Reds should be drunk cool.

Bandol: By law red wines are produced from a minimum of 50% Mourvèdre and must spend 18 months in cask before bottling. They have great ageing ability.

WHITE WINE

White under £4.50

La Carignano Chardonnay VdP d'Oc 95   13
Dunnes Stores
Ripe apple fruit flavours with enough acidity to add freshness to the medium long finish.

White £4.50–£5.25

Calvet Chardonnay VdP d'Oc 94   13
Grants
A ripe fruit style with a whiff of honey over the apple. Good fruit and acidity balance.

Chais Cuxac Chardonnay VdP d'Oc 95   14
Superquinn
Offers good-value drinking with its slight buttery texture and fruit appeal.

Chardonnay VdP d'Oc 95 13
United Beverages
A well-rounded wine with good fruit, hints of creaminess and balanced acidity.

Domaine de Gourgazeaud Chardonnay VdP d'Oc 95 14
Dunnes Stores
Deep yellow-gold with delicious hints of pineapple cut through with citrus-type acidity.

Domaine de la Tuilerie Chardonnay VdP d'Oc 95 14
Quinnsworth
The 95 vintage is particularly fresh and crisp, with ripe lemon-peel aromas that expand on flavour.

Fortant de France Grenache Blanc VdP d'Oc 95 14
Fitzgerald
Delivers more on flavour than aroma, with greengage fruit appeal supported by lively acidity.

White £5.25–£6

Alexis Lichine Chardonnay VdP d'Oc 95 13
Greenhills
Water-pale. What it lacks in aroma it makes up for in flavour with a crisp nutty finish.

Baron Philippe de Rothschild Sauvignon Blanc VdP d'Oc 95
Findlater 14
Rhubarb nuances with a clean fresh appeal, good weight of fruit and medium long finish.

Chauvenet Chardonnay de France VdP d'Oc 94 14
United Beverages
Touches of ripe tropical fruits with medium acidity and good length of flavour. For those who like a fruity white.

Fortant de France Sauvignon Blanc VdP d'Oc 95 14
Fitzgerald
The 95 vintage has the same pleasant citrus appeal as the 94. A

ripe style of Sauvignon with a nice bite of acidity adding freshness.

La Baume Philippe de Baudin Sauvignon Blanc VdP d'Oc 95

Quinnsworth ☆

A good zesty Sauvignon with a restrained herbaceous touch, good fruit flavours and extra-long finish.

Les Heritages Chardonnay VdP d'Oc 95 ☆

Dunnes Stores

Vinification and maturation in oak add a nice creamy touch to the exotic fruity finish.

Philippe de Baudin Chardonnay VdP d'Oc 94 14

Quinnsworth

Produced by BRL Hardy of Australian fame, this vintage has a creamy texture and exotic fruit tones with a harmonious extra-long finish.

White £6–£8

Baron Philippe de Rothschild Chardonnay VdP d'Oc 95

Findlater 14

Stony and steely with good tingling fresh apple appeal. Well-balanced crisp style.

Chais Baumière Chardonnay VdP d'Oc 94 13

Allied Drinks

A must for the oak lover with its creamy fruit tones and good weighty texture.

Chais Baumière Sauvignon Blanc VdP d'Oc 94 13

Allied Drinks

Easy drinking with fresh appeal. Smooth and round with lively acidity adding freshness.

Chardonnay VdP de l'Aude 94 12

Cassidy

Mild aromas with a hint of peachy fruit that carries through on flavour.

Château Roubaud AC Costières de Nîmes 94 ☆
Dalton
Offers something different. Stony fruit appeal, good palate
weight and enough structure to hold up the bone dry appealing
finish.

Domaine de Brau Blanc de Brau VdP Côtes de Lastours 94
Brangan **14**
Very appealing citrus fruit tones. Extremely well-made organic
wine with zesty acidity, making it a perfect match for grilled
fish.

Domaine du Bosc Sauvignon Blanc VdP d'Oc 94 **13**
Cassidy
Reasonable length and good balance. Slight grapefruit tone.

James Herrick Chardonnay VdP d'Oc 94 **14**
Wines Direct
Peachy/apricot aromas and flavours. Smooth and rich on the
palate. Long lingering finish.

La Serre Chardonnay VdP d'Oc 94 **13**
Searson
A very appealing style with lots of fruit backed up with fresh
acidity and weighty mouth texture.

Laroche L Chardonnay VdP d'Oc 94 **12**
Allied Drinks
Deep gold in colour. Nutty aromas followed by apple fruit
flavours. Good weighty wine with a slightly bitter finish.

Laroche Sauvignon Blanc VdP d'Oc 94 **12**
Allied Drinks
Deep yellow-gold. Good citrus attack. Not much fruit develop-
ment. Clean fresh finish.

Ryman Viognier VdP d'Oc 95 ☆
Quinnsworth
A luscious oak-matured wine with medium acidity and a long

succulent finish. Enjoy it young while it retains its appealing fruit characteristics.

White £8–£10

Château St James AC Corbières 94   12
Callaghan
Doesn't give much on aroma, but has pleasant stewed apple flavours and a reasonable finish.

Fortant de France Collection Chardonnay VdP d'Oc 93
Fitzgerald
Deep green-yellow in colour, with interesting aromas of lemon and ripe grapefruit peel. Mouthfilling well-rounded style with a smooth creamy finish.

White £10–£12

Château Haut Gléon AC Corbières 95
Jenkinson Wines
New oak dominates, but mango-type fruits come through on flavour. The long finish has a nice creamy touch.

White £12–£15

Domaine de Terre Mégère 'La Galopine' AC Coteaux du Languedoc 94
Brangan
Deep green-gold with very impressive aromas of vanilla and ripe peach giving way to a fat weighty texture. The balance and finish are superb.

RED WINE

Red under £4.50

Abbaye St Hilaire AC Coteaux Varois 94
Superquinn
This really delivers on taste. It has an appealing ruby red colour, cherry aromas and flavours, and a surprisingly lengthy finish.

La Carignano Cabernet Sauvignon VdP Cassan 94   12
Dunnes Stores
Purple has turned to crimson, but the stalky red berry fruit appeal is still there. A good food wine.

La Carignano Merlot VdP Cassan 94   14
Dunnes Stores
Pleasant easy-drinking style with jammy-type flavours and a
nice bite of acidity.

La Carignano Syrah VdP Cassan 94   14
Dunnes Stores
Garnet in colour, with a hint of jammy liquorice taking over
from the fruit appeal.

Labouré-Roi Cabernet Sauvignon VdP d'Oc 95   13
Quinnsworth
A chewy wine with a pleasant crimson colour and slight bite of
spice on the finish.

Labouré-Roi Merlot/Syrah VdP d'Oc 95   13
Quinnsworth
Plummy cherry appeal. Easy-drinking fruity style with a
medium long finish.
Red £4.50–£5.25

Calvet Cabernet Sauvignon VdP d'Oc 95   14
Grants
Plummy and jammy. Fresh fruit and soft tannic structure.

Calvet Merlot VdP d'Oc 95   ☆
Grants
Good structure, pleasant leafy blackcurrant aromas and good
fruit development. Its bite and grip make it a good choice with
food.

Calvet Syrah VdP d'Oc 94   14
Grants
A little bottle maturation has helped highlight the spicy jammy
fruit appeal.

Cordier Cabernet Sauvignon VdP d'Oc 95   13
United Beverages
Easy drinking with blackberry jam touches and a good bite of

acidity. Still young—the tannins are obvious but should soften with a little time.

Cuvée Antoine de Montpezad AC Coteaux du Languedoc 94

Dunnes Stores   14

Since last tasted, the wine, produced from Syrah, has assumed a whiff of tobacco. Soft fruity attack with good structure for enjoying now.

Domaine Ste Nathalie AC Faugères 94   14

Dunnes Stores

Nicely balanced, the wine has depth of flavour with supple harmonious tannins and acidity.

Fontaine de Cathala Cabernet Sauvignon VdP d'Oc 94   13

Dunnes Stores

Deep purple in colour, with chunky ripe berry fruit appeal. A pleasant, surprisingly long satisfying finish.

Fortant de France Grenache VdP d'Oc 94   13

Fitzgerald

Ruby pink in colour, with juicy fruit appeal. Good value, in an easy-drinking style. At its best served cool.

Laperouse VdP d'Oc 94   ☆ ☆

Quinnsworth

Has developed extremely well since tasted last year. Its classic structure and some bottle age add up to a wine which has it all at an extremely competitive price.

Red £5.25–£6

Alexis Lichine Merlot VdP d'Oc 95   14

Greenhills

Deep purple in colour, with raw blackcurrant jelly aromas. Good fruit on the palate, with a soft supple finish.

Arnaud de Villeneuve AC Côtes du Roussillon 94   14

Allied Drinks

Inky black in colour, with lots of jammy fruits. A robust chunky wine in an easy-drinking style.

[145]

**Baron Philippe de Rothschild Cabernet Sauvignon VdP d'Oc
95**   *Findlater*   **14**
Crimson in colour, with leafy herbaceous appeal and good
tannic structure. Still young.

Baron Philippe de Rothschild Merlot VdP d'Oc 95   **14**
Findlater
Deep ruby in colour. Shows better on flavour than aroma. Good
mouthfilling red berry fruit appeal with a harmonious finish.

Barton & Guestier Cabernet Sauvignon VdP d'Oc 94   **14**
Dillon
The herb-like tone of the 95 vintage is very attractive. The taste
holds up from first impression to last.

Barton & Guestier Merlot VdP d'Oc 95   **14**
Dillon
A modern red wine in both presentation and flavour. The
pleasant red berry fruit tones hold up right through to the
finish, with a nice stalky bite at the end. Serve cool. Good lunch
wine.

Château Cazal Viel AC St Chinian 94   ☆
Quinnsworth
The 94 vintage is a complex example of this appetising wine. It
has classic restraint due to its young vintage, with assertive
tannins. Should be drunk with food. Delicious.

Château de Clapier AC Côtes de Lubéron 93   **12**
Wines Direct
Deep purple in colour, with strawberry fruit aromas. Good
attack of sweet ripe fruit supported by supple tannins.

Château de Flaugergues AC Coteaux du Languedoc 94   ☆
Dunnes Stores
Dense savoury spicy aromas. Good weight of fruit extract with
lively acidity and tannin add up to a long savoury lipsmacking
finish.

Château de Gourgazeaud AC Minervois 92 ☆☆
Dunnes Stores
As this wine has matured, the herbs and spices win over the
fruit. Cloves, bay leaf, rosemary—the list is endless to describe
this attractive wine which has a nice long supple finish.

**Château Milhau-Lacugue Cuvée des Chevaliers AC St Chinian
93**   *Quinnsworth*   14
Inky in colour. This red wine from the Languedoc is a chunky
style with a 'mineral' backbone produced from a blend of
grapes including Carignan, Grenache and Cinsaut.

Chauvenet Cabernet Sauvignon de France VdP d'Oc 94
United Beverages   ☆
Deep crimson in colour, with a very attractive aroma of spice
which converts to peppers on flavour. Good value.

Cheval-Quancard Merlot VdP d'Oc 94   14
Brangan
Crimson in colour. Delivers on stalky fruit flavours with a nice
bite of tannin adding structure. Good food wine.

Chevalier AC Côtes du Ventoux 95   13
TDL
Appetising fruity aromas of raspberry which carry through on
flavour. Nice bite of cherry on the finish.

**Cuvée Harmonie, Domaine la Condamine L'Êvêque VdP des
Côtes de Thongue 94**   13
Searson
Deep purple with red berry fruits overlain with spice.

Domaine Coste Rouge AC Coteaux du Languedoc 94   ☆
Dunnes Stores
A real treat, with its appealing black cherry fruit. Packs a punch
of flavour, backed up with smooth tannins and a long supple
finish. Hard to beat at the price.

Domaine de Moulines Merlot VdP de l'Hérault 94   14
Terroirs
Terrific green pepper appeal. Fruit shows through on flavour,
with drying tannins and balanced acidity adding good structure.

Domaine St Martin AC Côtes du Roussillon Villages 94
Searson   12
Blackcurrant leafy aromas that carry through in flavour in an
easy-drinking style.

Fortant de France Cabernet Sauvignon VdP d'Oc 94   14
Fitzgerald
The 94 vintage has a deep saturation of purple-crimson, with
dense aromas of wild red berry fruits. A chewy style with
pronounced tannins.

Fortant de France Merlot VdP d'Oc 94   14
Fitzgerald
Deep crimson with smoky brambly fruit appeal. Has good
structure, with flavour holding up through the mouth-coating
yet supple tannins. A 'cool' red.

La Baume Domaine de la Baume VdP d'Oc 94   14
Quinnsworth
Nicely presented. Ribena in colour, with hot berry fruit appeal.
An opulent style with lots of fruit and that little austere touch
that young Merlot imparts to a wine.

La Baume Philippe de Baudin Merlot VdP d'Oc 94   14
Quinnsworth
This wine has wonderful extract with rich squashed red berry
fruit appeal and a silky opulent finish.

La Baume Philippe de Baudin Syrah VdP d'Oc 95   ☆ ☆
Quinnsworth
French grapes vinified by an Australian winemaking expert
have resulted in a big wine in every sense. Deep in colour, with

dense savoury aromas and flavours. A rich, chunky, satisfying wine.

Merlot VdP de l'Aude 94   13
Cassidy

Easy-drinking jammy style, with supple tannins and a little austere twist on the finish.

Philippe de Baudin Cabernet Sauvignon VdP d'Oc 93
Quinnsworth

This vintage has matured well in bottle since last tasted. It demands attention with its blackberry fruit appeal which has developed a hint of mint. Smooth and silky—delicious on its own or with a snack.

Red £6–£8

Chais Baumière Cabernet Sauvignon VdP d'Oc 93
Allied Drinks

Super mouthfilling flavours of blackcurrant and spice. Another example of good Australian winemaking in a classic French style.

Château Cap de Fouste AC Côtes du Roussillon 94
McCabes

A big rich red. The bright crimson colour is extremely appealing. The aromas are all about spice, coffee and fruit with a hint of vanilla. The finish is impressive and packed with savoury appeal.

Château de Brau Cabardes VDQS 95   14
Brangan

Crimson in colour, this organic wine smacks of earthy tones. It has an intriguing underripe fruit appeal with a whack of tannin and a very smooth finish. An interesting wine.

Château de la Liquière AC Faugères 94   14
Wines Direct

Ox-blood red with hints of nutmeg and clove. Good bite of savoury herbs with plenty of tannin and acidity to add structure. Appealing savoury style.

Château de Mattes AC Corbières 92   14
Dalton
A big style with spicy new oak appeal, medium tannins and
flavours that persist with a characteristic bite of pepper.

Château du Donjon AC Minervois 93   14
Wines Direct
A top example of a fruity yet spicy South of France wine. Note
the hint of damson fruit followed by drying tannins and good
acidity. Good food wine.

Château Pech-Céleyran AC Coteaux du Languedoc 94
Findlater   ☆
Robust earth and mint tones, impressive structure, mouth-
drying tannins and lots of fruit hidden behind. Extra-long
finish.

**Château Peche-Redon La Clape Cuvée Reservée AC Coteaux
du Languedoc 94**   14
Quinnsworth
More savoury than fruity in style with herby tones, a super rich
colour and assertive tannins.

Château Roubaud AC Costières de Nîmes 94   14
Dalton
Dense smoky fruit ending in a slightly meaty finish. A savoury
wine with a long finish.

Château St Auriol AC Corbières 93   ☆
Searson
A super vintage with its hot baked aromas. Delivers even more
on flavour, with mouth-puckering tannins and wonderful
herbal touches. A savoury, meaty wine.

Cuvée de l'Arjolle VdP des Côtes de Thongue 94   ☆ ☆
Brangan
Produced from 70% Cabernet Sauvignon and 30% Merlot, this

vintage exhibits a rich saturation of colour with aromas of tea and coffee mingling with chocolate. The first impression of sweet ripe fruit is outweighed by assertive tannins. A super vintage.

Delaunay Syrah VdP d'Oc 94   14
Brangan
Pleasant deep crimson colour with wine-gum aromas and a chewy, fruity finish.

Domaine Clavel 'La Méjanelle' AC Coteaux du Languedoc 94
Wines Direct   ☆
Produced from a blend of 50% Grenache and 50% Syrah, this interesting wine has cooked red berry fruit aromas and flavours. Fermentation in oak adds vanilla and spice to the long pleasant finish.

Domaine d'Aupilhac AC Coteaux du Languedoc 93   14
Searson
Closed on aroma, with savoury rather than fruity tones. A good food wine.

Domaine de l'Hortus AC Coteaux du Languedoc 93   14
Wines Direct
Ruby red with lots of jammy fruits. Traditional method with extended maceration on skins gives good depth of flavour and helps round out the drying tannins on the finish.

Domaine de Limbardie Cabernet Sauvignon VdP Coteaux de Murviel 94   ☆
Brangan
Attractive soft creamy opulence more reminiscent of Merlot than Cabernet. The drying tannins give the game away, adding structure to this young wine.

Domaine de Terre Mégère 'Les Dolomies' AC Coteaux du Languedoc 94   ☆
Brangan
A long-time favourite with chocolate and prune aromas.

Chunky, chewy appeal ending in a hint of spice.

**Domaine des Chênes Les Grands-Mères AC Côtes du
Roussillon Villages 94**   *Wines Direct*   ☆
Deep purple-crimson in colour; loaded with cherry and
liquorice. Very balanced with supple harmonious tannins. A
super example of its style.

Domaine du Bosc Syrah VdP de l'Hérault 94   12
Cassidy
Raspberry-coloured with a slight pungent stalky aroma. A wine
that needs food.

Domaine du Grand Crès AC Corbières 93   13
Wines Direct
Deep purple in colour, with herb-like aromas and flavours.

La Serre Merlot VdP d'Oc 94   14
Searson
Chunky, with smoky liquorice, Merlot fruit, gum-drying
tannins and balanced acidity.
Red £8–£10

Campagne de Centeilles AC Minervois 92   14
Brangan
Showing maturity with its tawny reflections. An ideal choice
for the Sunday roast, with its mature aromas and flavours of
herbs and beefy appeal. Enjoy now.

Chapelle Haut Gléon AC Corbières 93   14
Jenkinson Wines
The strawberry fruits are deliciously complemented by a
chocolate creamy touch. Nice oak influence adds to the long
succulent finish.

Château Flaugergues La Méjanelle AC Coteaux du Languedoc

94   *Dunnes Stores*   ☆☆

This vintage is powerful and chunky with a tight-knit structure.
The raspberry fruit is overtaken by the tannins. The finish is
impressive.

Fortant de France Collection Cabernet Sauvignon VdP d'Oc 94

Fitzgerald   ☆

Deep blackberry in colour. Rich and plummy with a delicious
attack of fruit supported by balanced acidity. A smooth style
with good length.

Red £10–£12

Château Haut Gléon AC Corbières 93   ☆

Jenkinson Wines

Deep cherry red, the wine has a delicious bite of high acidity
with good red berry fruit development and a long rich finish

Domaine l'Aguilière Grenat AC Coteaux du Languedoc 95

Brangan   ☆☆

Full of squashed red berry summer fruits and cream.
Mouthfilling flavours are supported by good tannic structure.
Very well-made wine with a delicious bite of ripe fruit flavour
in mid-palate.

Red £12–£15

Château Vignelaure (David O'Brien) AC Coteaux d'Aix en

Provence 86   *Febvre*   ☆

Produced from old vines of Cabernet Sauvignon, Syrah and
Grenache, this is the top wine in the range of this famous
Provence wine. It oozes red berry and herb appeal. Showing
maturity it has classic structure and a long complex finish.

Domaine Bunan Mas de la Rouvière AC Bandol 89   ☆

Mackenway

Since last tasted this wine has developed extremely well.
Produced from a blend of Mourvèdre, Grenache, Syrah and
Cinsaut, its powerful herby influence is still apparent, but the

flavours have mellowed into a smooth opulent finish.

**Domaine Richeaume Cuvée Columelle AC Côtes de Provence
92**   *Karwig*   ☆☆

Inky black in colour with complex aromas of cedar and herbs.
Huge concentration of flavour on the palate ending in a
delectable spicy tannin finish. Provence at its best from an
organic wine producer.

Domaine Richeaume Syrah AC Côtes de Provence 93   ☆
Karwig

Big, powerful and spicy, with all the herby tones associated
with Provence. Savoury opulent finish.

Mas de Daumas Gassac VdP de L'Hérault 93   ☆☆
Allied Drinks

Has developed well since tasted last year. The mineral touch
has softened, with the blackcurrant of Cabernet Sauvignon
beginning to show. Merlot, Syrah and Malbec help contribute
spice, plum and tobacco scents. A classy wine in every way.

Red £15–£20

Château de Pibarnon AC Bandol 92   ☆☆
Terroirs

Produced principally from the Mourvèdre grape. 'Wow' again.
Herby aromas give way to a big fruit attack of plums and
cherries. Long concentrated finish. Still young.

Château Pradeaux AC Bandol 90   14
Karwig

Deep crimson in colour, with an intriguing aroma of tar and
violets. Still young and needs a little more bottle age to allow
the promise of fruit tones to emerge.

**Domaine de Trévallon Les Baux AC Coteaux d'Aix en Provence
93**   *Brangan*   ☆☆

The 93 vintage is as wild and wonderful as the 92. Still very
young, it has a superb attack of sweet ripe chewy fruit. The
tannins dominate at this stage, but notice how rich and

appealing this youthful wine is.

Domaine Tempier Cuvée Spéciale la Migoua AC Bandol 90
Brangan ☆☆☆

Rich, powerful and concentrated, with warming plum and cedar tones. A big, bold wine produced principally from the Mourvèdre grape and aged by law for a minimum of 18 months. A shining example of the most serious red wine of Provence.

Red £20–£30

Clos d'Ière Cuvée 1 AC Côtes de Provence 92 ☆☆
Brangan

Aroma of freshly picked mushrooms with a smoky tone. The flavour is of ripe opulent fruit overlain with herbs ending in an interesting concentrated finish.

Domaine Ott Longue Garde AC Bandol 90 ☆☆
Mitchell

Concentration of figs, prunes and spice. Rich and complex, the flavours swirl around the palate. First-class winemaking and a top example of its style. Shows just how well Mourvèdre can age.

ROSÉ WINE

Rosé £5.25–£6

Château de Flaugergues AC Coteaux du Languedoc 95 **13**
Dunnes Stores

Hints of baby pink with pleasant sherbet and jammy fruit aromas. A slight bitter twist to the dry finish makes it a good choice with summer lunches.

Fortant de France Rosé de Syrah VdP d'Oc 95
Fitzgerald

A modern dry rosé with raspberry and cherry fruit aromas and flavours. Very attractive fresh style with a hint of spice. Enjoy young and fresh.

France—South-West

Principal grape varieties

Similar to Bordeaux, the region also has many native vines, some of which are listed below.

White	Red
Gros Manseng	Tannat
Mauzac	Négrette
Len de l'El	Malbec (Auxerrois)
Petit Courbu	Abouriou
Petit Manseng	Fer
Ugni Blanc	
Colombard	

Labelling guide

AC wines include:

Bergerac (the best known): Merlot often dominates in the blend of red wines. Crisp white and dry rosé styles are also produced.

Pécharmant: considered one of the best red wines of the region.

Côtes de Duras: white and red styles are produced.

Gaillac: more white is produced than red, along with a style known as perlé (faintly bubbly).

Côtes de Montravel: dry to sweet.

Monbazillac: the most famous sweet wine of the region.

Buzet: red wine dominates.

Irouléguy: white, red and rosé.

Côtes du Frontonnais: the local grape Négrette dominates in the blend of this red wine.

Côtes du Marmandais: red is produced from a variety of grapes; white and rosé also produced.

Cahors: from one of the oldest vineyards in France. Traditionally known as the 'black wine of Cahors' due to its dark colour. Malbec dominates. Two styles are produced: traditional robust one and lighter modern.

Madiran: the local grape variety Tannat is used extensively in blended red wines. Madiran rivals Cahors as one of the deepest-coloured and longest-lived wines of South-West France.

Jurançon: dry white wines are produced chiefly from the Gros Manseng grape, while Petit Manseng dominates in the production of sweet wines.

Vins de Pays des Côtes de Gascogne: produced from Ugni Blanc and Colombard, the whites are very fresh, crisp and lively.

WHITE WINE

White £5.25–£6

Côtes de St Mont VDQS 94   13
Findlater
Water-pale, with a slight nutty overtone and dry finish. The grape varieties are interesting and include Gros Manseng, Petit Manseng and Petit Corbu.

Domaine du Rey VdP Côtes de Gascogne 95   14
TDL/Searson
Gooseberry and nettles all the way! Fresh and zippy with an extra-long finish.

La Coudette VdP Côtes de Gascogne 95   12
Findlater
Bone dry with crisp even tart acidity, making it an ideal choice for oily fish.

White £6–£8

Blanc de Blancs AC Jurançon Sec 95   14
Searson
This vintage, although still very young, has a pleasant touch of honeysuckle backed up with lemon-type acidity giving interest to the finish.

Château de la Jaubertie AC Bergerac Sec 95   ☆
Mitchell
A very well-made example of a fresh zippy style with a nice bite of stony fruit.

Château Jolys AC Jurançon Sec 94   14
Wines Direct
This 'nutty' dry white wine is produced from Gros Manseng, Petit Manseng and Courbu. It has good length of flavour with a slight tobacco finish.

Château le Bost AC Bergerac Sec 95 14
Hugan
Pale in colour. Very clean and flinty with fruit flavours
emerging. Cut through with zippy acidity.

Domaine du Tariquet VdP Côtes de Gascogne 95 14
Brangan
Straw-yellow in colour. Neutral on aroma. Delivers much more
on flavour, with lively acidity adding a fresh finish to the ripe
apple-fruit character.

RED WINE

Red £5.25-£6

Côtes de St Mont VDQS 94 13
Findlater
Tannat and Fer Servadou are blended with Cabernet Franc and
Sauvignon to produce a fairly tannic wine still hiding the fruit.

La Coudette VdP Côtes de Gascogne 95 13
Findlater
Pale crimson, this well-made modern red has good light red
berry fruit appeal with supple tannins adding structure.

Red £6–£8

Château Bellevue La Forêt AC Côtes de Frontonnais 94 14
Mackenway
Produced principally from the Négrette grape, which gives
good structure, and Gamay and Syrah, which add fruit and
spice. All round, a supple fruity wine with a touch of spice.

Château de la Jaubertie AC Bergerac 94 14
Mitchell
Crimson with hints of purple. Clean fresh fruity aromas of
plum and damson are still hidden under mouth-drying tannins.
The structure and classic style make it a better choice than some
94 Bordeaux styles.

Château le Bost AC Bergerac 93 ☆
Hugan
An attractive 'solid' wine with herb-like aromas. Fruit emerg-

ing on the palate and a nice hint of spice make this a serious well-balanced wine.

Château Montauriol 'Les Hauts de Montauriol' AC Côtes du Frontonnais 95　　　*Brangan*　　　14
Still very youthful, with its purple-cerise colour. It has a wonderful bite of cherry fruit with assertive tannins overtaking fruit which fights back on the finish.
Red £10–£12

Domaine de Mignaberry AC Irouléguy 90　　　13
Brangan
Deep ruby. Full of summer fruit tones with a touch of stalkiness. A nice bite of tannin adds structure, with good acidity supporting the fruit.
Red £12–£15

Clos de Gamot AC Cahors 90　　　14
Brangan
Showing maturity in colour and aroma, this wine exhibits tar and cedar tones with a hint of liquorice. A mature style.

Germany

Main wine regions

Ahr
Mittelrhein
Mosel-Saar-Ruwer
Rheingau
Nahe
Rheinhessen

Pfalz
Franken
Hessische Bergstrasse
Württemberg
Baden
Sachsen Saale-Unstrut

Principal grape varieties

White
Müller-Thurgau
Riesling
Silvaner
Kerner
Scheurebe
Gewürztraminer
Ruländer (Pinot Gris)
Weissburgunder (Pinot Blanc)
Bacchus

Red
Spätburgunder (Pinot Noir)
Portugieser
Trollinger
Dornfelder

Labelling guide

Quality is classified by the ripeness of the grapes at harvest.

Deutscher Tafelwein (DTW): table wine, usually sweet.

Deutscher Tafelwein Landwein (LTW): can be compared to the French country wine category. Produced from one of twenty designated zones in dry or semi-dry styles.

Qualitätswein bestimmter Anbaugebiete (QbA): indicates quality wine from one of the 13 designated quality regions.

Qualitätswein mit Prädikat (QmP): This category includes the finest and most long-lived of all German wines (six grades).

Kabinett: wines produced from fully ripened grapes.

Spätlese: wine produced from late harvested grapes, traditionally sweeter than Kabinett wines, but more are now being produced in a drier style.

Auslese: wines produced from a harvest of very ripe grapes. Can be sweet or dry.

Beerenauslese: the high natural sugar content of these grapes ensures intense sweet wines.

Trockenbeerenauslese: unctuous concentrated rich dessert wines produced from grapes affected by noble rot.

Eiswein: grapes picked when frozen, producing superb sweet wines with a long life span.

Anbaugebiet indicates a specific region.

Bereich on the label indicates a collective term for a large area within a region, e.g. Bereich Johannisberg.

Grosslagen: name given to a group of vineyards within a region.

Ursprungslagen: a recent introduction, meaning a specific site of origin of a particular style of wine produced from specific grapes. More precise than Grosslagen.

Einzellage: single individual vineyard sites.

Hochgewachs: top-quality Riesling from the Mosel-Saar-Ruwer.

Charta: a group of Rheingau wine estates making and marketing top-quality Riesling.

Moseltaler: QbA wines from traditional grapes from the Mosel-Saar-Ruwer.

Trocken: dry

Halbtrocken: medium dry.

Weingut: wine estate.

AP number (Amtliche Prüfungsnummer): a quality control number appearing on quality wines and composed of 10–12 digits. The digits or numbers represent specific things such as the quality control station where the wine was tested, year of testing, vineyard location and year of bottling.

Liebfraumilch, Germany's biggest-selling easy-drinking semi-sweet wine, can be produced from four specific regions (Rheinhessen, Pfalz, Nahe and Rheingau) and four grape varieties (Riesling, Silvaner, Kerner or Müller-Thurgau).

Sekt: German term for sparkling wine.

Weissherbst: rosé wine.

Süssreserve: unfermented grape juice permitted as a sweetener, added to wine before bottling. Very strictly controlled.

Wine styles

Whites range from dry to medium to rich dessert styles. Rated for their light alcohol and elegance.

Rosés: fresh and fruity. Not widely available.

Reds: improving all the time. Light in colour and style. Oak-aged are interesting. Deeper coloured wines are produced from the Dornfelder.

Sweet: some of the longest-lived and greatest sweet wines, especially in the Beerenauslese, Trockenbeerenauslese and Eiswein styles.

Vintages

White

95 Very good to superb, especially Mosel.
94 Superb Riesling from top estates. Long keeping sweet wines.
93 Very good to superb, especially Mosel, Pfalz and sweet.
92 Very good. QbA for early drinking. Some classic QmP.
91 Very good QmP for early drinking.
90 Superb.
89 Superb, especially Mosel late harvested. Drinking well.
88 Superb. Lively and fruity. Drinking well now but can keep.
87 Very good. Light. Drinking well now.

Good older vintages: 83 superb, 76 superb, 71 classic.

WHITE WINE

White under £4.50

Schmitt Söhne Rheinbaron Kabinett Rheinhessen QmP 94
Dunnes Stores   13
Hints of green. Stony-fruit Riesling character on aroma. Fresh, fruity flavours end in a medium dry, medium long finish.

White £4.50–£5.25

Goldener Oktober Riesling Qba 94   13
Grants
Has held up well on flavour since tasted in 95. Pleasant, light and fruity in an off-dry style. Perfect choice for the newcomer to wine drinking. Drink chilled.

Schmitt Söhne Spätlese Mosel Gold QmP 94   14
Dunnes Stores
Showing plenty of pleasant fruity tones, this off-dry Riesling is balanced with a lively kick of acidity supporting the fruit.

White £5.25–£6

Deinhard Riesling Dry Rheinhessen QbA 94   13
Mitchell
Pleasant aromas of pithy grapefruit with good fruit develop-

ment on the palate, finishing in a fruity yet dry style.
White £6–£8

Kirchheimer Schwarzerde Gewürztraminer Kabinett
halbtrocken QmP 94 *Wine Barrel*
Spicy floral fruity flavours with a slight hint of spritz mingle
with zesty acidity and finish on a high note of fruit in an-off dry
style. Delicious.

Piesporter Treppchen Kabinett Riesling QmP 95 14
Quinnsworth
A perfumed Alpine flower Riesling with a steely core. The off-
dry finish and tingling acidity make it a must for poultry,
especially turkey. Modern labelling adds appeal.

Ungsteiner Honigsäeckel Ehrenfelser Kabinett QmP 95
Wine Barrel 14
Ehrenfelser is a crossing of Riesling and Silvaner. This example
is very deep yellow, with intense tropical and citrus fruit
aromas. Long flavoursome yet lively finish.

Ungsteiner Nussriegel Riesling Kabinett Trocken QmP 95
Wine Barrel
Deep yellow in colour with delicious apple and lime touches.
Top quality with an attractive zesty fruity finish.
White £8–£10

Ungsteiner Honigsäeckel Scheurebe Kabinett QmP 95 14
Wine Barrel
Not often seen on the Irish market. Deep yellow in colour, with
pleasant asparagus aromas. Tingling acidity gives way to a
slight spiciness on the finish.

Ungsteiner Weilberg Riesling Spätlese halbtrocken QmP 94
Wine Barrel
A wonderful tasting experience marked with orange and
grapefruit peel. Excellent flavours are wrapped around citrus
acidity. Shows the class of German Riesling.

White £10–£12

Hochheimer Königin Victoria Berg Kabinett QmP 91   14
Mitchell
Green-tinged with fresh delicate floral aromas, waxy texture
and a rich tangy finish.

White £12–£15

Ockfener Bockstein Riesling Spätlese QmP 94   13
Karwig
Medium sweet, fresh, with low alcohol (7.5%) and lots of
refreshing spritz.

Greece

Main wine regions

Côtes de Meliton (classic European red styles), Náoussa, Nemea, Cephalonia, Samos (island famous for its sweet wine), Mantinia, Pátras.

Principal grape varieties

Greece produces wine from the classic grape varieties but also has a myriad of native grapes, including:

White

Assyrtiko: light dry to luscious styles.
Malvasia: dry peachy whites.
Muscat: bone dry to rich dessert styles.
Robola: citrus-type lively wines.
Savatiano: aromatic white used for blending and in retsina production.

Red

Agiorgitiko: top red, producing rich supple wines.
Limnio: rustic herby wines.
Mavrodaphne: dry and fortified wine styles.
Xynomavro: burgundian styles with some sparkling and rosé.

Labelling guide

Epitrapezeos Oenos: table wines. Some wineries work outside the quality control system in order to experiment with different grapes and styles.
Topikos Oenos: Vin de Pays regional wines produced from well-known European or classic grapes.
OPAP: the abbreviation for nineteen appellations from proven regions of superior quality.
Appellation by tradition: this covers retsina, the famous Greek wine flavoured with pine resin and recognised by the EU as an exclusive Greek product.
Reserve: white or red wine with a total ageing period of two years.
Grand Reserve: whites with a total ageing period of three years and reds with a total ageing period of four years.
Cava (not to be confused with the Spanish sparkling wine of the same name): a range of aged table wines very popular in Greek

restaurants and tavernas.

Wine styles

Whites should be drunk young and fresh. Classic-style reds have ageing ability. Dessert wine should be consumed young.

WHITE WINE

White £4.50–£5.25

Boutari Retsina 95   14
Taserra
Retsina is made from Savatiano, Rhoditis and Assyrtikos with some Alep pine resin added to the must. Think of lemon curd and pine needles. This is a good example of the style.

Kretikos (Boutari) VdP de Crète 95   14
Taserra
Produced from the Vilana grape (a speciality of Crete) this is an interesting, lively wine with a delicate almond touch. Enjoy young and fresh.

Lac des Roches (Boutari) 95   14
Taserra
Pale green in colour with perfumed aromas. Well rounded on the palate, with more pungent fruit flavours emerging to add interest.

White £8–£10

Domaine Carras Mellisanthi 95   13
Parsons
Looking for a new taste? Then try this. Clean in style with a touch of oak.

RED WINE

Red £4.50–£5.25

Cava Tsantalis 91   13
Quinnsworth
Produced from Cabernet Sauvignon and the common Greek red wine grape Xynomavro, the 91 vintage is ruby red and delivers on ripe fruit flavours with a good whack of supple tannins.

Kourtaki Vin de Crète 95 ☆

Findlater

Deep cherry red—robust and beefy in style with a whack of
tannin. A big wine for a small price. Offers something different.

Kretikos (Boutari) VdP de Crète 95 13

Taserra

Bright pale ruby in colour. Juicy and fruity with a hint of
creaminess. Produced from Kotsifali, which gives softness, and
Mandelaria, which adds structure. A speciality of Crete.

Nemea (Boutari) 94 14

Taserra

Produced from the noble Greek variety Agiorgitiko, also known
as St George, this is a fruity wine reminiscent of raspberry jelly.
Medium acidity makes it an easy wine to drink on its own.
Red £5.25–£6

Naoussa (Boutari) 94 14

Taserra

Pale cherry in colour, this delicious wine, produced from the
Xynomavro (meaning acid black) and aged in oak casks, is an
impressive example of how good the grape can be. Fruit holds
up to the finish with drying tannins and acidity adding
structure.

Paros (Boutari) 94 14

Taserra

Deep ruby in colour, with a very pleasant spicy touch and
good, ripe fruit appeal. Think of raspberry and blackcurrant.
Red £8–£10

Château Carras 93 ☆☆

Parsons

A heady exotic wine with a distinctly savoury quality that
shouts its youth but can be appreciated now. Classic in style it
shows just how good Greek wines can be.

Domaine Carras Limnio 94 14

Parsons

Shows what top-class winemaking can do. It has subtle aromas

of red berry fruits overladen with an interesting earthy touch.
Red £12–£15

Domaine Carras Syrah 94 ☆
Parsons
Firm fleshy Syrah with good depth of colour. Everything comes
together on this one—colour, aroma and taste. Flavour persists
with a slightly baked fruit finish.

Hungary

Main wine regions

Tokaj-Hegyalja
Eger
Villány-Siklós
Sopron

Dél-Balaton
Mór
Mátra Foothills
The Great Plain

Principal grape varieties

Interesting native grape varieties include:

White
Furmint
Hárslevelü
Olaszrizling (Welschriesling)
Leányka
Szürkebarát (Pinot Gris)
Ezerjó
Mezesfehér (used for dessert wine production)
Classic varieties such as Sauvignon Blanc, Chardonnay and Pinot Blanc are also grown.

Red
Kadarka
Kékfrankos
Pinot Noir
Merlot
Cabernet Sauvignon

Labelling guide

Wines are named by district followed by the name of the grape, for example Egri Bikavér is Bikavér (Bull's Blood) from the town of Egri.

Minöségi Bor on the label indicates a quality wine.

Tokaji, the most famous golden wine of Hungary, has several wine styles: Szamorodni can be dry or sweet, Aszu indicates a sweet wine, and Eszencia, which is rare, is an extremely concentrated rich wine.

Wine styles

Modern fresh crisp white wines should be consumed young.

Bull's Blood and Kékfrankos are at their best drunk cool within one to three years. Classic red styles can be enjoyed from two to four years. Wonderful botrytised dessert wines have good ageing ability.

WHITE WINE

White under £4.50

Dunavár Prestige Chardonnay Minôségi Bor 95   14
Dunnes Stores
Intense aromas of a fresh floral nature. Delivers on fresh fruity
appeal with a hint of bitter almond.

Dunavár Prestige Sauvignon Blanc 95   13
Dunnes Stores
Hugh Ryman is head of the winemaking team. A grassy
Sauvignon style with good attack of fruit, crisp acidity and
lively finish.

White £4.50–£5.25

Bátaapátí Estate Chardonnay 94   13
Grants
Deep yellow-gold in colour, with a slight floral touch that
continues on the palate. Finishes in a clean fresh style.

Bátaapátí Estate Tramini 95   ☆
Grants
Intense grapey Muscat aromas in a young zippy style. Good
roundness of fruit and length. Easy to enjoy.

Chapel Hill Balatonboglár Chardonnay 95   14
Barry & Fitzwilliam
The younger vintage is far more appealing, with a fresh limey
character and tangy crisp finish.

Hungarian Country White Pinot Gris/Riesling 95   14
Gilbeys
Seawater tingling fresh on aroma with earthy apple flavours.
An interesting mix of grapes in an appealing style.

White £6–£8

Disznoko Estate Tokaji Dry Furmint 94   14
Searson
This vintage is a wine to make you ponder! Note the clear
yellow colour; it delivers more on taste than aroma. Enjoy the
lively lemon-like acidity and touch of tropical fruit flavours.

RED WINE

Red under £4.50

Vineyards of Eger Cabernet Sauvignon 94   14
Quinnsworth
Intriguing tea leaf aromas with a white pepper spice appeal
make this a good buy for the price.

Vineyards of Eger Merlot 94   14
Quinnsworth
Ruby in colour, with vegetal aromas and flavours. A good food
wine for the money. Has good classic structure.

Red £4.50–£5.25

Bátaapátí Estate Kékfrankos 93   14
Grants
A cool red that has developed with some bottle age. Liquorice
and cherries spring to mind, not unlike an Italian red.

Chapel Hill Balatonboglár Cabernet Sauvignon 93   14
Barry & Fitzwilliam
The 93 is ruby red with cherry and liquorice appeal. Good
attack and development, with tannin and acidity holding the
fruit together.

Hungarian Country Red Kékfrankos 95   14
Gilbeys
Peppery spicy Kékfrankos that offers cool red-wine drinking at
a very fair price.

Red £5.25–£6

Bátaapátí Estate Möcsényi Special Reserve 94   ☆
Grants
Stalky fruit appeal from the blend of Cabernet Sauvignon and
Cabernet Franc. Quite classic in structure and good at the price.

Italy

Main wine regions and some of their wines

Piedmont: The most famous red grape is Nebbiolo, producing Barolo, which has to be aged for three years, two of them in cask, and Barbaresco, which has two years' ageing. Barbera, grown around the town of Asti, is the most common red grape and can produce fresh fruity styles or more full-bodied styles when grown around the town of Alba. The red Dolcetto grape produces vibrant fruity reds. Gavi and Cortese di Gavi are the best-known whites.

Valle d'Aosta: Small production.

Trentino-Alto Adige: Red and white wines are based on classic grape varieties. Schiava, a local variety, dominates red wine production.

Lombardy: particularly noted for top sparkling wine production.

Veneto: best-known white wine is Soave. Best-known reds are Valpolicella and Bardolino. Recioto Amarone della Valpolicella, produced from half-shrivelled sun-dried grapes, is noted for its bittersweet twist on the finish.

Friuli-Venezia Giulia: dry tannic reds suitable for ageing are produced from the Refosco grape. Noted for good whites and fruity reds.

Emilia-Romagna: famous for Lambrusco, the medium-sweet gurgling wine.

Tuscany: home of Chianti and Brunello di Montalcino. All Chianti is red and Sangiovese dominates production. Two styles are produced, the easy fruity styles and the more full-bodied styles of Riserva. There are seven sub-regions, but only one, Rufina, appears named on the label. Most Chianti comes from the Classico sub-region.

Brunello di Montalcino, one of Italy's most expensive wines, is matured in cask for four years (five if Riserva) before being bottled. Vino Nobile di Montepulciano, also produced from the Sangiovese (known here as Prugnolo Gentile), can often rival top-quality Chianti. Vernaccia di San Gimignano is the most famous white wine of Tuscany.

Umbria: most famous white is Orvieto. Most famous producer is Lungarotti, who created the red DOC Torgiano.

Latium: Frascati is this region's most famous white, produced from the Trebbiano grape.

Marches: Verdicchio produces crisp white styles of which Verdicchio dei Castelli di Jesi is the most noted. Rosso Conero is a robust red.

Abruzzo: Montepulciano d'Abruzzo is the best-known red wine.

Puglia (Apulia): produces over 24 DOC wines, with Salice Salentino the most popular red.

Basilicata: Aglianico del Vulture is one of Italy's best-known reds.

Campania: Taurasi is the best known red wine produced from the Aglianico grape.

Islands of Sicily (noted for the fortified wine Marsala) and *Sardinia:* white wine production dominates.

Principal grape varieties

As well as classic varieties, Italy boasts hundreds of native grapes including:

White	Red	Red
Trebbiano	Canaiolo	Aglianico
Malvasia	Barbera	Bonarda
Moscato	Dolcetto	Lagrein
Garganega	Montepulciano	Nero d'Avola
Grechetto	Nebbiolo	Negroamaro
Vernaccia	Sangiovese (Brunello,	Primitivo
Pinot Bianco	Prugnolo, Gentile)	Corvina
Pinot Grigio	Rondinella	
Verdicchio	Molinara	
Verdello	Refosco	

Labelling guide

Wine laws are modelled on the French AC laws. There are four categories:

Denominazione di Origine Controllata e Garantita (DOCG): the highest-quality designation granted only to the following wines: Albana di Romagna, Asti Spumante, Moscato d'Asti, Barbaresco, Barolo, Brunello di Montalcino, Carmignano, Chianti, Franciacorta, Gattinara, Montefalco Sagrantino, Taurasi, Torgiano Rosso Riserva, Vernaccia di San Gimignano and Vino Nobile di Montepulciano.

Denominazione di Origine Controllata (DOC): this quality designation applies to over 250 wines.

Indicazione Geografica Tipica (IGT): a new category similar to Vin de Pays but causing much confusion.

Vino da Tavola: basic table wine. Some innovative winemakers opt for this quality status because they produce outside the strict rules of DOC.

Labelling terms

Blanco: white.
Rossa: red.
Rosato: rosé.
Secco: dry.

Abboccato: slightly sweet.
Dolce: sweet.
Vecchio: old.
Spumante: sparkling.

Classico: best part of a wine-producing area.
Riserva: wines that have been matured longer.

Wine styles

Most Italian whites are pale, light, very fresh and ideal for matching with food or just sipping. Examples are wines such as Orvieto, Gavi, Soave, Frascati and varietals such as Chardonnay, Pinot Grigio, Pinot Bianco and Sauvignon Blanc from the north-east and Emilia-Romagna.

Light quaffing red wines include Valpolicella and Bardolino.

Fruity red wines for early consumption include Dolcetto, Valpolicella Classico, non-Riserva Chianti, Rosso Conero, Montepulciano d'Abruzzo and varietals such as Cabernet Sauvignon, Merlot and Pinot Nero from the north-east.

Big full-bodied reds capable of long maturation in bottle include: Barolo, Barbaresco and some Barberas (mainly oak-aged examples) from Piedmont; Valpolicella Amarone from Veneto; Brunello di Montalcino, Vino Nobile di Montepulciano, Chianti Classico and Chianti Rufina Riservas from Tuscany; Torgiano from Umbria; Taurasi from Campania; most wines produced from the local Negroamaro and Nero d'Avola grapes, such as Salice Salentino from Puglia and the islands. Vin Santo is produced mainly in Tuscany and Umbria. High in alcohol, its style varies from dry to sweet.

Vintages

North Italian Red

95 Barbera. Average. Barolo. Very good.
94 Dolcetto. Very good. Choose carefully.
93 Dolcetto and Barbera. Good. Barolo and Barbaresco.
92 Average early drinking all round.
91 Average to good especially Barolo, Barbaresco and Barbera.
90 Superb, ripe and long ageing especially Barolo and Barbera.

89   Superb. Rich and concentrated all round.
88   Very good to classic. Well structured. Look for top
     producers.
Good older vintages: 85 and 82.

Tuscany/Chianti:

95   Choose carefully
94   Good to very good
93   Good
92   Average to good
91   Average to very good. Drink now.
90   Superb, classic. Concentrated and powerful. Drink
     now or keep.
89   Average
88   Superb. Rich and elegant. Drink now.
87   Average to good
86   Good to very good. Well structured if tannic.
85   Superb. Rich and concentrated.

WHITE WINE

White under £4.50

Cavatina Frascati Superiore DOC 95   12
Quinnsworth
Stony fruit aromas. Malvasia, Trebbiano and Greco combine to
make this a fresh, easy-drinking style.

White £4.50–£5.25

Badia Alle Corti Orvieto Classico DOC 95   12
Dunnes Stores
Crisp and fresh with the slight nutty tone characteristic of this
style of wine.

Botter Chardonnay VdT Tre Venezie nv   14
Barry & Fitzwilliam
Hints of apple peel aromas and flavours with a good crisp
finish add up to easy drinking.

Botter Pinot Grigio VdT Tre Venezie nv   14
Barry & Fitzwilliam
Cool summer drinking with a nutty tone and lively fresh finish.

Cecchi Orvieto Classico DOC 95　　　　　　　　13
Quinnsworth
Lively and fresh for the price. Ideal party wine.
White £5.25–£6

Antinori Campogrande Orvieto Classico DOC 95　　13
Grants
Pale straw in colour. Crisp and fresh, marked by zesty acidity
and subtle fruit tones.

Conti Serristori Orvieto Classico Secco DOC 95　　13
Dillon
Typical nutty nuances. Fresh clean and easy-drinking.

Folonari Pinot Grigio VdT 95　　　　　　　　　　14
Dillon
Water-pale with just a hint of green. Modern style, well made
with crisp acidity and enough fruit. Drink young and fresh.

Folonari Soave DOC nv　　　　　　　　　　　　　14
Dillon
A good example of this style with good weight and texture in
an easy-drinking style.

La Vis Riesling Trentino DOC 95　　　　　　　　　14
Febvre
A subdued Riesling in aroma but lively and fresh on the palate
with some length.

Pinot Grigio della Luna DOC 95　　　　　　　　　13
TDL
Pleasant summer drink. Pale yellow with definite spritz and
veggy aromas. Nice attack of acidity adds freshness to the
medium long length.

Ponte Tevere Frascati Superiore DOC 95　　　　　13
Dunnes Stores
This easy-drinking wine of the Romans has a typical slightly
bitter almond touch and medium long finish.

Ricasoli Orvieto Classico DOC 94   14
Fitzgerald
Showing some development, this traditional wine has a pithy
character with a touch of oiliness. The finish is good, supported
by crisp acidity.

Tre Venezie Chardonnay Pétillant nv   12
TDL
Served chilled on a summer's day, this spritzy wine will refresh
and offer easy uncomplicated drinking.

Villa Pigna Verdicchio dei Castelli di Jesi Classico DOC 95
Fine Wines   13
Water-pale in a light style with lots of lemon appeal finishing
in a note of crisp acidity.

White £6–£8

Alasia Muscaté Sec VdT 95   14
Findlater
From Piedmont, this delicious drinks smack of ripe grapefruit.
Unusual style. Offers something different.

Arione Gavi DOC 95   14
Ecock
Seashell aromas. Young acidity with a slight herbaceous tone
make this a good choice with seafood.

Bigi Vigneto Torricella Orvieto Classico DOC 95   14
Findlater
This Orvieto has more flavour than most with a good impact of
nutty touches, hint of spritz and a touch of spice on the finish.

Bolla Soave Classico DOC 95   13
Dillon
Crisp and fresh with citrus fruit tones and good zesty finish.

Carpineto Orvieto DOC 95   13
Taserra
A good example of this particular style. Don't look for complex-

ity, simply enjoy its refreshing crisp appeal.

Colli de Catone Frascati Superiore DOC 95   13
Febvre
Note the distinct lemon tang of acidity and nutty tones with a
waxy mouth-feel. Finishes a little short. Good example of this
style.

Cortegiara Trebbiano Del Veronese 95   14
Wine Vault
Sherbet/sorbet aromas with good weight and fruit in a zippy
dry new fresh style.

Di Majo Norante Greco VdT 94   14
Burgundy Direct
Delicious limey aromas continue on the palate as citrus fruit
flavours fan out, backed up with pleasant acidity. Good lengthy
finish.

Falanghina VdT 94   14
Burgundy Direct
Interesting wine. Had a slight touch of 'Elastoplast' aroma
which gave way to super, lemony flavours. Good texture and
weight. Delivers much more on taste than aroma.

La Vis Chardonnay Trentino DOC 94   13
Febvre
Rolls on the palate with a whisper of green apple fruit. Steely
acidity with fruit flavours expanding, finishing crisp and clean.

La Vis Pinot Grigio Trentino DOC 94   12
Febvre
Offers very pleasant crisp fresh drinking. Golden in tone with
leafy aromas and hints of nuttiness.

Leonildo Pieropan Soave Classico Superiore DOC 93   ☆
Superquinn
Yellow-gold in colour. From a top producer in Veneto in North

East Italy, this wine, with its cool fresh appeal, is a top example
of its DOC.

Macrina Verdicchio dei Castelli di Jesi Classico DOC 94
Febvre   13
Tangy fruit appeal with good weight on the palate and a
medium long finish.

Masi Serègo Alighieri Bianco di Garganega é Sauvignon 95
Grants   ☆
The elderflower of Sauvignon comes through with lots of
crunchy green apple behind. Pale white-gold in colour this is a
perfect seafood wine.

Masi Soave Classico Superiore DOC 94   14
Grants
A very good example of its style. Gulpable with a perfect crisp
finish ending in a nutty overtone.

MezzaCorona Moscato Giallo Trentino DOC 93   14
Mitchell
Pale lemon in colour. Orange blossom aromas. Perfect served
chilled as an apéritif or with fruity desserts.

MezzaCorona Pinot Grigio Trentino DOC 95   13
Mitchell
Light and refreshing with a hint of spritz and lively finish.
Good with seafood.

Monteleone Soave Classico Superiore DOC 94   12
Febvre
Light in style with good acidity, pleasant grapefruit skin
aromas and flavours with a nice bitter twist on the end.

Orlandi Contucci Ponno Ghiaiolo Sauvignon 95   ☆
Findlater
Zippy style, with a steely character and lively crisp finish. A
modern, fresh wine.

Umani Ronchi Verdicchio dei Castelli di Jesi Classico DOC 95
Wine Vault **14**
Deep yellow gold with nutty tones and very pleasant lemon/
lime citrus acid appeal.

Vigneto Ca'Nova Lugana DOC 95 ☆
Molloy's
Produced from the Trebbiano di Lugana this water-pale wine is
tingling fresh both in aroma and flavour. It demonstrates the
lively tangy refreshing appeal of this grape when properly
produced. Perfect for fish.

Villa di Canlungo Late Harvested Pinot Grigio DOC 95
Ecock **14**
A good example of this grape with its stony aromas opening up
on flavour and fruit emerging through the crisp dry finish.

Zonin Aquileia Chardonnay DOC 95 ☆
Italfood
Restrained stony fruit. Very fresh and crisp with enough
slightly underripe peach fruit coming through the zesty acidity.
A well-made wine typical of its birthplace.
White £8–£10

Alois Lageder Alto Adige Südtirol Chardonnay DOC 92
Febvre **13**
Very good balance between fruit and acidity. Fresh and
extremely drinkable with a hint of vanilla pods.

**Alois Lageder Pinot Bianco Weissburgunder Alto Adige Südtirol
DOC 92** *Febvre* **13**
Apple peel aromas and flavours. Fresh summer drinking shot
through with steely acidity.

Alois Lageder Pinot Grigio Alto Adige Südtirol DOC 95
Febvre
A super example of the style with its hazelnut aromas. Bal-
anced, crisp, easy-drinking wine.

Carpineto Querciabella Orvieto Classico DOC 94   14
Taserra
This oak-influenced style offers more substantial drinking than
the 93 tasted last year. The subtle nutty aromas are there but
this vintage offers more apple fruit appeal.

I Frati Lugana DOC 95   14
Superquinn
A perfect summer wine with its delicate nutty aromas and
refreshing hint of spritz on the lively finish.
White £10–£12

Bucci Verdicchio dei Castelli di Jesi Classico DOC 92   13
Karwig
Straw coloured. Delicate nutty tones persist to the pleasant,
slightly austere finish. A good example of Verdicchio

Pio Cesare Gavi DOC 95   13
Cassidy
With its surprising steely tone overladen with apples, this is a
good wine to serve with fish.

Planeta La Segreta VdT 95   14
Wine Vault
Modern style—crisp and clean with all the appeal of a young
fresh wine. A perfect partner for seafood.

RED WINE

Red under £4.50

Coppiere Montepulciano d'Abruzzo DOC 95   13
Quinnsworth
Displays good cherry type fruits with a characteristic, appeal-
ing bittersweet finish.
Red £4.50–£5.25

Botter Cabernet VdT Tre Venezia nv   12
Barry & Fitzwilliam
A savoury wine, better on flavour than aroma. Needs food.

Botter Merlot VdT Tre Venezia nv 14
Barry & Fitzwilliam
A very pleasant wine with intense fruit, vibrant acidity and
long finish.

Cecchi Chianti DOCG 95 14
Quinnsworth
Deep ruby in colour. Classic Chianti touch with bittersweet
chocolate cherry aromas and flavours that linger.

Sartori Amarone della Valpolicella Classico DOC 90 14
Dunnes Stores
Deep garnet in colour with heady prune aromas. Good attack of
fruit followed by characteristic high acidity ending in a
pleasant austere finish.

Villa di Vetrice Chianti Rufina DOCG 94 13
Findlater
Ruby red. A crisp juicy Chianti style with cherry flavour
characteristics.
Red £5.25-£6

Antinori Santa Cristina VdT Tuscany 94 14
Grants
From a master winemaker this 'cool' red has hints of leather
and liquorice aromas. For those who prefer the slight austerity
of Italian wines to up-front jarring fruits.

Cantina Tollo Montepulciano d'Abruzzo DOC 95 14
Febvre
Ruby red. Closed on aroma but opens up in taste with hints of
Morello cherry. The touch of tannin on the finish adds interest.

Conti Serristori Chianti DOCG 95 13
Dillon
Cherry red with cherry aromas. Good fruit cut through with a
bite of fresh acidity. A smack of tannin adds interest to this
young fruity style.

Folonari Valpolicella DOC nv　　　　　　　　　　　**12**
Dillon
Delivers more on taste than aroma. A modern style with easy
appeal, good cherry fruit and a slightly bittersweet finish.

Ricasoli Chianti DOCG 94　　　　　　　　　　　**14**
Fitzgerald
Deep crimson in colour with plenty of damson and cherry
aromas. Flavours carry through on palate with a pleasant
austerity on the finish. Good food wine.

Red £6–£8

Agricole Vallone Salice Salentino DOC 93　　　　**13**
Karwig
Blackberry toned. Produced principally from the Negroamaro
grape. Morello cherry flavours with a bite of acidity and a
pleasant bitter finish.

Allegrini Valpolicella Classico DOC 95　　　　　**14**
Superquinn
A lively fruit-driven style, light and refreshing with raspberry
and cherry fruit echoing on the finish.

Antinori Badia a Passignano Chianti Classico DOCG 94　　**14**
Grants
Deep crimson in colour with dry, earthy tones and typical black
cherry fruit finish. Still needs a little time to harmonise the fruit
and tannin.

Arione Nebbiolo d'Alba DOC 93　　　　　　　　**14**
Ecock
An interesting example of the Nebbiolo grape. Ignore the
medium ruby colour which contrasts with the meaty savoury
style with high acidity and tangy finish. A wine that needs
food.

Badia Alle Corti Vino Nobile di Montepulciano DOCG 92
Dunnes Stores　　　　　　　　　　　　　　　　☆
Big in colour aroma and taste. The mouth-drying tannins take
over the delicious cherry fruit. A hearty wine.

Bolla Valpolicella DOC 95   14
Dillon
Crimson in colour with fresh vibrant fruit. A good luncheon
wine, at its best served cool. Medium long finish.

Boscaini San Ciriaco Valpolicella Classico DOC 95   14
Febvre
From a single vineyard. Deep crimson in colour, plum/cherry
fruit appeal and juicy, vibrant finish.

Candido Salice Salentino Riserva DOC 92   ☆
Findlater
Smoky, spicy aroma with a hint of tar. On the palate, acidity is
first noticed followed by cherry fruit. Tannins assert themselves
on the finish. An interesting wine, produced from the
Negroamaro and Malvasia Nera grapes.

Cecchi Chianti Classico DOCG 94   13
Quinnsworth
Has developed since last tasted. Showing a slight orange tinge
so characteristic of the Sangiovese grape. Still has the sweet
cherry and chocolate tones. Enjoy now.

Colle Secco Montepulciano d'Abruzzo DOC 93   ☆
Febvre
This vintage shows complex aromas of cherry and tar with a
spicy cinnamon tone. Not for the faint-hearted.

Colli Senesi Chianti DOCG 93   14
Febvre
Very balanced wine on flavour with lots of cherry fruits and
distinct bitter twist. Surprisingly drying tannins on the finish.

Conti Serristori Chianti Classico DOCG 94   14
Dillon
A good example of the youthful zippy style of Chianti with
cherry appeal and a pleasant austere finish.

Di Majo Norante Aglianico DOC 92   13
Burgundy Direct
Robust wine with baked fruit aromas from the Aglianico grape
that imparts high acidity. A definite food wine.

Di Majo Norante Ramitello Riserva DOC 92   ☆
Burgundy Direct
Wonderful jammy aromas of blackberry overladen with
cinnamon spice. Fruit expands on the palate with tannins
rolling in behind. A nice bite of acidity adds interest to the extra
long finish.

La Vis Cabernet Sauvignon Trentino DOC 93   12
Febvre
Wonderful blackcurrant fruit aromas, but disappointing
flavour; Cabernet Sauvignon from this region can be a little
'green'. Better with food.

La Vis Merlot Trentino DOC 94   14
Febvre
Dense fruity creamy aromas reminiscent of plum. Super attack
of fruit on the palate which fans out and kicks in at the end
with a hint of spice. Pleasant supple tannins.

Lungarotti Rubesco Rosso di Torgiano DOC 93   ☆
Findlater
From a famous family estate in central Italy this unique wine
produced from Sangiovese and Canniolo grapes has tobacco
and mushroom aromas and fulfils on taste what it promises on
aroma with a high acidic finish.

Marano Valpolicella Classico Superiore DOC 93   13
Febvre
Deep ruby. Tarry liquorice aromas which all blend together on
the palate. Very Italian in style with a smoky spicy finish.
Perfect with meat-based pasta.

Masi Valpolicella Classico Superiore DOC 94 ☆

Grants

Ruby red. Amazing mashed banana aromas and flavours. Fresh fruit attack, balanced acidity and tannin. Very classic in a lively, appealing style.

Melini Chianti Classico DOCG 94 14

Gilbeys

A vibrant style—ruby red in colour with quaffable cherry fruit appeal. Very pleasant hint of austerity on the finish.

MezzaCorona Merlot Trentino DOC 94 13

Mitchell

A good example of the lean slightly herbaceous style of North Eastern Italian reds. Enjoy it with food especially pasta and pizza.

Piancarda Rosso Conero DOC 94 14

Febvre

Has all the hallmarks of well-made Italian wine from the Marches region. Extremely appealing bittersweet finish.

Podere La Regia Specula Montepulciano d'Abruzzo DOC 94

Findlater ☆ ☆

Amazing wild herb tones that explode with flavour on the palate. There is no in-between with this wine, a smoky Italian classic.

Rèmole Chianti (Rufina) DOCG 94 ☆

Allied Drinks

Wild, wonderful, and young. Typical cherry aromas with a bite of acidity finishing with a slightly bitter twist. Extremely satisfying.

Tacchetto Bardolino Classico DOC 95 14

Fitzgerald

One of the best examples of the style. Savoury aromas with lots of white pepper spice and a hint of lively spritz on the finish.

Teroldego Rotaliano DOC 94   14
Fcbvrc/Molloy's
Wonderful black cherry colour. Creamy, cherry fruit assails the
nostrils. Big attack of fruit with surprisingly balanced tannins
and a nice bite of acidity.

Villa Cerna Chianti Classico Riserva DOCG 93
Quinnsworth
Deep ruby in colour, the 93 vintage oozes fruit appeal. Very
balanced in an austere way with plenty of fruit supported by
tangy acidity. Calls for food. Delicious.

Villa Rizzardi Poiega Valpolicella Classico Superiore DOC 93
Fitzgerald
From a single vineyard site this delicious wine has wonderful,
typical tar and dark chocolate aromas. The taste is even better
with a bite of spice and a lean, austere yet vibrant finish.
Red £8–£10

Arione Barolo DOCG 92   13
Ecock
Light in colour with a tawny edge this is a definite food wine
with high acidity, high alcohol and a bittersweet finish.

Avignonesi Vino Nobile di Montepulciano DOCG 92
Searson
Good choice for an average vintage. Drinking well now with a
good attack of sweet berry fruits. Enjoy the lingering cherry
fruit flavours on the medium long finish. Perfect with pasta.

Badia a Coltibuono Chianti Classico DOCG 94
Findlater
What a wine! Rustic in style the 94 vintage is a classic with
blackcurrant/cherry aromas and flavours and a tantalising bite
of acidity with obvious tannins on the finish.

Carpineto Dogajolo VdT 95
Taserra
Full of personality with sweet ripe juicy fruit. Extremely

appealing in a vibrant rather than classic style.

Castello d'Albola Chianti Classico DOCG 94   14
Italfood
This youthful wine has echoes of cherry fruit with a comple-
mentary bite of acidity indicating that it's good with food.

Conte Contini Bonacossi Barco Reale di Carmignano DOC 95
Wine Vault   14
Purple toned with delicious ripe raspberry aroma. A gulpable
style, lively and fresh. Good luncheon wine.

Fattoria del Corno Vino Nobile di Montepulciano DOCG 91
Febvre   14
Delivers much more on flavour than aroma. Acidity still masks
the fruit but plenty of tannin will ensure good maturation in
bottle.

Giribaldi Dolcetto d'Alba Vigna Bataijen DOC 94   ☆
Kelly
Deep purple in colour with vibrant fruity appeal. A chewy
chunky style with well-developed flavours and a bite of zesty
acidity. Satisfying, long finish.

Masi Campo Fiorin Ripasso VdT 91
Grants
Wonderful sweet and sour fruit appeal unique to Italy. The
tight-fisted fruit emerges on the palate and finishes in a
thought-provoking style.

Masi Serègo Alighieri Valpolicella Classico Superiore DOC 92
Grants   ☆ ☆
A top example of its style. The amazing ruby colour is followed
by black Morello cherry fruit aromas and flavours. Ageing in
cherry wood adds a roundness. Note the wonderful bite of
austerity on the finish.

Ronchi di Castelluccio Le More VdT 93   14
Burgundy Direct
Classic restrained aromas of plum and fig. The fruit is longing
to emerge but needs more time for tannins to soften.

**Ronco de Gramogliano Colli Orientali del Friuli Cabernet DOC
93**   14
Febvre
Big bold and wild with lots of liquorice and mint tones. Long
flavoursome finish with a hint of spice.

Ruffino Ducale Chianti Classico Riserva DOCG 91
Dillon
A sturdy wine. This vintage is a little shy on aroma but has a
nice touch of spice and smooth generous fruit. A top quality
vintage needing time to mature.

San Jacopo da Vicchiomaggio Chianti Classico DOCG 94
Mitchell   14
A delicious smoky cherry and fig wine with mouthfilling
flavours and long exciting finish.

Taurino Salice Salentino Riserva DOC 93
Ecock
The Negroamaro grape adds spice, the oak influence a touch of
vanilla. A savoury rather than fruity wine that merits its star on
flavour and sheer individuality.

Villa Antinori Chianti Classico Riserva DOCG 93
Grants
The 93 vintage has all the colour and flavour expected from this
style. Offers much more on flavour than aroma with an
appealing bite of dark chocolate on the finish.

Villa di Capezzana Carmignano DOCG 92   14
Searson
Brick-toned, with cedar, spice and clove aromas and flavours.
Enjoy now.

Red £10–£12

Agontano Rosso Conero Riserva DOC 92   14
Febvre
Dominated by the Montepulciano grape with some Sangiovese
this has robust herb-like tones. A big chewy wine.

Caparzo Rosso di Montalcino DOC 92   14
Febvre
Intense ruby red with a slight cheesy aroma bursting into wild
cherry on the palate. A definite food wine.

Carpineto Chianti Classico DOCG 94   13
Taserra
Crimson in colour with typical 'soapy' aromas and soft ripe
sweet fruit emerging on the palate. Medium long finish.

Carpineto Rosso di Montalcino DOC 93   ☆
Taserra
This pure Tuscan wine has hints of dark chocolate, a wonderful
bite of ripe, zappy fruit with lively acidity and very good tannic
structure.

Castello di Nipozzano Chianti Rúfina Riserva DOCG 92
Allied Drinks   ☆ ☆
Chianti at its best with its deep crimson colour and dense
aromas of cherry. The tang of bittersweet fruit on the finish,
with mouth-drying tannins, indicates a wine which will
continue to develop.

Fattorio Petrognano Pomino DOC 93
Karwig
Ribena in colour. Wonderful smoky capsicum and nutmeg
tones. Packs a punch of ripe fruit with a very pleasant bite of
acidity on the finish. Super drinking.

Parrina Riserva DOC 91   14
Wine Vault
Garnet in colour with attractive dried fruit and delicious sweet

and sour appeal. A savoury wine which is drinking well now.

Pio Cesare Barbera d'Alba DOC 93

Cassidy

Juicy, fruity, plummy. Big in everything—fruit, acidity, and cherries, with gripping tannins. A top wine of its particular style.

Pio Cesare Dolcetto D'Alba DOC 95 14

Cassidy

Note the appealing cerise colour and attractive brambly fruit appeal followed by gum-smacking tannins. Big and juicy.

Scassino Terrabianca Chianti Classico DOCG 92 14

Karwig

Dense ruby red with Liquorice Allsorts aroma overladen with spicy cinnamon. The immediate attack of ripe fruit is delicious but is quickly overtaken by acidity and tannin.

Volpi Barolo DOCG 92

Dunnes Stores

A wine with a characteristic orange hue at the edge. Note the spice and Morello cherry appeal overlain with a hint of tobacco. Not for the faint-hearted. Big and bold.

Zonin Amarone della Valpolicella (Il Maso) DOC 92 ☆

Italfood

Naturally dried grapes impart dried fig and prune tones to this powerful wine. Open it one hour before serving to bring out its savoury qualities.

Red £12–£15

Alois Lageder Mazon Pinot Nero Alto Aldige Riserva DOC 93
Febvre 13

Light ruby in colour with stalky aromas. The fruit emerges on the palate with chewy tannins and medium long finish.

Bernadette et Renzo Bolli Montecalvi 92　　　　14
Parsons
Layers of elusive fruit flavours that range from cherry to
raspberry. Very appealing in style.

Bolla Amarone della Valpolicella Classico DOC 89　　　14
Dillon
Another example of classic Amarone with dense chewy fig and
prune flavours and a super, austere, bittersweet finish.

Capitel de Roari Amarone della Vallipolicella Classico DOC 91
Karwig　　　　14
Extraordinary aromas of cough medicine, plums and cherries.
Much better on the palate with a delicious sour/sweet fruit
tone finishing bone dry. High alcohol (15%) renders it port-like.

Carpineto Chianti Classico Riserva DOCG 91　　　14
Taserra
Crimson in colour with fresh ripe cherry fruit appeal. Perfumed, with good, concentrated fruit flavours and typically
austere finish.

Carpineto Farnito Cabernet Sauvignon di Toscana VdT 91
Taserra　　　　14
Deep ruby. A top example of just how good Cabernet
Sauvignon is from Tuscany. Deep capsicum aromas followed
by a rich savoury palate. Has matured extremely well since last
tasted.

Castello Vicchiomaggio Petri Chianti Classico Riserva DOCG 93
Febvre　　　　14
Crimson in colour. Subtle aromas of raspberry with a smoky
touch. Super balance between fruit, acidity and tannin that all
come together in a harmonious, mouthfilling flavour.

La Caduta Rosso di Montalcino DOC 92　　　14
Febvre
Well-structured wine with all elements fighting to assert

themselves. Tannins win out but the acidity and dense cherry fruits leave their impact on the finish.

Marano Amarone della Valpolicella Classico DOC 91 ☆ ☆
Febvre
Complex aromas of fig and liquorice. Raisined fruit attack that explodes in flavour and is cut through by balanced acidity. Tannin fights back gently on the long, flavoursome finish.

Masi Amarone della Valpolicella Classico DOC 91 ☆ ☆ ☆
Grants
Since last tasted this vintage has mellowed into an awesome wine. Italian at its best. Big on everything—note the bitter-sweet chocolate and cherry fruit appeal with a tight-knit structure.

Nicolello Barolo DOCG 91   14
Mitchell
Produced from 100% Nebbiolo. Not an easy wine to understand but this is a fair example of what it's all about—high acidity, tannin and fruit content overlain with a smack of tar.

Terrabianca Vigna Della Croce Chianti Classico Riserva
DOCG 91   *Karwig*   14
A chewy, chunky wine with dense, smoky, inky tones and that delicious characteristic sweet/sour bite to the finish.

Villa Borghetti Amarone della Valpolicella Classico DOC 90
Woodford Bourne ☆
Traditionally made this deep ruby coloured wine has elegant restrained aromas of plum and cedar. The immediate attack of fruit is also restrained but quickly opens up to roll around the palate followed by very balanced acidity and tannin.
Red £15–£20

Avignonesi Grifi VdT di Toscana 88 ☆ ☆
Karwig
What a stunner! This blend of Prugnolo (Sangiovese) and Cabernet Franc is deep and dense with creamy mocha tones. It

flows on the palate with a super attack of raspberry and strawberry fruits. A simply delicious super-Tuscan aged in oak.

Banfi Col di Sasso VdT 95
Gilbeys
Light in style, this wine is extremely balanced and harmonious. First taste smacks of a Beaujolais style but taste and taste again to appreciate its subtle class. Balanced and elegant but expensive.

Pio Cesare Barolo d'Alba DOCG 92   14
Cassidy
Tobacco and liquorice assail the senses with reticent strawberry fruits ending in a delicious sweet/sour finish. Big, strapping wine.

Produttori di Barbaresco Barbaresco DOCG 90   13
Karwig
Showing hints of brick this wine produced from the Nebbiolo grape takes its name from the province of Barbaresco. Austerity is its hallmark with tart acidity and tannins hiding the strawberry fruit.

Ronco della Simia (Sangiovese Cru) 92
Burgundy Direct
The label may embarrass but this will surprise and delight the drinker who wants a wine with attitude! Still very young which is obvious from the mouth-puckering tannins hiding the rich, succulent fruit.

Terrabianca Piano del Cipresso VdT di Toscana 90
Karwig
Aromas of chocolate and cream are followed by extremely pleasant toasty tones. This wine shows what super-Tuscans are all about.

Red £20–£30

Brunello di Montalcino DOCG 88   14
Febvre
Tawny coloured, with an amazing bouquet of figs and gorse.

Intense and rich with a meaty overtone and a very strong sweet and sour finish.

Tenuta Trerose Vino Nobile di Montepulciano DOCG 92
Mitchell   **14**
Ruby turning to brick at the rim. Complex, slightly medicinal, aromas. Mellow fruit tones emerge on the palate with good tannins and a strong finish.

New Zealand

Main wine regions

North Island
Northland
Bay of Plenty
Auckland
Gisborne/Poverty Bay
Hawke's Bay
Martinborough
Wairarapa

South Island
Nelson
Marlborough
Canterbury
Otago

Principal grape varieties

White
Müller-Thurgau
Chardonnay
Sauvignon Blanc
Riesling
Chenin Blanc

Red
Cabernet Sauvignon
Pinot Noir
Merlot

Labelling guide

A system of Certified Origin is being introduced which will indicate on the label precisely where the grapes are grown. The grape variety and region of origin of the wine are nearly always mentioned.

Wine styles

Sauvignon Blanc styles are crisp, lively and pungent. Chardonnay-based wines have superb intensity of fruit flavours and lively crisp acidity. Red wine-making is improving. Top-class Pinot Noir is being produced. Top-class dry sparkling wines are also produced.

Vintages

96	Superb	94	Very good to good
95	Very good	93	Good to very good

WHITE WINE

White £6–£8

Aotea Sauvignon Blanc 95

Parsons

Deep green-gold. This vintage is all about nettles and gooseberries. The fruit appears riper on the palate, which is typical of the North Island style. Sip, savour and enjoy.

Cooks Gisborne Chardonnay 95 13

Fitzgerald

Fresh fruit salad aromas and flavours with rounded fat texture. Good ripe Chardonnay with a touch of spice on the finish.

Cooks Gisborne Sauvignon Blanc 94 14

Fitzgerald

Pale yellow with grassy tones, a slight hint of spritz and long fruity appeal. Easy style.

Esk Valley Hawkes Bay Sauvignon Blanc 95 14

Barry & Fitzwilliam

Crisp and fresh with restrained gooseberry appeal. Has an elegant long finish.

Montana Marlborough Chardonnay 95 14

Grants

Nicely structured; fresh and clean with touches of exotic fruit.

Montana Marlborough Sauvignon Blanc 95 ☆

Grants

It never disappoints. With some bottle development the wine appears less pungent, but still has the rhubarb and gooseberry appeal. Drink now to enjoy at its tangy best.

Philip Rose Estate Sauvignon Blanc 95 14

Fine Wines

Extremely attractive in its style. The herbaceous quality is all there, but without the screeching acidity of some.

St Clair Marlborough Chardonnay 95   **14**
Barry & Fitzwilliam
Has grapefruit appeal in a fresh tangy style.

St Clair Marlborough Sauvignon Blanc 95   **14**
Barry & Fitzwilliam
Deep gold in colour, with delightful elderflower and nettle
aromas. Very good palate development and finish.

Stoneleigh Vineyard Marlborough Chardonnay 94   **14**
Fitzgerald
Deep yellow in colour, this oak-aged, creamy, buttery Chardonnay has lemon citrus acidity with good length of flavour. Enjoy
it at its best now.

Stoneleigh Vineyard Marlborough Sauvignon Blanc 95
Fitzgerald   ☆
Exactly how this style should be, with its nettles, dry, earthy
tones and gooseberry fruit. Mouthfilling pungency with good
length.
White £8–£10

Esk Valley Hawkes Bay Chardonnay 93   **14**
Barry & Fitzwilliam
Spicy with fresh citrus fruit appeal and a pleasant toasty finish.

Hunter's Sauvignon Blanc 95   ☆ ☆
Gilbeys
Always a star—the 95 is another classic full of gooseberry and
cream appeal. Everything comes together—the fruit, acidity
and alcohol. Stunning.

Matua Gisborne Chardonnay 93   ☆ ☆
Woodford Bourne
Yellow-gold with very pleasant subtle oak appeal. Packed tight
with exotic fruit flavours that carry right through to the long
finish.

Matua Hawkes Bay Sauvignon Blanc 95   ☆
Woodford Bourne
Pale with a hint of lemon. Zippy green fruit flavour with an

attractive citrus touch. Fresh, clean and delicious.

Morton Estate Hawkes Bay Sauvignon Blanc 95 ☆
Dillon
The 95 screams its variety with a wonderful pungent tone. A real signature style for anyone looking for crisp Sauvignon Blanc.

Morton Estate Hawkes Bay White Label Chardonnay 94
Dillon **13**
Since last tasted this wine has developed a slight nutty tone. The kiwi fruit style is still obvious, with a clean, medium-long finish.

Morton Estate Hawkes Bay Yellow Label Chardonnay 94
Dillon **14**
Pale with a tinge of green. A slight lactic touch comes through the ripe melon-type fruit. A very approachable wine with lots of flavour and a pleasant crisp finish.
White £10–£12

Babich Hawkes Bay Sauvignon Blanc 95 ☆
Mitchell
A must for those who like the pungency of Sauvignon. With its nettle earthy aromas, it has a more restrained fruit character than other examples of this style.

Cloudy Bay Chardonnay 94 ☆☆☆
Findlater
The wonderful spicy oak and citrus fruit aromas are still obvious since tasted last year. These are followed by a tingling fresh lively attack, with flavours expanding and developing. Leaves the palate whistle clean.

Coopers Creek Chardonnay 94 ☆
Mackenway
Fermentation in American oak adds a touch of vanilla to this peachy wine, supported by good acidity. Round and full with great flavour.

Grove Mill Sauvignon Blanc 94   13

Cassidy

Extremely pungent raw gooseberry aroma, extending on the
palate. Has quite a short finish, but the lover of New Zealand
Sauvignon will enjoy this style.

Redwood Valley Sauvignon Blanc 95   ☆

Parsons

Wonderful blackcurrant leafy aromas that don't disappoint on
flavour. A classy style, not overbearing.
White £12– £15

Coopers Creek Sauvignon Blanc (Oak Aged) 95

Mackenway

Smooth and creamy with the characteristic bite of gooseberry.
A treat to drink. Offers something different.

RED WINE

Red £6–£8

Cooks Hawkes Bay Cabernet Sauvignon 94   14

Fitzgerald

An interesting style of wine with aromas of pea-pod. Full-
flavoured with plenty of stalky fruit character well supported
by balancing tannins.

Montana Cabernet Sauvignon 94   ☆

Grants

Deep ruby with lots of cinnamon and clove appeal. A wonderful example of the huge improvement in New Zealand reds.
The appealing aromas continue straight through on flavour,
finishing on a rich high note of ripeness.

Stoneleigh Vineyard Marlborough Cabernet Sauvignon 94

Fitzgerald   ☆ ☆

A top example of just how good New Zealand's reds are
becoming. The 94 vintage is deep crimson in colour with
delicious ripe blackberry jelly appeal that spills over on to the
palate. The tannins are smooth with a hint of spice. A long,
silky finish.

Red £8–£10

Esk Valley Hawkes Bay Merlot/Cabernet Franc 93
Barry & Fitzwilliam
A top example from New Zealand. Everything comes together—fruit, acidity and alcohol. A wholesome satisfying finish.

Morton Estate Hawkes Bay Cabernet/Merlot 95   14
Dillon
The 95 vintage has riper fruit than the 93, with a very pleasant touch of Mocha. Youthful acidity adds a lean lively touch to the medium-long finish.
Red £12–£15

Babich Mara Estate Cabernet Sauvignon 94
Mitchell
An exciting style, with its subtle yet exquisite fruit balance. Harmonious in a classic way with a lively bite of acidity and fruit on the finish.
Red £20–£30

Rippon Vineyard Pinot Noir 94
Dalton
This wine really offers something different for the wine drinker. Everything combines, the fruit reminiscent of squashed strawberry and raspberry, the hint of spice and extra-smooth succulent finish. Delicious.

Portugal

Main wine regions seen on the Irish market

Vinho Verde, Douro, Dão, Bairrada, Torres, Ribatejo, Setúbal Peninsula, Alentejo, Algarve.

Principal grape varieties

Portugal is noted for its large selection of native varieties.

White	Red
Alvarinho	Baga
Arinto	Bastardo
Bical	João de Santarém (also known
Loureiro	as Periquita, Moscatel and
Fernão Pires	Castelão Frances)
Chardonnay	Tinta Pinheira
Sercial	Tinta Roriz
	Touriga Nacional

Labelling guide

Vinho de Mesa: table wine.

IPR: equivalent to French country wines. There are over forty throughout the country.

DOC (Denominação de Origem Controlada): highest-quality category based on French AC laws.

Selo de Garantia: a stamp located over the neck of the bottle guaranteeing that strict quality controls are carried out. Also guarantees the authenticity of the wine.

Garrafeira: indicates wines of high quality of a particularly good vintage. Red wines must be aged for a minimum of two years in cask and one in bottle. Whites are aged for a minimum of one year, including six months in bottle. Most producers age for much longer.

Tinto: red.	*Velho:* old.
Rosado: rosé.	*Reserva:* outstanding quality.
Adega: winery.	*Espumante:* sparkling.
Colheita: vintage.	

Quinta: an individual wine-making estate.

Wine styles

Vinho Verde: spritzy, young, fresh, zippy white style for very
young drinking.

Oak-influenced Chardonnays are rich and creamy with the ability
to age for a few years.

Moscatel adds an aromatic marmalade style to easy-drinking
whites.

Quality dry sparkling wines offer value for money.

Fruity reds always have a marked slightly austere edge, making
them good food wines.

Oak-influenced reds are classic in style and can age.

Regions to look out for are Alentejo and Douro for modern
affordable styles and Bairrada and Dão for beefier, more
traditional styles.

WHITE WINE

White under £4.50

Aliança Bairrada DOC 95   13
Reynolds
A modern well-made wine from traditional varieties including
Bical, Sercial and Maria Gomes. Perfect seafood wine. Drink
young and cool.

Barra Vinho Branco Vinho de Mesa nv   14
Dunnes Stores
Marmalade-type aromas and medium long finish in an easy-
drinking style.

J. P. Branco Vinho de Mesa nv   14
Reynolds
Hint of grapey Muscat. At its best served chilled. For those who
like fruity whites.

Porta dos Cavaleiros Dão DOC 94   13
Reynolds
Crisp, clean and easy-drinking. A good party wine.

Medal Winners
The 1996
International
WINE Challenge

RED WINE OF THE YEAR

Bright Brothers *Douro* red 1995

GOLD MEDALS

Bright Brothers *Douro* 1995
Fiuza & Bright *Cabernet Sauvignon* 1994
J. P. Vinhos *Tinto da Anfora* 1991

SILVER MEDALS

Fiuza & Bright *Cabernet Sauvignon* 1994 (Bordeaux Style)

BRONZE MEDAL

Esporao *Cabernet Sauvignon* 1992

COMMENDED

White
Bright Brothers *Arinto/Sercial* 1995
Fiuza & Bright 'Campo dos Frades' *Chardonnay* 1995
Red
Bright Brothers *Estremadura* 1994
Fiuza & Bright 'Campo dos Frades' *Cabernet Sauvignon* 1995
Fiuza & Bright *Merlot* 1994
J. P. Vinhos *Quinta da Bacalhoa* 1993

Widely available T. P. Reynolds & Co. Ltd

White £4.50–£5.25

Alandra (Herdade do Esporão) Vinho Regional 94   12
Reynolds
Aromatic with a hint of ripe fruit. Pleasant easy drinking on a summer's day.

Aliança Angelus Bairrada DOC 93   13
Reynolds
Indigenous grapes such as Bical, Maria Gomes and Sercial produce this easy-drinking style with citrus appeal.

Bright Brothers Sercial Arinto Ribatejo DOC 95   14
Reynolds
A super example of what modern winemaking can do with traditional styles. Steely, with stony fruits and a crisp clean finish.

Casal Garcia Vinho Verde DOC nv   12
Dunnes Stores
Typical light slightly spritzy style with high acidity. Good choice for oily fish. Low alcohol.

Terra Franca Bairrada DOC 94   ☆
Dillon
Very pleasant greengage fruit appeal with enough lemon-like acidity to add a crisp finish. A star in its style.
White £5.25–£6

Albis Terras do Sado Vinho Regional 95   13
Mitchell
Produced from native Arinto, Malvasia and Moscatel grapes, the flavours and aromas are all about spice and a pleasant orange tang. Drier on flavour, the wine finishes on a crisp fresh note.

Campo dos Frades Chardonnay Vinho Regional 95   14
Reynolds
Nutty aromas and flavours with a good fresh tone and long clean finish.

Catarina Vinho Regional 94   13
Reynolds
Local variety Fernão Pires combines with Chardonnay to give a
pale yellow appearance, slight citrus aromas and waxy citrus
flavour.
White £6–£8

Fiuza Chardonnay Vinho Regional 95
Reynolds/Superquinn
Delicious lemon and lime appeal with more ripe fruit showing
through on flavour and ending in a long creamy finish. Top-
class winemaking.

Fiuza Sauvignon Blanc Vinho Regional 95
Reynolds
Delightful blackberry leaf aromas with mouthfilling flavour
and a nice bite of acidity. An unusual and interesting style.

João Pires Vinho Regional 95   14
Reynolds
Tangy and fresh with hints of peach and orange. Good length of
flavour.

Monte Velho Alentejo VQPRD 95   14
Reynolds
An appealing style with hints of grapefruit and peach. Good
strong finish.

Vinha da Defesa Alentejo DOC 93   13
Reynolds
Pale lemon in colour, the 93 continues to have a lemon peel
touch underlined with apples.
White £10–£12

Cova da Ursa Chardonnay Vinho Regional 94
Reynolds
A delicious wine with lots of classic toasty, nutty aromas with a
good attack of fruit that develops and lingers. Smooth succulent
finish.

RED WINE

Red under £4.50

Aliança Reserva Bairrada DOC 92
Reynolds
Produced from the Baga grape. Meaty extract and nice bite on
the finish make it perfect with pasta with meat sauce. A top
example of its style.

Barra Vinho Tinto Vinho de Mesa nv 12
Dunnes Stores
Reasonable length of flavour with some plum and herb appeal.

Porta dos Cavaleiros Dão DOC 92 ☆
Reynolds
Warm earthy aromas of wild mushroom spill over on to the
palate. Packs a punch of acidity and tannin with hearty fruit
behind.

Serradayres Vinho Regional 93 13
Reynolds
Well structured with plenty of fruity appeal and a nice bite of
tannin on the end.
Red £4.50–£5.25

Alandra Vinho Regional 94 14
Reynolds
Deep crimson with damson and plum aromas. Very fruity,
jammy attack.

Aliança Angelus Reserva Bairrada DOC 92 14
Reynolds
Garnet in colour. This older vintage has pleasant strawberry
fruit touches in an easy-drinking style.

Aliança Reserva Dão DOC 92 14
Reynolds
Deep crimson. Has developed well since last tasted. The
plummy fruit is still obvious. Good food wine.

Bright Brothers Baga Beiras Vinho Regional 94
Superquinn
Rich in extract with white pepper spice aromas and flavours. A big wine in every sense with spice and fruit mingling in harmony right through to the long finish.

Charmaba Douro DOC 94
Reynolds
The 94 vintage is still young, with a deep crimson colour. A bite of tannin hides the fruit. Offers something different. An interesting choice.

Mandos Dão DOC 92   14
Quinnsworth
Delicious whole ripe blackberry appeal and a long, slightly austere finish.

Mandos Douro DOC 92   14
Quinnsworth
A mature style with brick nuances of colour. Mature inky aromas. Acidity is obvious, but the fruit holds its own, ending with a smack of tannin. Needs food.
Red £5.25–£6

Aliança Alabastro Alentejo Vinho Regional 92   14
Reynolds
Developing nicely, the wine still has a liquorice appeal with chewy fruit.

Campos dos Frades Cabernet Sauvignon Vinho Regional 95
Reynolds
Extremely appealing with its deep crimson colour. Lots of blackcurrant fruit aroma that comes through on flavour, ending in a long classic finish.

CR&F Alentejo Vinho Regional 92   14
Reynolds
Ruby red in colour. The red berry fruity aromas are gentle but obvious. Has a pleasant austere finish. Perfect meat wine.

Mateus Signature Douro DOC 93   13
Dillon
Crisp and fruity in an easy-drinking style.

Monte Velho Reguenos VQPRD 93
Reynolds
The 93 vintage is deep crimson in colour from the talented
winemaker David Baverstock. Packed with cherry fruit flavours
and a soft supple finish.
Red £6–£8

Cabeça de Toira Reserva VQPRD 91   14
Reynolds
A big style of wine with mature aromas of oil and prune.
Robust and solid with good length.

Carvalho, Ribeiro and Ferreira Garrafeira Ribatejo DOC 00
Reynolds
Be careful opening the waxy capsule! Worth the mess as this
tawny-hued wine has fragrant floral tones with good balance.
A classic Portuguese style.

D'Avillez Portalegre VQPRD 90
Mitchell
Great depth of seductive prune and dark chocolate aromas with
good mature fruit flavour appeal. Wonderful drinking.

Falcoaria Almeirim VQPRD 95 ☆
Reynolds
Austere, with a big structure, this wine is produced from the
Trincadeira Preta and Periquita. It has lots of savoury tones
with good structure and extra-long finish.

Fiuza Cabernet Sauvignon Vinho Regional 94   14
Reynolds/Superquinn
Super-ripe cassis overlain with a stalky character. Good balance
of fruit and tannin. Still has time to mature.

Fiuza Merlot Vinho Regional 94 ☆
Reynolds
A modern style with great depth of colour. Ripe, red-berried
fruit that lives up to its promise on taste. Appealing long finish.

Foral Garrafeira Douro DOC 90 ☆
Reynolds
Has matured since last tasted into a lovely approachable drink.
The fruit is pushing its way through the obvious tannins. A
super food wine.

João Santarém Torres Vedras Reserva VQPRD 89 13
Reynolds
Well made with firm structure and a nice touch of earthy
woodland fruit appeal.

Meia Pipa Vinho Regional 91 14
Reynolds
Appealing blackberry-type aroma. Flavours fan out on the
palate, ending on a high note of fruit.

Tinto da Talha Alentejo DOC 94 13
Dunnes Stores
Easy uncomplicated wine with cold tea and herb aromas. More
stewed fruit in flavour, with balanced tannins and a long easy
finish.
Red £8–£10

Cabernet Sauvignon do Esporão Vinho Regional 93 14
Reynolds
Produced from 100% Cabernet Sauvignon. American oak adds
an interesting coconut tone. Long flavoursome finish.

Esporão Reguengos Reserva VQPRD 91 ☆
Reynolds
The wine has developed wildflower and herb aromas since last
tasted. The attractive lush finish is still obvious. A delicious
example of modern Portugal.

Porta dos Cavaleiros Reserva Dão DOC 89   **14**
Reynolds
Earthy touch overlain with hints of cinnamon. Solid core of
fruit that follows through to the long austere finish. Enjoy now.

Trincadeira do Esporâo Vinho Regional 94   **14**
Reynolds
Named after the grape variety, this wine developed a ripe
fruity tone over cold tea aromas when left open for a while
before drinking. A smack of vanilla adds interest.
Red £10–£12

José de Sousa Garrafeira, Reguengos de Monsarraz VQPRD 91
Mitchell
Traditionally fermented in clay pots and produced from
traditional grapes including Trincadeira, Aragonez and
Castelão Francês (Periquita), this has bags of sweet ripe fruit
appeal overlain with tarry tones and an unmistakable austere
finish.

Quinta do Poço do Lobo Barraida DOC 87   **14**
Reynolds
A host of native grape varieties produce a robust wine with
ageing potential. This example is showing its age and should be
enjoyed now.

ROSÉ WINE

Rosé under £4.50

Casal Mendes Rosé Vinho de Mesa nv   **13**
Reynolds
A lively fresh style with a hint of spritz. Good summer
drinking.

Romania

Main wine regions

Dealul Mare   Cotnari
Murfatlar   Tîrnave

Principal grape varieties

As well as classic European there are many native or indigenous
varieties.

White   *Red*
Welschriesling   Cabernet Sauvignon
Gewürztraminer   Pinot Noir
Feteascâ Albâ   Merlot
Pinot Gris   Feteascâ Neagrâ
Tâmaîioasâ
Chardonnay

Labelling guide

Similar to the German wine laws.
   VS: superior quality.
   VSO: superior quality and appellation of origin.
   VSOC: top of the range with three quality categories.
   CMD: late harvest.
   CMI: late harvest with noble rot.
   CIB: selected late harvest with noble rot.

Wine styles

Whites should be drunk young. The best reds are matured in the
winery and released for sale when ready to drink.

WHITE WINE

White £4.50–£5.25

Posta Romana Classic Chardonnay 95   ☆
Barry & Fitzwilliam
From the Black Sea coast area, this water-pale wine has
pleasant sherbet aromas. The finish has a limey peel attraction.
Good balance between fruit and acidity.

ROMANIAN WINES

'Outstanding'
Wine Magazine

'Glorious'
Moveable Feast RTE

'Stunning'
Sunday Tribune

'Wonderful'
Oz Clarke BBC Food and Drink

'BLOODY GREAT WINES'
The Examiner

Imported by Barry & Fitzwilliam Ltd.
Cork and Dublin

RED WINE

Red £4.50–£5.25

Posta Romana Classic Cabernet Sauvignon 90 ☆
Barry & Fitzwilliam
Fermented and matured in oak, this is a good buy with its
pleasant tar and liquorice tones and good palate development.
Nice vanilla touch kicks back on the end.

Posta Romana Classic Pinot Noir 91 14
Barry & Fitzwilliam
The 91 vintage has more spicy fruit appeal. Good quality at the
price.

Special Reserve Cabernet Sauvignon 92 14
Barry & Fitzwilliam
This barrel-matured wine offers great drinking pleasure with
smoky leafy tones and lots of blackberry jam flavours. Hard to
beat at the price.

South Africa

Main wine regions

Constantia, Stellenbosch, Paarl, Worcester, Robertson, Klein Karoo, Orange River, Walker Bay.

Principal grape varieties

White	*Red*
Steen (Chenin Blanc)	Pinotage (a crossing of Pinot
Chardonnay	Noir and Cinsaut)
Sauvignon Blanc	Shiraz
Colombard	Cabernet Sauvignon
Ugni Blanc	Merlot
	Cabernet Franc
	Ruby Cabernet

Labelling guide

Wine of Origin is the quality designation.

Vintage: 75% of the wine must be from the vintage stated on the label.

Varietal: if a grape variety is stated, it must be made from 75% of that variety.

By law, the term 'estate' on a label means that grapes must be grown and vinified on the estate.

Cultivar: South African name for vine variety.

Wine styles

Whites continue to improve. A good example is wine produced from the attractive fruity Steen, which is lively and full of zesty acidity. Chardonnay, especially with oak influence, can be top quality.

Varietal reds such as Cabernet Sauvignon offer an attractive concentrated fruity style. Top-quality reds are very much influenced by traditional French styles and offer classic structure with the ability to mature.

Pinotage can be fruity and juicy or full-bodied and complex. It helps to know the producer.

WHITE WINE

White under £4.50

Culemborg Chenin Blanc 95   13
Dunnes Stores
Lots of pleasant pungent aromas. Good fruit development and
length of flavour.

Culemborg Dry White 95   12
Dunnes Stores
Easy-drinking modern white with a floral touch and zesty
acidity adding freshness.
White £4.50–£5.25

Culemborg Sauvignon Blanc/Chardonnay 95   14
Dunnes Stores
Very pale green. A crispy, crunchy wine with a clean correct
finish.

Helderberg Sauvignon Blanc 96   14
Quinnsworth
Better on flavour than aroma, with good weight of fruit
balanced by a spicy touch on the finish.

Kumala Chenin Blanc/Chardonnay 95   13
Barry & Fitzwilliam
Good fruity attack backed up with zesty acidity. The short
finish is fresh and balanced.

Kumala Colombard/Sauvignon Blanc 95   13
Barry & Fitzwilliam
Easy-drinking style with a good bite of fruit on the finish.

Long Mountain Chenin Blanc 95   13
Greenhills
A clean citrus style with lively acidity and fruity finish.

Long Mountain Dry Riesling 95   14
Greenhills
Another modern style with ripe fruit character supported by
crisp acidity.

Long Mountain Sauvignon Blanc 94   14
Greenhills
The stony fruit appeal is enticing, with a crisp clean finish. Lean
and lively with enough fruit to add interest.

Namaqua Colombard 95   13
Findlater
Yellow-toned with a hint of lemon drops. Flavour fills out very
well on the palate.

Van Riebeeck Chenin Blanc 95   14
Fitzgerald
The 95 vintage is livelier than the 94 tasted last year, with good
fruity Chenin in a slightly off-dry finish.
White £5.25–£6

Bellingham Blancenberger 95   13
Dunnes Stores
This blend of Sauvignon Blanc and Chenin Blanc in its distinc-
tive squat bottle is lively and fresh with a hint of spritz.

Culemborg Chardonnay 95   13
Dunnes Stores
Unusual, very ripe apple aromas and flavours, with fruit
holding up to the end.

KWV Chenin Blanc 95   14
Fitzgerald
With its delightful aromas, this vintage is much more tangy
than the 94, with lots of fruity flavours and a slightly off-dry
finish. Perfect aperitif.

KWV Sauvignon Blanc/Chardonnay 94   13
Fitzgerald
Since last tasted, the Chardonnay is showing more than the
Sauvignon. The apple fruits are still obvious, with a nice
rounded weight and good finish.

Long Mountain Chardonnay 95   14
Greenhills
Green leafy aromas giving way to mouthfilling flavours
echoing the ripe fruits of summer.

Nederburg Chardonnay 95   13
Dillon
Pale gold in colour, with good fruit and balanced acidity.

Paarl Heights Chenin Blanc 95   14
Gilbeys
Very good fruit and acidity balance. Clean, fresh and crisp on
the finish.

Van Riebeeck Sauvignon Blanc 95   14
Fitzgerald
This new vintage is all about lemon and limes. A well-rounded
style with good fruit and balance.

Villiera Estate Blanc 95   14
Grants
Yellow-gold, with pleasant ripe apple fruits giving way to a
creamy texture that packs a punch of fruit on the balanced
finish.
White £6–£8

Bellingham Chardonnay 95   14
Dunnes Stores
Subtle oak influence adds complexity and interest to the kiwi-
type fruit. The long finish has a smack of toast on the end.

Boschendal Chenin Blanc 95   13
Grants
Pale straw in colour and much better on taste than aroma. Note
the hint of spritz and good attack of fruit finishing in an
approachable easy style.

De Wetshof Estate Bon Vallon Chardonnay nv   ☆
Findlater
A good example of unoaked Chardonnay. Maturation on the
lees adds a nice nutty nuance. Enjoy the creamy finish with
crisp acidity.

Douglas Green Sauvignon Blanc 95   13
Cassidy
Obvious pungent aromas of rhubarb. Good attack of fruit and
acidity giving a medium long finish.

Fleur du Cap Chardonnay 95   14
Febvre
Creamy apricot aromas and flavours in a classic oak-matured
style. Nothing hollow in the middle—just good fruit from start
to finish.
White £8–£10

Boschendal Chardonnay 94   ☆
Grants
Apple and custard—fresh toast—this has it all, with lots of
fresh acidity. A classic style that delights the weary palate.

De Wetshof Estate Lesca Chardonnay 95   14
Wine Vault
Clean fresh aromas with sherbet. Delicious fresh apple fruit
attack with enough fruit to hold up to the last tasty mouthful.

Wildekrans Sauvignon 95   14
Barry & Fitzwilliam
Easy-drinking style with smoky bacon aromas and good flavour
development.

White £10–£12

Plaisir de Merle Chardonnay 94 ☆☆
Dillon
Pale with hints of green. Mouth-watering apple, peach and
spicy oak tones. Fruit shines through before oak influence takes
over on the long finish.

RED WINE

Red under £4.50

Culemborg Dry Red 95 13
Dunnes Stores
Easy drinking with plenty of fruit and good flavour carry-
through with some structure on the end.

Culemborg Pinotage nv 14
Dunnes Stores
Crisp and slightly spicy with blackberry jelly touches.

Helderberg Cabernet Sauvignon/Merlot 95 14
Quinnsworth
Still a little closed. Well balanced with appealing smoky, spicy
tones.

Helderberg Cinsault/Shiraz 96 13
Quinnsworth
Strawberry in colour, with a mineral backbone and hint of mint.
Needs a little more bottle age to show fruit.
Red £4.50–£5.25

Helderberg Cabernet Sauvignon 96 14
Quinnsworth
Pleasant ripe green and red peppers with a touch of pea-pod. A
smoky touch enters on flavour. An interesting vegetal-style
Cabernet.

Helderberg Pinotage 95 13
Quinnsworth
Really delivers on fruity appeal in a tingling, fresh, approach-
able style.

Helderberg Shiraz 96   14
Quinnsworth
Ruby pink with fruit-gum aromas and the familiar minty touch.
Easy-drinking style.

Kumala Cinsault/Pinotage 95   13
Barry & Fitzwilliam
Ruby pink in colour, this fruity, jammy style is easy both on the
palate and the pocket.

Kumala Shiraz/Cabernet Sauvignon 95
Barry & Fitzwilliam
Crimson in colour, with delicious blackcurrant jelly aromas.
Lots of grip with a spicy touch. Supple tannins add interest to
the long finish.

Long Mountain Cabernet Sauvignon 95
Greenhills
A star with its delicious deep blackberry appeal which carries
through in flavour. Offers good drinking pleasure at a reasonable price.

Van Riebeeck Pinotage 92   13
Fitzgerald
This fruity wine has held up well since last tasted. Good choice
for a party.
Red £5.25–£6

Bellingham Pinotage 94   14
Dunnes Stores
An elegant wine with blackberry and cream appeal. Good
balance between fruit and acidity. Good gripping finish.

KWV Cabernet Sauvignon WO 92   14
Fitzgerald
Has assumed cedar and leather aromas since last tasted. The
fruit is still apparent in flavour, with a hint of oak and good
tannins adding structure.

Long Mountain Shiraz 94   14
Greenhills
Everything comes together in this one—the jammy fruit appeal,
supple texture and long finish.

Nederburg Cabernet Sauvignon 93   14
Dillon
Deep cherry-red in colour, with good depth of flavour of
bramble-type red berry fruits. Good structure.

Nederburg Pinotage 94   14
Dillon
The 94 vintage is far more vibrant than the 92 tasted last year,
with very pleasant jammy-type fruits, a good bite of acidity and
a little smack of tannin to add structure.

Paarl Heights Red 96   13
Gilbeys
Strawberry-coloured with a tinge of purple. Better on flavour
than aroma, with juicy, fruity, red berry appeal.

Van Riebeeck Cabernet Sauvignon 93   13
Fitzgerald
Since last tasted, this wine has developed a hint of prunes with
a touch of smoke. It certainly has improved with some bottle
age. Enjoy now.

Villiera Estate 94   ☆
Grants
A star buy for the money, with its deep saturation of colour,
creamy fruit appeal and hint of aniseed. Flavour holds up from
start to finish in a soft plummy style.
Red £6–£8

Cardouw Cabernet Sauvignon 90   13
Verlings
Blackberry jam appeal. Soft-centred with a pleasant supple
fruity finish.

Cardouw Pinotage 91　　　　　　　　　　　14
Verlings
This wine has developed interesting savoury aromas and
flavours. Good development and finish.

Douglas Green St Augustine 93　　　　　　14
Cassidy
Garnet in colour, showing some maturity. Creamy plummy
aromas carry through on flavour with good length.

Fleur du Cap Merlot 93　　　　　　　　　　☆
Febvre
Deep dense colour is followed by wonderful aromas of pea-pod
and cassis overlain with vanilla. The fruit is well supported by
good acidity and tannins.

KWV Cabernet Sauvignon/Shiraz WO 92　　13
Fitzgerald
Oak-aged for 15 months, this vintage has assumed smoky
liquorice tones since last tasted. Enjoy now, as it is just beginning to show its age.

Swartland Pinotage 95　　　　　　　　　　☆
Wine Vault
Deep purple, with sweet fruit-gum appeal. Deliciously soft-
centred with tannins coming behind. A nice chunky style
ending in a long flavoursome finish.

Villiera Estate Cabernet Sauvignon 94　　14
Grants
Deep ruby in colour. Fresh red berry fruit sings its way right
through to the long fruity finish.
Red £8–£10

Fleur du Cap Cabernet Sauvignon 89　　　14
Febvre
The 89 has intense cassis fruit appeal, well supported by smoky
oak tones. Good length of flavour. A classic style.

La Motte Shiraz 93   14
Febvre
Classic in style, this wine is an example of how good Shiraz can
be from South Africa. Note the herby savoury quality fanning
out in flavour, with a nice tart structure held up by good
acidity.

Villiera Estate Merlot 94   ☆
Grants
Very classic in style, with lots of ripe red berry fruits and a hint
of chocolate to add interest. The high acidity is held in check,
with supple tannins allowing the fruit to fight back on the
finish. An interesting wine.

Wildekrans Pinotage 95   14
Barry & Fitzwilliam
Medium-bodied with supple fruity flavours reminiscent of
wine-gums.
Red £10–£12

Beyerskloof 93
Dunnes Stores
Cabernet Sauvignon full of rich warm fruit tones overlain with
spice. Intense rich flavoursome finish that lingers on and on. A
classic South African style.

Plaisir de Merle Cabernet Sauvignon 94
Dillon
Concentrated dairy chocolate with ripe cherry behind. Opulent
and rich with balanced fruit and acidity, assertive tannins and
long classic finish.

Spain

Main regions

Rioja, Navarra, Cariñena, Somontano, Penedès, Costers del Segre, Tarragona, Toro, Rueda, Ribera del Duero, Rias Baixas, Valencia, La Mancha, Valdepeñas.

Principal grape varieties

White	Red
Airén	*Garnacha*
Garnacha Blanca	Tempranillo (Cencibel, Ull de
Albariño	Llebre, Tinto Fino)
Verdejo	Cabernet Sauvignon
	Moristel

Labelling guide

Denominacion de Origen Calificada (DOC) Rioja only

Denominacion de Origen (DO) Just below Rioja in status

Vino de Mesa (VdM) Table wines

Vino de la Tierra (VdlT) Similar to the French Vin de Pays

Vino Comarcal (VC) Table wines with specific regional status

Tinto Red *Viejo* Old *Bodega* Winery

Sin Crianza Vino Joven or young wine with very little ageing

Crianza 12 months' ageing in cask and some months in bottle

Reserva Red. Minimum 36 months' ageing in cask and bottle. Released from the *bodegas* five years after the vintage. White and Rosé. Two years' ageing with 6 months in cask

Gran Reserva Red. 24 months' ageing in cask and 36 in bottle or vice versa, released from the *bodegas* 6 years after the vintage. White and Rosé. Four years' ageing with a minimum of 6 months in cask

Cava Quality sparkling wine produced by the traditional method

Wine styles

Rioja Dry white styles, fruity rosés and reds. Tempranillo dominates red wine production and wines are released from the bodegas when ready to drink.

Navarra Good value white, rosé and red wines. Garnacha dominates red wine production. Particularly noted for dry rosé styles produced for early drinking. European varieties such as

Cabernet Sauvignon are becoming more popular and a major re-planting programme is on-going.

Cariñena is dominated by co-operatives and is a source of good quaffing red wines.

Somontano Moristel and Garnacha dominate red wine production 80% of which is controlled by one co-operative. Classic grape varieties are producing some very interesting wines. An area to keep an eye on.

Penedès Known principally for sparkling wine (Cava) production the area is a source of excellent rosé and exciting classic red and white wines.

Conca de Barberà is another small area with full bodied tannic red wines from the Cabernet Sauvignon.

Rueda is a good source of dry white wines from the Viura grape. Drink young and fresh to enjoy their slight nutty aromas.

Ribera del Duero Bodegas Vega Sicilia produces one of Spain's most famous red wines, 'Unico', the top wine which is only produced in top vintages and aged for up to ten years before release for sale. It is the most expensive red wine of Spain.

Valencia, La Mancha and *Valdepeñas* are sources of good value wines. Whites should be drunk young. Reds are medium bodied and fruity with some oak influence and can be produced in Reserva styles.

Vintages

Rioja

95	Potentially superb.
94	Superb.
93	Average.
92	Very good.
91	Very good to superb.
90	Rich and tannic. Very good.
89	Very good. Well balanced.
88	Good to very good. Medium bodied.
87	Very good to superb.

WHITE WINE

Whites under £4.50

Campo Verde Cariñena DO nv   13
Greenhills
Star-bright in a clean fresh style, with a nice kickback of green
fruit.

Castillo de Liria DO nv   12
Quinnsworth
Easy-drinking modern-style white, with a slight bitter almond
finish.

San Valero White DO nv   13
Dunnes Stores
Good weight of tropical fruit plus balancing acidity add up to a
good-value fruity white.

Señorio de Urdaix Navarra DO 94   13
Reynolds
Water-pale, the fruit has held up since tasted in 95. Medium-
long finish in an easy-drinking, well-made modern style.
White £4.50–£5.25

Las Campanas Chardonnay/Viura DO 95   12
Dunnes Stores
Clean and fresh in a modern easy-drinking style.

Marqués de Riscal Rueda DO 95   ☆
Findlater
A star buy for the money. Grassy and lively in a Sauvignon
Blanc style. The lemon tang gives a delicious bite to the finish.

Viña Marcos Navarra DO 94   13
TDL
Produced from the principal white grape of Rioja, Viura, this
wine has a whisper of apricot fruit. A gentle attack of acidity
with fruit expanding, and finishing with a touch of bitter
grapefruit.

"Campo Viejo: Spain's No. 1 selling Rioja"

RIOJA WINE EXPORTERS' GROUP

CASSIDY WINES LTD.
Unit 1b, Stillorgan Ind. Park.
Tel: 01-2954157

Viña Tito Blanco DO nv   14
Greenhills
Produced from 100% Macabéo, this a light spritzy style with
fresh appeal.
White £5.25–£6

Coto De Hayas Campo de Borja DO 95   13
Greenhills
Water-pale. Aromatic with hints of banana, pear and apricot.
Barrique fermentation and maturation give it the lift it needs.

Las Gruesas Yecla DO 95   13
Grants
Yecla is known more for its reds, but this is a good example of
modern Spanish white wine in an easy-drinking style.

Marqués de Cáceres Rioja DOC 95   14
Grants
This well-balanced wine is a good example of white Rioja. The
lemon appeal is obvious, with a good bite of fruit and medium-
long finish.

Marqués de Griñon Durius Vino de Mesa 94   13
Fitzgerald
Offers something different. The 94 vintage has quite a waxy
texture with good limey acidity and stewed apple fruit.

Viña Hermosa Rioja DOC 95   14
Reynolds
Clean fresh modern style. This 95 vintage has a pleasant hint of
nuttiness which adds interest.
White £6–£8

Enate Blanco Macabéo/Chardonnay DO 95   14
Febvre
A zippy wine—fresh and clean with greengage fruits and a
long lively finish.

Faustino V Rioja DOC 95   13
Gilbeys
Surprisingly pale, this wine has good stony fruit appeal with a
slight earthy lemony taste. Good fish wine.

Genoli Rioja Blanco DOC 95 ☆
Greenhills
Crisp, fresh and well made from 100% Viura. If the wine
doesn't impress, the presentation certainly will.

Hermanos Lurton Rueda DO 93   14
Febvre
A tangy wine with good balance. The ripe grapefruit tone adds
interest. Good length and a medium-long fresh finish.

Marqués de Alella Chardonnay DO 95 ☆
Jenkinson Wines
For something different this delivers, with its good stony fruit
tones, lively acidity and fruity finish.

Marqués de Alella Classico DO 95   13
Jenkinson Wines
Clean and fresh with a spicy touch that will appeal to the off-
dry wine drinker.

Marqués de Alella Seco DO 95   14
Jenkinson Wines
Interesting wine with its stony fruit and zesty limey acidity
cutting through the finish. Better on taste than aroma.

Montecillo Viña Cumbrero Rioja DOC 95   13
Dillon
The 95 vintage has more fruit appeal than the 93 tasted last
year. Rhubarb springs to mind. Pleasant summer wine for
drinking young.

Olarra Rioja DOC 93   13
Allied Drinks
Deep golden in colour, with the typical oily lemon tone of the
modern-style white Rioja. Big finish with lots of oak tones and a
whack of kerosene. Offers something different.

Príncipe de Viana Chardonnay DO 95 ☆
Febvre
Deep yellow-gold in colour, this oak-fermented wine has a rich

crunchy aspect with a little hazelnut and fresh toast finish. Rich and full.

Raimat Chardonnay DO 95

Grants

Very attractive melon-type aromas and enough fruit to cut through the zesty acidity.

Royal Soledad Rioja DOC 95 14

Jenkinson Wines

A fresher vintage makes all the difference. The grapefruit appeal is still there, with a lively crisp clean finish.
White £8–£10

Conde de Valdemar Viñedo Rioja DOC 94 13

Febvre

Deep golden-yellow with lots of ripe melon fruit. Very obvious oak which cuts through everything and is inclined to mask the fruit on the finish.
White £10–£12

Enate Chardonnay DO 95 ☆

Dunnes Stores

Pale gold with a nutty character and pleasant floral overtones. Has a nice kickback of acidity and a long toasty finish.
White £15–£20

Gran Feudo DO Navarra 94 ☆

TDL

Subtle but obvious hazelnut aromas. Classic structure in a big opulent style. Nutty creamy finish that goes on and on. Super stuff.

RED WINE

Red under £4.50

Campo Rojo Cariñena DO nv 14

Greenhills

Tasted this year, the wine still has a modern quaffable fruity appeal with a hint of plums. Good value.

Ed's Red Tempranillo DO La Mancha 94 13

Quinnsworth

A youthful wine with cold tea aromas developing into damson

and chocolate flavours.

San Valero Red DO nv   13
Dunnes Stores
If you like a soft, supple easy-drinking red with jammy fruits, give this a try.

Señorio de los Llanos Reserva Valdepeñas DO 92
Superquinn
A super buy for the money. The Tempranillo grape known as Cencibel in this region of Spain has wonderful strawberry and tobacco appeal with a lovely bite of fruit well supported by good acidity and harmonious tannins. Drinking extremely well now.

Señorio de Urdaix DO 95   13
Reynolds
Easy-drinking red with a soft centre.

Viña Albali Tinto Reserva Valdepeñas DO 89
Superquinn
This wine proves what a good source the Valdepeñas region is for quality wine at reasonable prices. Extremely pleasant raspberry jelly aromas and flavours with a lively finish make this a star at the price. Enjoy now.
Red £4.50–£5.25

Berberana D'Avalos Tempranillo Rioja DOC 95   14
Quinnsworth
This younger vintage is still very closed. The fig-like fruit tones are overlain with a slight mineral touch.

Cermeño Toro DO 95
Reynolds
A robust wine with savoury meaty tones. Another variation of Tempranillo, it offers something different.

Don Ramón Campo de Borja DO 93
Greenhills
This 80% Garnacha and 20% Tempranillo wine is extremely

pleasant to drink, with freshly picked strawberry appeal and a hint of spice.

Fuente del Ritmo Tempranillo La Mancha DO 94
Quinnsworth
Still offering value for money, with more of an aniseed tone on this vintage combining with the blackcurrant and chocolate.

Las Campanas Crianza Navarra DO 92
Dunnes Stores
In a young Rioja style, this wine from neighbouring Navarra is crimson in colour, with shredded coconut aromas hiding the smack of strawberry fruits. It has a good flavoursome finish.

Marqués de Aragon Garnacha Puro Calatayud DO 95 ☆
Searson
Wonderful deep crimson in colour, with heady aromas of plum and spice. Skips down the throat easily, leaving lingering fruity flavours and a bite of acidity.

Viña Marcos Navarra DO 95 14
TDL
Easy drinking with cherry and plum aromas. A fruity red wine with medium acidity and little tannin.

Viña Tito Tinto DO 95 13
Greenhills
Ruby red. Closed on aroma but better on the palate. Easy-drinking spicy style.
Red £5.25–£6

Berberana Tempranillo Rioja DOC 94 14
Quinnsworth
A fruity friendly wine with coconut and strawberry fruit appeal. Attractive labelling adds interest.

Campo Burgo Tempranillo Rioja DOC 95 13
Reynolds
Soft plummy Tempranillo pleasantly presented at a good price.

Castaño Monastrell DO 95   14
Grants
Youthful looking. Strawberry and cream with a pleasant hint of
sherbet. Zippy fruit will appeal to the novice red wine drinker.
Serve cool.

Castillo de Almansa Reserva DO 89   14
Wine Barrel
Showing great depth of colour with wine-gum aromas. The
good structure and length of flavour make this very suitable for
red meat dishes.

Conde Bel Rioja DOC 95   13
Jenkinson Wines
Easy-drinking style which will appeal to the red wine drinker
who likes fruit.

Coto De Hayas Crianza DO 93   14
Greenhills
Mainly Garnacha with a dash of Tempranillo, this cherry-red
wine has a smack of damson and plum.

Gran Feudo Crianza Navarra DO 93   ☆
TDL
Blood-red with hints of spice and vanilla. Spice continues right
through to the end. Tannins and acidity are harmonious. Good
structure. Great drinking for the price.

Jaume Serra Tempranillo DO 94   14
Mackenway
The 94 vintage is a real 'smoothie', full of squashed strawberry
fruit and creamy coconut tones. Long succulent finish.

Las Campanas Cabernet Sauvignon DO 90   14
Dunnes Stores
Lots of herbaceous brambly fruit appeal which carries through
to the long finish and ends in a whack of tannin making it a
good choice with food.

Las Gruesas DO 94   14

Grants

Better on flavour than aroma. Note the spice and Marmite-like flavours in a chunky style.

Marqués de Griñon Durius Toledo DO 93   ☆

Fitzgerald

The fruit has really emerged in this vintage. Balanced tannins and acidity make for delicious drinking. Cherry and chocolate in the finish with supple tannins.

Montaraz Tierra de Barros nv   14

Reynolds

Garnacha and Tempranillo produce a wine with hints of liquorice in an easy-drinking style.

Mósen Cleto Crianza DO 92   14

Greenhills

Bananas and cream! Interesting presentation, giving the impression of a dust-covered bottle. Produced from 75% Garnacha and 25% Tempranillo.

Navajas Rioja DOC 94   14

Searson

Super drink for the money, with its delicious touch of coconut and strawberry fruits. Long concentrated finish.

Ochoa Tempranillo-Garnacha Navarra DO 95   14

Kelly

Damson jam appeal with a delicious silky touch. Smooth and generous in a youthful style.

Viña Hermosa DOC 95   14

Reynolds

Pleasant aromas of creamy vanilla. This wine has a good bite of acidity and fruit.

Viña Mayor Ribera del Duero DO 95   14

Reynolds

A black cherry colour, with intriguing leafy bramble aromas.

More fruit-driven than other examples of this style. Needs
more time, as fruit is still hidden.
Red £6–£8

Bordón Rioja Crianza DOC 93   14
Jenkinson Wines
Showing the giveaway tile tone of a mature wine, this style will
appeal to the Rioja drinker who likes structure and tannin with
spice on the finish. Drink up and enjoy.

Castillo de Montblanc Conca de Barberá DO 94
Dunnes Stores
Totally fruit-driven, with a deep dense purple colour. Blackberries and cream spring to mind. Rich and opulent, with
mouth-watering tannins and length of flavour.

Chivite Reserva Navarra DO 91
TDL
Coconut and strawberries all the way from the first sniff to the
last swallow. A good introduction to Navarra red wine, which
will appeal to those who like Rioja.

Conde de Valdemar Crianza Rioja DOC 93   14
Febvre
Deep cerise in colour, with super balance between the fruit,
acidity and soft tannins. Note the sweet vanilla touch typical of
ageing in American oak.

Cune Rioja DOC 93   14
Findlater
Lots of cherry and tar aromas, with good layers of fruity
development. Good drinking now.

Duque de Sevilla Reserva Campo de Borja DO 90   14
Greenhills
Marmite aromas with Garnacha and Tempranillo blending well
to produce a savoury wine.

Enate Tinto DO 94   14
Febvre
Produced from Moristel, a speciality of the Somontano region,

which imports lively red berry fruit flavours, and Tempranillo, which adds colour and structure. Enjoy young for its super fruity appeal.

Faustino V Reserva Rioja DOC 91 ☆

Gilbeys

A big savoury wine that is always consistently good in quality. Rich and satisfying.

Gran Cermeño Toro Crianza DO 91 14

Reynolds

Another beefy style with good drying tannins and a pleasant kickback of ripe fruits.

Guelbenzu Crianza DO 93 ☆

Searson

Cabernet Sauvignon, Tempranillo and Merlot combine to produce a big savoury wine with meaty tones. It's all about tannin with fruit fighting hard to break through. Offers something really different.

Guelbenzu Jardin Navarra DO 95 ☆

Searson

Top-class wine produced from 100% Garnacha from 30–40-year old vines. Sauerkraut-like aromas that give way to spicy blackberry fruit and gum-smacking tannins. Note the amazing colour.

Marqués de Cáceres Rioja DOC 92 ☆

Grants

Still tight-knit on aroma. Better on flavour with savoury tones and good tannic structure. A classic style.

Marqués de Griñon Rioja DOC 92 ☆

Fitzgerald

Lipsmacking good! This wine has really developed well since last tasted, with the fruit dominating the tannins. Long finish with oaky tones right on the end.

Rioja Bordón

Marqués de Vitoria Crianza Rioja DOC 91   **14**
Remy
Typical of its style—fruity, creamy, smooth, with a very
pleasant long finish.

Monasterio de Tentudia Tierra de Barros 90
Reynolds
The classic presentation is followed by classic rustic tastes. A
solid wine from this little-known area, which produces a lot of
cork.

Montecillo Viña Cumbrero Rioja DOC 93   **14**
Dillon
A fresh example and good introduction to fruity Rioja. Straw-
berry fruit touches.

Múrice Crianza Rioja DOC 93   ☆
Greenhills
80% Tempranillo produces a super opulent wine with a big
silky texture. The wine's presentation can't fail to impress
either.

Olarra Rioja DOC 93   **14**
Allied Drinks
Ruby red with hints of raspberry overlain with a slight herby
tone. Sweet fruit attack ends in a beefy Oxo-like finish. Overall
more savoury than fruity, making it a good food wine.

Pozuelo Crianza DO 92
Grants
Deep ruby red, immediately suggesting mashed strawberries
and cream. Delicious chunky fruit with lots of grip and bite. A
decent drink with good structure and length.

Príncipe de Viana Cabernet Sauvignon Crianza DO 92   ☆
Febvre
Deep garnet in colour, with a heady mix of oak and spicy
aromas. Mouthfilling rounded fruit style with smoothness and
yet enough harmonious tannins to add interest. Great follow-
through and finish.

Príncipe de Viana Garnacha de Viñas Viejas DO 95   ☆ ☆ ☆
Febvre
An important grape variety in Navarra, this example has
amazing fresh-picked squashed raspberry fruit appeal. A
lovely, lively wine with balance and vibrancy.

Príncipe de Viana Tempranillo DO 95   ☆ ☆
Febvre
A big deep purple-crimson savoury wine. Dive into the aromas
of this smoky style with rich, full chewy fruit flavours and
wonderful supple tannins. Super wine for the money.

Raimat Abadia DO 91   ☆ ☆
Grants
Brick reflects through the deep garnet colour. Serious oak
influences knit together the sweet fruit, combining to give a
long silky balanced finish.

Royal Rioja DOC 94   14
Jenkinson Wines
This vintage has even more appeal than the 93 tasted last year
with its supple smooth oak tones overlain with a hint of spice.

Scala Dei Priorato DO 94   14
Karwig
Something different with its intense purple-black colour. Full of
herby flavours such as sage and a hint of thyme. Mouth-drying
tannins denote its youth. Lots of acidity.

Torres Gran Sangre de Toro Reserva Penedès DO 92   ☆
Woodford Bourne
Deep garnet in colour, with very pleasant liquorice and
redcurrant fruits. Mouthfilling flavours linger with vanilla
overtones.

Viña Hermosa Rioja Crianza DOC 92   13
Reynolds
Bright crimson in colour. The fruit is still hidden by the tannin.

Viña Las Torres Merlot Penedès DO 95
Molloy's
This wine shows how Merlot from this part of Spain can excel.
Its bright crimson colour and ripe fruit appeal are overlain with
plum and chocolate tones. The smooth silky finish is a bonus.

Viña Real Crianza DOC 91   14
Findlater
Crimson with a hint of tawny. This concentrated wine, pro-
duced from Tempranillo and Garnacha, and matured in
American oak, has a rich smooth texture.
Red £8–£10

Artadi Viñas de Cain Crianza Rioja DOC 93 ☆
Febvre
Well-balanced example of its style. Typical strawberry and
coconut appeal of young Rioja. The finish lingers long after the
last swallow

Berberana Gran Reserva Rioja DOC 87
Quinnsworth
Dominated by Tempranillo with some Garnacha and released
for sale from the winery in 93, this is a stunner at the price. Its
sweet fruit aroma with a mineral edge explodes on the palate
into a rich mature fruit character. Enjoy now.

Colegiata Reserva Toro DO 89
Mackenway
Since last tasted the oak has integrated extremely well. The
chunky fruit, smooth tannins and good acidity all add up to a
smooth, complex, mature wine.

Conde de Valdemar Reserva Rioja DOC 91 ☆
Febvre
This younger vintage has got it all, with super ripe red berry
fruits overladen with delicious grapefruit tone. Good length
and finish.

Enate Crianza Tempranillo/Cabernet Sauvignon DO 93
Febvre **14**
A big mouthful of ripe blackberry fruits supported by supple
tannins and good acidity add up to very fine wine drinking.

Ijalba Reserva Rioja DOC 90 **14**
Greenhills
Two years' ageing in oak adds a silky texture to the chocolate
and strawberry cream aromas. The wine lives up to its designer
bottle shape.

Marqués de Murrieta Reserva Rioja DOC 91 ☆
Gilbeys
Developing prune-like fruits since last tasted, this wine,
produced from 95% Tempranillo and aged in American oak, is
still an all-time favourite with a rich luscious finish.

Marqués de Riscal Reserva Rioja DOC 91 ☆
Findlater
This vintage has a touch more cigar-box aromas—the flavour is
still big and opulent with a delicious dash of coconut.

Marqués de Vitoria Reserva Rioja DOC 90 ☆
Remy
Oaky spicy tones mingle with strawberry fruit flavours and
round out to a long classic smooth finish.

Montecillo Viña Monty Gran Reserva Rioja DOC 87 ☆ ☆
Dillon
Wonderful complex aromas of tar and liquorice. The oak and
spice mingle in a rich smooth finish.

Muga Reserva Rioja DOC 91 ☆
United Beverages
Cherry liqueur aromas open up and expand on the palate with
a delightful salty tang. Excellent example of a traditional Rioja
bodegas.

Ochoa Gran Reserva Navarra DO 87
Kelly
A forward wine with mouth-watering strawberry fruit and
vanilla tones. Amazing smooth generous finish.

Ochoa Reserva Navarra DO 90
Kelly
A vibrant wine produced from Tempranillo and Cabernet
Sauvignon. Spanish winemaking at its very best, with ripe fruit
character, lively acidity and good length to the velvet textured
finish.

Pago de Carraovejas DO 94
Searson
A super example of this type of wine, with its deep blood-red
colour and green leafy vegetable aroma. Flavours of spice and
herbs fan out on the palate, ending in a rich well otructured
fluish. A very interesting wine.

Scala Dei Crianza Priorat DO 91
Karwig
Deep garnet in colour. Sweet vanilla and warm red berry fruit.
Good acidity and tannins add structure. Good solid wine
drinking.

Viña Hermosa Reserva Rioja DOC 89 14
Reynolds
The 89 vintage is showing maturity, but the fruit is still
generous with a bittersweet finish.

Viña Mayor Reserva Del Duero DO 91 14
Reynolds
Meaty and earthy, this wine takes understanding. Produced
from the Tinto Fino (a variation of Tempranillo) it has a long, if
tough, finish. Needs food.
Red £10–£12

Barón de Oña Reserva Rioja DOC 89 13
Karwig
Tile-brick in colour. Not for the faint-hearted, with its leather

type aromas. Softer on the palate, it has some fruit, but finishes in an austere style.

Cerro Anon Gran Reserva Rioja DOC 87   **14**
Allied Drinks
Orange glints reflected through the brick tones denote age. Smoky, jammy aromas and flavours also indicate maturity. Drinking extremely well now.

Chivite Gran Reserva 125 Anniversario Navarra DO 88
TDL
Ageing for 24 months in French oak and 18 months in bottle ensures a spicy touch to this complex, well-matured wine. The Tempranillo gives delicious tangy red berry fruit flavours and ageing in bottle rounds out the palate. Long persistent finish.

Enate Reserva Cabernet Sauvignon DO Somontano 92
Dunnes Stores
One of Spain's new and interesting DO areas located in Aragon in north-east Spain. This 100% Cabernet Sauvignon is garnet in colour, with undertones of very ripe cassis. Rich and satisfying, with a definite 'wow' factor.

Guelbenzu Evo Crianza DO 92
Searson
French oak, 30-year-old vines, Cabernet Sauvignon, Tempranillo, Merlot and top-class winemaking all add up to a classic red wine with strong spicy overtones.
Red £12–£15

Conde de Valdemar Gran Reserva Rioja DOC 86
Febvre
Succulent and ripe, with lots of blackberry jam tones. Luscious fruit is balanced by supple tannins and a nice hint of spice. An opulent wine.

Les Terrasses Alvaro Palacios DO 93
Febvre
An impressive wine. Deep ruby in colour, the aromas are all about new wood and spice. Lots of fruit hit back on flavour, with well-knit tannins and a good long finish.

Marqués de Cáceres Reserva Rioja DOC 89

Grants

Very deep ruby. Tight-knit on aroma, but the promise of
excellence lies in the taste. The whole impression is one of
harmony with seductive fruit appeal. A wine to linger over.

Marqués de Vitoria Gran Reserva Rioja DOC 89 14

Remy

Hints of brick in the garnet colour denote its age. Supple, silky
and smooth. Big fruity attack. Extra-long finish.

Pesquera Crianza DO 92

Searson

Dense concentrated aromas of herbs and ripe red berry fruits
with hints of vanilla. Classy ripe fruit attack. Big bold and
enjoyable. This wine has it all!

Red £15–£20

Baron de Chirel Rioja DOC 88 ☆ ☆ ☆

Findlater

A very serious wine with a super presentation. It smacks of
coffee and Mocha with gum-drying tannins and good acidity.
Balanced structure with a long elegant finish.

Red £20–£30

Clos Mogador Priorato DO 92 ☆ ☆

Karwig

Expensive, but worth it for the drinker who wants to explore
complex aromas and flavours. Subtle aromas of figs and spice
fan out on the palate. Tannins grip the front of the gums.
Classic style; only 800 cases produced every year from 18 ha.

ROSÉ WINE

Rosé £4.50–£5.25

Gran Feudo DO Navarra 94 14

TDL

Strawberry-tinged in colour. Good fruit development, but has a
dry finish with a slight apple flavour.

Viña Tito Rosé DO nv   12
Greenhills
This spritzy pale strawberry-coloured wine produced from
100% Grenache is easy to drink and refreshing, especially on a
summer's day.
Rosé £6–£8

Faustino V Rioja DOC 95   14
Gilbeys
Pale strawberry in colour, with earthy raspberry fruit character.
A nice example with a dry finish.
Rosé £8–£10

Enate Cabernet Sauvignon Rosado DO 95   ☆
Febvre
From innovative winemakers, this rosé is deep salmon-pink in
colour, with fresh crushed strawberry fruit and a long fruity
finish.

USA—California

Main wine regions

North of San Francisco
Mendocino
Napa Valley
Sonoma Valley
Los Carneros
Sierra Foothills

South of San Francisco
Livermore Valley
Monterey
Santa Cruz
Santa Barbera
Santa Clara Valley

Principal grape varieties

White
Chardonnay
Sauvignon Blanc (known as
Fumé Blanc when oak aged)
Chenin Blanc
Riesling
Emerald Riesling
Colombard
Viognier
Gewürztraminer
Pinot Blanc

Red
Cabernet Sauvignon
Zinfandel
Syrah
Pinot Noir
Merlot
Sangiovese
Nebbiolo
Grenache
Barbera
Petite Sirah (not to be
confused with Rhône Syrah)
Carignan
Cabernet Franc
Gamay

Labelling guide

Over 60 AVAs (Approved Viticultural Areas) define particular growing regions but not the type of grapes grown, 85% of the wine must come from the region named on the label.

Varietal: if a wine states the name of the grape variety on the label, it must be produced from 75% of the specified grape.

Vintage: wine must be made from 95% of grapes grown in the stated year on the label.

Reserve: usually indicates a special selection from the winery.

Estate bottled: to use this term the winery must own or be in control of the vineyards from which the wine is produced.

Rosé wines became even more popular when the Californians used the term 'blush' to describe the style.

Wine styles

Varietal red and white wines from classic grape varieties are produced for early drinking.

Classic wine-making influenced by European immigrants includes oak-influenced Chardonnay whites, varietals such as Cabernet Sauvignon and blended reds with great ageing ability.

Zinfandel: produces a vast array of styles from easy-drinking to full-bodied port-like wines.

White Zinfandel: term used to describe a pink-tinged wine produced from this grape.

'Meritage' is the term used to describe wines produced from the blend of classic Bordeaux varieties, e.g. Cabernet Sauvignon, Merlot, Malbec and Cabernet Franc.

California produces top-class sparkling wines, with Champagne houses investing in vineyards and wineries.

Vintages

Cabernet Sauvignon based wines

95   Good to very good.
94   Very good to superb.
93   Good to very good.
92   Good to average. Drink early.
91   Superb, intense and rich.
90   Superb. Rich and complex, especially Napa.
89   Very good to superb. Some too tannic.
88   Very good.
87   Superb. Rich and complex.
86   Superb.
85   Superb.

Chardonnay

95   Good to very good.
94   Superb. Will keep.
93   Very good.
92   Very good.
91   Superb. Concentrated and rich.
90   Very good to superb.

WHITE WINE

White £4.50–£5.25

Sutter Home Sauvignon Blanc 94   14
Quinnsworth
Tingling fresh acidity, stony-fruit appeal with a clean fresh
finish.

Vendange California White 94   13
Barry & Fitzwilliam
Attractively presented with peachy hints and a touch of spritz.
White £5.25–£6

Blossom Hill Chardonnay nv   13
Gilbeys
Well-made wine with hints of mango. Fresh and appealing.

Domain Hill and Mayo Chardonnay 93   13
Superquinn
From Mendocino County, this wine has some bottle maturity,
with appealing ruby grapefruit tones and medium finish.

Ernest & Julio Gallo Chardonnay nv   13
Fitzgerald
Still good straightforward drinking with kiwi fruit and some
length on the finish.

Glen Ellen Proprietor's Reserve Chardonnay 95   14
Grants
Lemon-tinged with citrus fruit and peach appeal. Good
weighty style with a pleasant buttery touch and long finish.

Glen Ellen Proprietor's Reserve Sauvignon Blanc 94   13
Grants
Ripe fruit appeal—the gooseberry tasted in this vintage in 95
has given way to ripe apricot and peach with a creamy
influence. Drinking well now.

GEYSER PEAK

THE SILVERADO TROPHY
for the best Sauvignon Blanc

Awarded to

GEYSER PEAK WINERY

1995 Sauvignon Blanc

** Best of Show **

The UK International Wine & Spirit Competition is recognised worldwide as one of the most prestigious wine judgings. 1,400 of the finest wines from 38 countries were entered.
Only 14 US wines received gold medals.
Geyser Peak wines were awarded three!

For further information on Geyser Peak's Award Winning Selections, please contact
Peter Dalton, Dublin (01) 295 4945
Geyser Peak Winery, Geyserville, California 95441
USA

Sutter Home California Chardonnay 95   13
Quinnsworth
From the Napa Valley, this is a fruity, easy-drinking style with a hint of nutmeg.

Vendange California Chardonnay 94   14
Barry & Fitzwilliam
Good fruit appeal in the form of apple and greengage fruit with medium acidity.
White £6–£8

Ernest & Julio Gallo Turning Leaf Chardonnay nv   14
Fitzgerald
This green-tinged wine has gentle hints of vanilla, with lively exotic fruit appeal and excellent use of oak adding a touch of creaminess.

Wente Vineyards Chardonnay 95   13
Dunnes Stores
A waxy mouthful of ripe generous fruit flavours with a smack of oak and medium acidity.

Wente Vineyards Sauvignon Blanc 94   ☆
Dunnes Stores
Elderflower aromas give way to ripe fruit flavour. Great depth and toastiness.
White £8–£10

Clos du Val Le Clos Chardonnay 93   14
Terroirs
Fermentation in French oak adds butter tones to the apricot-style fruit flavours. Supple with an enticing, lingering finish.

Ernest & Julio Gallo Sonoma Chardonnay 93   14
Fitzgerald
Green-gold in colour. Pleasant sherbet aromas with fresh fruit salad appeal supported by citrus acidity. The oak influence adds roundness and creaminess to the long finish.

Geyser Peak Sauvignon Blanc 95   14
Dalton
Water-pale. Clean aromas of Sauvignon fruit less pungent in style than some. More fruity than herbaceous.

Sebastiani Sonoma County Chardonnay 94   14
Barry & Fitzwilliam
Ripe apricots with good depth of flavour and subtle toasty tone from maturation in French oak. Medium acidity and high-alcohol finish.
White £10–£12

Heitz Cellar Napa Valley Chardonnay 94   14
Terroirs
Deep gold in colour, with an intriguing floral tone which comes through on the palate. Note the freshly made toast finish.
White £12–£15

Acacia Caviste Chardonnay 94
Searson
Deep golden yellow. The oak influence adds subtle aromas to the pineapple flavours. A hint of spritz adds a lively finish to the expanded fruit tone.

Beaulieu Carneros Chardonnay 94
Gilbeys
Oak-fermented and matured, this is a rich wine reminiscent of peach and melon-type fruits. Long toasty finish with elegance and good structure.

Château Woltner Howell Mountain Chardonnay 95
Terroirs
Subtle oaky aromas with a distinctive buttery tone carry through on flavour. Acidity fights back. At 13.5% the alcohol is noticeable. Still young.

Robert Mondavi Coastal Chardonnay 94   ☆
Woodford Bourne
Strong nutty character with a lively mouthful of creamy fruits. The nutty tones win out on the end.

Sequoia Grove Chardonnay 94   ☆
Mitchell
A well-made harmonious wine with creamy oak tones impart-
ing an extra-long toasty finish to the peachy fruit.
White £15–£20

Sonoma-Cutrer Russian River Ranches 94   13
Terroirs
Spicy oak dominates the melon-type fruits. Weighty, oily mouth
feel with a long interesting finish.

RED WINE

Red £4.50–£5.25

Vendange California Red 94   ☆
Barry & Fitzwilliam
Chocolate and plums! An opulent style—very easy on the
palate and pocket.
Red £5.25–£6

Blossom Hill Collection Cabernet Sauvignon nv   14
Gilbeys
Leafy liquorice aromas with flavour that holds up to the
medium long finish.

Ernest & Julio Gallo Cabernet Sauvignon 94   14
Fitzgerald
Smooth and silky. Easy to drink with a medium long, fruity
finish.

Glen Ellen Proprietor's Reserve Cabernet Sauvignon 93
Grants   14
A good introduction to Californian Cabernet, with its beetroot
colour and smoky blackcurrant flavours cut through with
supple tannins.

Glen Ellen Proprietor's Reserve Merlot 94   13
Grants
Strawberry red in colour. Good fruit and a smack of liquorice
that adds interest to the long finish.

Glen Ellen Proprietor's Reserve Red nv   14
Grants
Aromas of mint leaves with summer fruit flavours breaking
through. Well-made balanced wine.

**Paul Masson Vintners Selection Reserve Cabernet Sauvignon
nv**   *Dillon*   13
Easy delicate drinking with a nice touch of opulence on the
finish.

Sutter Home Cabernet Sauvignon 93   14
Quinnsworth
Very fruity, reminiscent of figs and aniseed. Smooth and supple
in taste, with a good long finish.

Sutter Home California Merlot 94   14
Quinnsworth
Purple in colour, with a spicy, almost nutmeg, aroma. Nice fruit
on the palate with a pleasant bite of acidity on the finish.

Vendange Cabernet Sauvignon 95   13
Barry & Fitzwilliam
A flavoursome wine—smooth and well rounded with an easy
finish.

Vendange Zinfandel nv   14
Barry & Fitzwilliam
Soft and supple with fresh fruity appeal. Easy-drinking
enjoyable style.
Red £6–£8

Ernest & Julio Gallo Turning Leaf Cabernet Sauvignon 94
Fitzgerald   14
Pleasant smoky fruit appeal developing into a round creamy
palate.

Ernest & Julio Gallo Turning Leaf Zinfandel 93   ☆
Fitzgerald
Aged for two years in oak, this ruby red wine has an attractive

cherry liqueur flavour with aromas of wood shavings. Delicious and different.

Monterey Vineyard Cabernet Sauvignon 94 ☆

Fine Wines
Rich, ripe and complex, with lots of flavours giving a range of sensations from cedar to savoury, wrapped together with toasty oak.

Wente Vineyards Cabernet Sauvignon 95 13

Dunnes Stores
Stalky aromas with moderate intensity of flavour ending in a bite of spice.
Red £8–£10

Cline Côtes D'Oakley 94 14

McCabes
Attractively labelled, this oak-matured wine is produced from old vines. Sweet fruit flavours are cut through with lively acidity. The oak influence adds a spicy touch to the finish.

Ernest & Julio Gallo Sonoma Cabernet Sauvignon 92 ☆ ☆ ☆

Fitzgerald
Top of the range. Deep black cherry in colour. Wonderful aromas of cassis and vanilla. Has a super smooth attack supported all the way by rich ripe red berry fruits and harmonious tannins. The finish is extra long and succulent.

Ernest & Julio Gallo Sonoma Zinfandel 93 ☆ ☆

Fitzgerald
Fifteen months' ageing in oak adds extra complexity to this concentrated chewy wine with intense ripe berry fruit overlain with spice. Flavours persist on the long finish.

Guenoc Lillie Langtry Cabernet Sauvignon 91 ☆

Remy
This vintage is top class, with wonderful depth of colour and big red berry fruit aromas overlain with spice. mint and eucalyptus. Big and bold in every sense.

Guenoc Lillie Langtry Petite Sirah 92 14
Remy
Plummy rich and ripe, with a robust fruit character, good
tannic structure and long fruity finish.

Robert Mondavi Woodbridge Barrel Aged Zinfandel 94
Molloy's
The drip-resistant bottle is appealing, but the liquorice and
woodland ripe spicy berry appeal even more. This wine is
stamped all over with the winemaking expertise of Mondavi. A
Zinfandel with structure and less 'hot berry' tone than others.

Sebastiani Sonoma County Cabernet Sauvignon 93
Barry & Fitzwilliam
Garnet with a hint of tawny. This wine has a core of savoury
meaty tones with a delicious sprinkling of spice. A super
wholesome style.

Sebastiani Sonoma County Zinfandel 92
Barry & Fitzwilliam
The wine has a very rich damson and wild berry fruit appeal.
The tastes are ripe and flavoursome with a bite of freshness on
the finish.
Red £10–£12

Fleur de Carneros 94
Parsons
A delectable vintage, still full of strawberry fruit appeal ending
in a fresh fruit flourish.

Pellegrini Sonoma Valley Barbera Old Vines 94
McCabes
This wine offers a good opportunity to taste the Californian
version of the versatile Barbera. It shows how vibrant the grape
can be, with whole blackberry fruit appeal in a thirst-quench-
ing, lively style.

Ravenswood Vintners Blend Zinfandel 94   **14**
Mitchell
Very attractive with its quaffable juicy red berry fruit appeal
and fresh silky finish.
Red £12–£15

Carneros Creek Pinot Noir 94
Parsons
A delicious ripe elegant style with strawberry flavours
intertwining with balanced acidity and supple tannins.

Franus Zinfandel 94
Terroirs
A delightful example of zippy Zin with its cooked fruit appeal,
supple tannins and toasty tone. Finishes with an opulent
flourish.

Mahoney Estate Carneros Las Piedras Vineyard Pinot Noir 94
Parsons
Crimson in colour, with wonderful aromas of rich red berry
fruit, creamy and seductive. Lives up to its promise on flavour
which carries right through to the lively vibrant finish.

Robert Mondavi Coastal Cabernet Sauvignon 93
Woodford Bourne
Minty tones with cherry fruit appeal. Not overpowering in
flavour—the fruit is obvious but still hidden by the gum-drying
tannins. Shows a lot of promise.
Red £15–£20

Acacia Carneros Pinot Noir 94
Searson
A wonderful stylish wine combining sweet fruit with the
special farmyard appeal of top Pinot. Soft ripe succulent attack
that explodes and finishes in a delicious smack of spice.

Robert Sinskey Vineyards Pinot Noir 93
Terroirs
Straight-to-the-heart Pinot style with glorious fruit and tannins

Take your pick from the best selection of wine in Ireland.

You'll find there's so many to choose from at Quinnsworth.
We've travelled the length and breadth of the world to bring you wine of the finest quality. But it's not just our superb wine selection that you'll find irresistible, our prices are pretty tempting too. It's this commitment to your palate and pocket which means that Quinnsworth now has the best selection of wine in Ireland.

REAL VALUE
Quinnsworth

doing their best to tame the richness. Fruit wins out on the end. Expensive—yes, but only 4,100 cases are produced. Definitely a special occasion drink.

Stag's Leap Wine Cellars Cabernet Sauvignon 93 ☆ ☆ ☆
McCabes
A real stunner! Rich, opulent and complex, with brambly fruit appeal overlain with good use of oak. Well-rounded fruit flavours with a delicious bite of acidity and supple tannins. A classic style.
Red £20–£30

Carneros Creek Signature Reserve Pinot Noir 94 ☆ ☆
Parsons
Ignore the aroma and just zoom in on the flavour. Delicious mouthfilling flavours in an elegant supple style. Nothing sticks out in this wine, it's all about harmony and balance.

ROSÉ WINE

Rosé £4.50–£5.25

Vendange California White Zinfandel 94 13
Barry & Fitzwilliam
Onion-skin colour. Very fruity with fresh acidity. Serve chilled on a summer's day.
Rosé £5.25–£6

Glen Ellen Proprietor's Reserve White Zinfandel 95 14
Grants
Very pale baby pink with vibrant young raspberry fruit appeal. A slight hint of spritz adds liveliness. Clean and crisp in an off-dry style.
Rosé £6–£8

Wente Vineyards White Zinfandel 95 14
Dunnes Stores
Very light baby pink. Refreshing and lively with a hint of spritz and nice raspberry fruit character. Off-dry.

Champagne and sparkling wines

An AC within itself, Champagne is a unique style of sparkling wine. It is strictly defined and legally protected. The word 'Champagne' must appear on the label and cork of each bottle.

Main regions

Montagne de Reims, Valée de la Marne, Côtes des Blancs, Aube. Within these areas there are 301 different 'crus' or villages.

Principal grape varieties

Chardonnay, Pinot Noir and Pinot Meunier
Each contributes its own special characteristics to the blend. For example, Chardonnay contributes finesse and elegance, Pinot Noir structure and flavour, and Pinot Meunier aroma.

Labelling guide

Non vintage: accounts for the vast majority of styles. Known by the name of the maker or house, blends of different wines and years are designed to produce a consistent house style. Aged for a minimum of fifteen months before release for sale.

Vintage: Produced from blends of a single year. Not every year is considered good enough to produce a vintage Champagne. Aged for a minimum of three years but most is aged for much longer before release for sale.

Blanc de Blancs: Produced exclusively from Chardonnay these are Champagnes with a light fresh flavour becoming deeper with some age.

Blanc de Noirs: Produced exclusively from one or both of the black grapes Pinot Noir or Pinot Meunier. The quite rare Bollinger's Vieilles Vignes is a superb example.

Prestige or deluxe cuvées: Moët et Chandon were the first to produce a *cuvée prestige*, the famous Dom Pérignon. Most houses now produce one. Some examples are Roederer's Cristal, Laurent-Perrier Cuvée Grand Siècle, Heidsieck Dry Royal, Taittinger Comtes de Champagne, and Veuve Clicquot's Grande Dame.

Single vineyard wines: Krug's Clos de Mesnil (a Blanc de Blancs) is an example. Usually aged in the winery for six years or more before release for sale.

Rosé or pink Champagne: Two methods are used. A small amount of red wine (from the Bouzy region) can be added to the blend. The juice (must) is allowed to remain in contact with the black grape skins for a short period during fermentation.

BOB or Buyer's Own Brand: Champagnes made to the requirements of special customers such as hotel groups, supermarkets or restaurants.

RD (recently disgorged): Champagnes left in contact with the sediment or lees for many years before disgorgement (the process by which sediment is removed from the wine).

Styles

Extra Brut	very dry	*Demi-sec*	sweet
Brut	dry	*Rich or doux*	very sweet
Sec	off dry		

Vintage

There is a general feeling that owing to superb quality 96 will be a declared vintage.

90 Superb—a very special vintage
89 Excellent, succulent and full bodied
88 Potentially a long lived vintage
86 Very good
85 Superb

OTHER SPARKLING WINES

France: Many regions in France, including the Loire (Saumur), Alsace, Bordeaux and the South (Blanquette de Limoux), produce quality sparkling wine, usually by the traditional method.

Germany: The tank method is used to produce the majority of German sparkling wine—'Sekt'. Important producers include Henkell and Deinhard.

Italy: North East Italy produces top quality traditional method sparklers. Asti Spumante (DOCG since 1994, now called simply Asti) is a sweet, low-alcohol sparkling wine produced by a unique method. Wine produced from the Moscato grape labelled Moscato d'Asti is of higher quality and is medium dry.

Spain: 'Cava' is the Spanish term for traditional method sparkling wine. Most Cavas are produced in Penedès, north of Barcelona, from Spanish grapes such as Parellada, Xarel-Lo and Macabeo. Quality producers include Freixenet, Codorniu and Parxet.

New World: California, New Zealand and Australia are producing top quality sparkling wine from Chardonnay, Pinot Noir and Pinot Meunier. This is usually indicated on the label. Otherwise the wines are known by their brand name. Many Champagne houses have invested in overseas vineyards and winery operations, for instance Miguel Torres in Chile, Mumm in California and Moët et Chandon with Green Point in Australia.

CHAMPAGNE

£12–£15

Comte L. de Ferrande Brut nv
Dunnes Stores
Top class for the price. Elegant floral aromas are supported by good acidity and a long creamy finish.

Raymond de Belval Brut nv
Superquinn
Hard to beat at the price, this well-structured Champagne has good fruit with a hint of biscuit and balancing acidity.

£15–£20

Bredon Brut nv   14
Fine Wines
Toasty and creamy with a nice bite of apple fruit and lively mousse. Fruitier than most.

Brossault Brut nv   14
Greenhills
A lively style with the emphasis on ripe apple fruits. Medium long finish.

Dravigny Demoizet 1er Cru Selection Brut nv
Burgundy Direct
Delicate fruit with good bubbly mousse and fresh acidity. Superb quality with a distinct yeasty flavour.

J. M. Gremillet Selection Brut nv   **13**
Allied Drinks
Easy-drinking style with good mousse and a dry finish, offering good value for money.

Jacquart Brut Tradition nv   **13**
Quinnsworth
A very pleasant drink with good apple fruit character, lively mousse and good length.

Princesse de France Grande Réserve nv   ☆
Bacchus
Produced from 60% Pinot Noir, 20% Chardonnay and 20% Pinot Meunier, the wine has an elegant delicate character with a fine bead of bubble. Marked by a pleasant toastiness on the finish, this is, as the producers say, a very 'seductive' Champagne.
£20–£30

Billecart-Salmon Brut nv   **14**
Brangan
Rich yet subtle fruit flavours, with characteristic biscuity tones.

Bollinger Cuvée Speciale Brut nv   ☆
Woodford Bourne
Stylish Champagne—big and bold with concentrated fruit aromas and flavour, finishing in a pleasant toasty aftertaste.

Bonnet Brut Heritage nv   ☆ ☆
Bacchus
Produced from 32% Pinot Noir, 50% Pinot Meunier and 18% Chardonnay, this wine has ripe fruit tones with good biscuit nuances, a fine bead of mousse and a clean, long finish. Not as dry as some.

Canard-Duchêne Brut   14
TDL
Fresh, clean and lively, with a hint of apple fruit, creamy
texture and buttery finish.

Charles Heidsieck Brut Reserve nv   14
Remy
Pleasant creamy biscuit tones follow through on flavour.
Elegant and stylish.

Delamotte Brut nv
Terroirs
Made from 50% Chardonnay, 30% Pinot Noir and 20% Pinot
Meunier, this is a finely balanced Champagne with floral and
fruity tones rounding off to a long finish.

Gosset Grande Réserve Brut nv
Best Cellars
Produced from 44% Chardonnay, 42% Pinot Noir and 14%
Pinot Meunier, this best-selling wine exhibits wonderful subtle
buttery fruit tones. Long and flavoursome with attractive
spritz.

Heidsieck Monopole Brut nv   14
Allied Drinks
Crisp and fresh. An easy-drinking style with a nice creamy
touch and appealing long finish.

Lanson Black Label nv   14
James Adams
Distinctive with delicate fruit flavours and a pungent yeasty
tone which is the hallmark of Champagne.

Laurent-Perrier Brut nv
Gilbeys
Always consistent in quality, with a good persistence of bubble
bead and light fresh apple flavours with a biscuity background.

Moët et Chandon Brut Imperial 90

Dillon

This vintage is all about rich, ripe yet subtle fruit flavours with
a fine bead of bubble and long elegant finish.

Mumm Cordon Rouge Brut nv

Barry & Fitzwilliam

Ripe fruit tones make this less dry. Good flavour development
and some length to the finish.

Pol Roger Extra Dry nv   14

Barry & Fitzwilliam

Appealing yeasty tones and a clean fresh finish.

Pommery Brut Royal nv

Mitchell

A very attractive style with a delicious subtle nutty tone, good
length of fruit and clean finish.

Roederer Premier Brut nv

Searsons

Superbly balanced, with lots of ripe citrus and apple fruit tones.
Creamy biscuity finish. Value for money.

Ruinart Brut nv   ☆

Hugan

A very well-balanced Champagne with good fruit, fine mousse
and a long satisfying finish.

Taittinger Brut nv   ☆

Gilbeys

Ripe fruit tones follow through on creamy mousse and end in a
yeasty bread-like finish.

Veuve Clicquot Ponsardin Brut nv

Findlater

The label was personally designed by this famous widow.
Creamy tones with a fine persistent bead of bubble make this an
extremely attractive drink.

£30–£50

Delamotte Blanc de Blancs 85

Terroirs

Produced from 100% Chardonnay, which imparts a fine,
elegant floral aroma. Five years' ageing on the lees gives a
creamy, biscuity character.

Veuve Clicquot Rich Reserve 88

Findlater

A style that is pitched between brut and demi-sec, this off-dry
vintage dominated by Pinot Noir, with one-third Chardonnay is
perfect with mildly spicy food.

Over £50

Dom Pérignon 88

Dillons

This superb vintage, produced from 55% Chardonnay and 45%
Pinot Noir, has an amazing creaminess and texture due in no
small measure to the skill of winemaker Richard Geoffroy.

Krug Grande Cuvée nv

Remy

Complex and elegant. The intense fruity aromas and buttery
biscuit tones are supported by a fine firm mousse. Superb
quality.

Roederer Cristal Brut 89 ☆☆

Searsons

Rich, deep, elegant—all words that suit this amazing wine with
its lemon-green colour and lively mousse. Pinot Noir dominates
this superb style, which was originally produced and reserved
for the Czars of Russia.

Salon 83

Terroirs

Salon produces only vintage wine, and then only in the greatest years. Noted for its remarkable ageing ability, it is made from 100% Chardonnay. The 83 has delicious fruity appeal with lively mousse.

Veuve Clicquot La Grande Dame 89

Findlater

With its embossed bottle and unique shape, this extremely elegant, delicate wine, produced from 60% Pinot Noir and 40% Chardonnay, is sheer class—subtle yet powerful at the same time.

ROSÉ CHAMPAGNE

Rosé £20–£30

Canard-Duchêne Brut Rosé nv ☆

TDL

Shows an attractive colour with a clean fruity palate, good fizz and length of flavour. A zippy style.

Rosé £30–£50

Billecart-Salmon Brut Rosé nv 14

Brangan

An attractive salmon colour. Lively fruit flavours reminiscent of strawberry and finishing with a pleasant lively acidity.

Billecart-Salmon Cuvée Elisabeth 89

Brangan

Beautifully presented, this is a delicious rosé from an equally delicious vintage. Squashed red berry fruit with a creamy texture and fine mousse combine to make an elegant style.

Delamotte Rosé nv

Terroirs

Produced from 100% Pinot Noir, the wine has a pale salmon colour with delicious wild strawberry fruit appeal and a hint of chocolate.

Moët et Chandon Rosé nv 14
Dillon
Delicate squashed strawberry aromas and flavours with good
follow-through on flavour—a fine gentle mousse and elegant
finish.

Veuve Clicquot Rosé Reserve 85 ☆ ☆
Findlater
Pale salmon in colour, with definite tantalising Pinot Noir fruit
characteristics and flavour reminiscent of cherries and crushed
strawberries. This is a top-class rosé.

SPARKLING WHITE

£6–£8

Carrington Brut nv (Australia) ☆
Fitzgerald
A top-quality sparkling wine offering real value for money.
Fruity with a good bite of acidity and medium long finish.

Cépage Chardonnay Frizzante nv (France) 13
Mitchell
Uncomplicated juicy fruity drinking. Ideal for large
celebrations where the event calls for an inexpensive bubbly.

£8–£10

Aliança Bairrada Bruto 94 (Portugal) 14
Reynolds
Light green-tinged colour with good mousse, fresh lively
acidity and some length to the finish.

Chevalier de France Chardonnay Brut nv (France) 14
TDL
Pleasant hints of butterscotch with good citrus acidity. Nicely
balanced with good mousse and spritz.

Codorníu Première Cuvée Chardonnay Brut nv (Spain) 14
Grants
Fresh and crisp with elegant mousse and a long subtle fruity
finish. Cava is at its best drunk young and fresh.

Freixenet Carta Nevada Semi-Seco nv (Spain)   **13**
Woodford Bourne
Crisp and fresh in style, with pleasant mousse and a touch of
nuttiness on the finish. Medium dry finish.

Freixenet Cordon Negro Brut nv (Spain)   **14**
Woodford Bourne
Rich and nutty in style, with some yeastiness and a medium
long finish.

Lancers Brut nv (Portugal)   **13**
Gilbeys
With its distinctive bottle shape, this is the ultimate 'quaffing'
medium sweet wine produced from the Periquita grape of
Portugal.

Mondoro Asti DOCG nv (Italy)   **14**
Grants
Beautifully presented. Considered one of the best examples of
Asti Spumante, this is for the drinker who likes the ripe, grapey
flavours of Moscato with a lively acidity cutting through the
medium long finish.

£10–£12

Château Moncontour AC Vouvray Brut 92 (France)   **14**
Febvre
Fine example of stylish sparkling wines. Apple aromas and
flavours with good mousse and a crisp finish.

Collavini Il Grigio Brut nv (Italy)   **14**
Ecock
Made from 100% Chardonnay, this wine has good-quality fruit
and great finesse.

Edouard Delaunay Chardonnay Brut nv (France)   ☆
Brangan
Stamped all over with classic winemaking, this sparkler offers
good drinking pleasure at a very affordable price. Crisp and
elegant with a fine long finish.

Lindauer Montana Brut nv (New Zealand) ☆

Grants

Hard to beat for value and style. Subtle fruity tones with lots of bubble and bite.

Mumm Cuvée Napa Brut nv (USA) ☆

Barry & Fitzwilliam

Exotic fruit tones with lively mousse and a good clean finish. Will appeal to those who like fruity sparkling wines.

Parxet Cava Brut Reserva nv (Spain) 14

Jenkinson Wines

Deep yellow-gold with lively bubbles. Heady bread-like aromas with high acidity.

Paul Cheneau Cava Blanc de Blancs Brut nv (Spain) 14

Bacchus

Fine bubbles with a lively tang of acidity and a creamy texture add up to very pleasant drinking at a fair price.

Seppelt Salinger Traditional Method 91 (Australia) ☆

Dunnes Stores

Attractively presented with fine bubbles, fragrant aromas and a creamy, fruity character.

Zonin Prosecco Brut nv (Italy) 14

Italfood

Produced from the Prosecco grape, this aromatic sparkling wine has a fruity tone, good acidity and a slightly bitter nutty finish typical of its style.

£12–£15

Bredif AC Vouvray Brut nv (France) ☆

Gilbeys

A zesty, well-made sparkling wine with good apple-type flavours and fine mousse produced from the Chenin Blanc grape.

Brown Brothers Pinot Noir/Chardonnay nv (Australia) ☆
Molloy's
A wine with very attractive fruit, creamy mousse and full
balanced finish.

Caves de Lugney AC Crémant de Bourgogne Brut nv (France)
Mackenway 14
Produced from 100% Chardonnay, this wine has a nice creamy
mousse with hints of peach. Classic presentation.

Deinhard Lila Riesling Brut nv (Germany) 14
Mitchell
A wine with flowery fruit character, lemony acidity and
medium long crisp finish.

Gratien & Meyer AC Saumur Brut nv (France) 14
Gilbeys
Good mousse which holds up in the glass and a dry finish.
From a famous house in the Loire.

Miguel Torres Brut Nature nv (Spain) ☆
Molloy's
From the king of Spanish winemaking, this is hard to beat at the
price. White-gold in colour, with a fine elegant mousse, a
slightly nutty tone and a dry classic finish.

Parxet Cava (Chardonnay) Extra Brut nv (Spain) 14
Jenkinson Wines
This well-balanced blend includes Parellada and Macabeo as
well as Chardonnay. Good fruit and lemon-like acidity with a
dry finish.

Rotari Brut DOC Trento 91 (Italy) 14
Mitchell
Light and elegant with a fine bead of bubble, good crisp acidity
and long, clean finish.

Seaview Pinot Noir/Chardonnay Brut 92 (Australia) ☆
Findlater
A decent drink at a decent price. It has good structure with
fruity appeal and a lively attractive lemon tang.
£15–£20

Gaston Huet AC Vouvray Brut nv (France) ☆
Brangan
Excellent buttery aromas and flavours—rich and smooth. Top-
class example of its style.

Green Point 93 (Australia) ☆ ☆
Febvre
A superb example of just how classic Australian winemaking
can be. The flavours are rich and structured, smacking of
butterscotch and peach. Extra-long finish.

Pelorus Cloudy Bay 91 (New Zealand) **14**
Findlater
Luscious texture, good depth of flavour and extra-long finish.

Yalumba Cuvée D 92 (Australia) ☆
Cassidy
Deliciously fruity with a hint of cream and peach. Elegantly
presented with a smooth tasty finish.
£20–£30

Mountadam Chardonnay/Pinot Noir 90 (Australia) ☆
Wine Vault
Very refreshing, with a classic structure, from one of the
Australian masters of Chardonnay. The Pinot adds delicious
fruit and the Chardonnay provides elegance.

SPARKLING RED

£5.25–£6

Seppelt Sparkling Shiraz 92 (Australia) **14**
Dunnes Stores
Reminiscent of raspberry mousse, this unusual fruity red
sparkling style is enjoyed by the Aussies drunk chilled with
turkey and other poultry.

SPARKLING ROSÉ

£8–£10

Yalumba Angas Brut Rosé nv (Australia) **13**
Cassidy
Easy drinking. Lots of bubble and zest, full of gooseberry and
apple-type flavours.

£10–£12

Gratien & Meyer AC Saumur Brut Rosé nv (France)
Gilbeys
Pale strawberry in colour. Plenty of red ripe berry fruit appeal
and a long lingering finish.

SPARKLING DESSERT

£12–£15

Parxet Cava Cuvée Dessert nv (Spain) ☆
Jenkinson Wines
Tinged with gold, this is a fine dessert sparkling wine with
pleasant sweetness and nuances of fruity flavours reminiscent
of raspberry. Serve chilled.

Fortified and dessert wines

SHERRY STYLES

Fino

Produced in Jerez and Puerto de Santa María, Fino is matured under a layer of flor yeast which helps preserve freshness and avoids oxidation. Very pale in colour; bone dry, elegant with a pungent delicate bouquet of almonds. Leaves the palate whistle clean. Drink fresh and chilled. Examples include:

Croft Delicado (Gilbeys)
Domecq La Ina (Fitzgerald)
Gonzalez Byass Elegante (Gilbeys)
Gonzales Byass Tio Pepe (Gilbeys)
Osborne Pale Dry (Barry & Fitzwilliam)
Pando (Woodford Bourne)
River Fly (Findlater)
Sandeman Seco (Dillons)
University Fino (Mitchell)

Manzanilla

A very dry Fino from the town of Sanlúcar de Barrameda. Style: very pale with characteristic pungency and nutty tones with a slight salty edge to the finish. Examples include:
Osborne (Barry & Fitzwilliam)
Lustau Papirusa (Mitchell)—this one is superb, delicate and very dry.

Amontillado

A style that has lost flor yeast. Light amber in colour with hazelnut/walnut aromas. Dry or medium dry. Examples include:
Croft Classic (Gilbeys)
Domecq Double Century (Fitzgerald)
Dry Fly (Findlaters)
Garveys (Kelly)
Gonzales Byass Caballero (Gilbeys)
Gonzalez Byass La Concha (Gilbeys)
Harveys Club (Grants)
Sandeman Medium Dry (Dillon)
University Amontillado (Mitchell)

Williams & Humbert Dry Sack (Woodford Bourne)

Palo Cortado

Falls between the styles of Fino, Amontillado and Oloroso. Dark amber in colour, with a roasted nut aroma. This is a rare and interesting style of Sherry. Highly prized, it is worth the extra cost. Examples include:

Lustau Peninsula (Mitchell)
Williams & Humbert Dos Cortades (Woodford Bourne)—an old Oloroso that has assumed Amontillado characteristics. The oldest wine in the blend is 100 years old.

Oloroso

A style of sherry that never developed flor and has been fortified up to 18°. In colour ranging from dark gold to rich amber; can be dry or sweet with a nutty, raisiny flavour. An example of a dry Oloroso is *Lustau Almacenista* (Mitchell). Cream Oloroso is deep brown with rich fruity aromas and deep caramel flavours in a sweet style. Examples include:

Garvey's (Kelly)
Lake Fly Sweet (Findlater)
Osborne Medium (Barry & Fitzwilliam)
Sandeman (Dillon)
Walnut Brown (Woodford Bourne)
Williams & Humbert A Winter's Tale (Woodford Bourne).

Pale Cream

Fino-based, pale in colour, rich, sweet and creamy with intense dried fruit flavours. Examples include:

Croft Original (Gilbeys)
Domecq Double Century (Fitzgerald)
Harveys Bristol Cream (Grants)
Osborne Cream (Barry & Fitzwilliam)
University Pale (Mitchell)
Williams & Humbert Canasta Cream (Woodford Bourne)

PORT STYLES

Vintage Port

Only declared in certain years of outstanding quality. Not every house declares a vintage in the same year. The wines do most of their maturing in bottle for up to twenty years, so they throw a heavy sediment in the bottle and have to be decanted. Noted for their deep crimson colour, smooth velvety texture and rich peppery finish. Generally declared vintages include 94, 92, 91, 85, 83, 82, 80, 77, 75, 70, 66, 63. Examples include:

Cálem 77, 83 (Cassidy)
Churchill 85, 91 (Findlaters)
Cockburns 83 (Grants)
Croft 82 (Gilbeys)
Dows 63, 66, 70 (Karwig)
Ferreira 77 (Reynolds)
Fonseca 91, 92 (Mitchell)
Fonseca-Guimaraens 76, 82, 87 (Mitchells)
Graham's Malvedos 84 (Fitzgerald)
Graham's Vintage 80, 83, 85 (Fitzgerald)
Osborne 70 (Barry & Fitzwilliam)
Pitters 53 (bottled 88) (Taserra)
Pocas 82 (Cassidy)
Sandeman 85 (Dillon)
Taylors 83, 85 (Woodford Bourne)
Warre's 77, 83, 85 (Febvre)
Warre's 75 (Grants)

Late Bottled Vintage (LBV)

A Port of a single year which has been matured in cask and bottled in its fourth to sixth year. The wine has already thrown its sediment in cask and does not require decanting. Full flavoured with velvet-like texture and smooth raisin fruit with a little tartness on the end. Examples include:

Cockburn's Anno 90 (Grants)
Croft 87 (Gilbeys)
Graham's 88, 90 (Fitzgerald)
Offley 88, 90 (Allied Drinks)
Porto Noval 88 (Barry & Fitzwilliam)
Sandeman 89 (Dillon)
Taylor's 88, 90 (Woodford Bourne)
Warre's Traditional 81 (Searson)

Aged Tawny Port

'True' tawny is aged in barrels for at least five but up to forty years; this explains the light amber colour of the wine, which is delicate and fragrant with delicious raisiny nutty flavours and aromas. Examples include:

Barros 10-year-old (Kelly)

Cockburn's Tawny 10-year-old (Grants)
Croft Distinction Tawny Reserve (Gilbeys)
Fonseca Tawny 10-, 20- or 40-year-old (Mitchell)
Ferreira Quinta do Porto 10-year-old Tawny (Reynolds)
Ferreira Duque de Bragarca 20-year-old Tawny (Reynolds)
Osborne Tawny (Barry & Fitzwilliam)
Warre's Nimrod Very Finest Old Tawny (Searsons)

Vintage character

A late-bottled vintage style blended from a number of years and aged in wood for five years. Having thrown their deposit in the cask, the wines need not be decanted. These robust wines have Christmas cake aromas and flavours. Examples include:
Cálem Vintage Character (Cassidy)
Churchill Finest Vintage Character (Findlater)
Delaforce Rich Vintage Character (United Beverages)
Fonseca Bin 27 Vintage Character (Mitchell)
Warre's Warrior Finest Vintage Character (Febvre)

Ruby

A blended uncomplicated style, aged for a few years. Sweet, with mouthfilling flavour reminiscent of plum pudding; high-alcohol finish. Examples include:
Cálem Ruby (Cassidy)
Cockburn's Fine Ruby (Grants)
Croft Fine Ruby (Gilbeys)
Ferreira (Reynolds)
Fonseca Ruby (Mitchell)
Graham's Fine Ruby (Fitzgerald)
Osborne Ruby (Barry & Fitzwilliam)
Offley Fine Ruby (Allied Drinks)
Sandeman 3 Star and 5 Star Fine Ruby (Dillon)
Warre's Fine Selected Ruby (Searsons)

White Port

May be dry or sweet. Dry white Port is good as an aperitif. High in alcohol and thick in texture, it benefits from being served very chilled. Examples include:
Churchill White (Findlater)
Ferreira Dry White (Reynolds)
Fonseca Sirocco (Mitchell)
Warre's Fine Selected White (Searsons)

If you find it difficult to locate vintage Port, try O'Briens of Donnybrook, Dublin 4, who carry an extensive range.

VINS DOUX NATURELS (VDN)

France

To produce a VDN grape spirit is added to the must to stop the fermentation at an early stage. This results in a naturally sweet wine with an alcohol content ranging from 15 to 21%. White VDNs are produced from the Muscat grape while dark/red ones are produced from Grenache.

Muscat de Beaumes-de-Venise: exhibits the aromas and flavours of Muscat and has a wonderful expansive fruit finish that goes on and on. Available in Ireland from négociants such as Chapoutier (Grants), Jaboulet (Gilbeys) and Perrin (Brangan).

Muscat de Rivesaltes: Arnaud de Villeneuve AC Muscat de Rivesaltes (Brangan) is a wonderful golden colour. Mouthfilling flavours of marmalade make this a delightful sweet aperitif or accompaniment to pâté or fruit-based desserts.

Banyuls is made chiefly from Grenache. *Domaine de la Rectorie* AC Banyuls (Brangan) is intense purple with aromas of raisins, plums and caramel. Rich and concentrated. *Rimage* AC Banyuls (Mitchell) is light golden amber with silky smooth dried plum and fig tones and a smooth concentrated flourish.

Rasteau is an aged VDN produced from old Grenache vines. *Signature* AC Rasteau (Dalton) is brick in colour, full of prune and dried fig flavours ending in a big port-like style.

Jurançon: produced mainly from the Petit Manseng grape, it is rich and honeyed. *Domaine Bellegarde* AC Jurançon (Wines Direct) has a hint of oak which adds interest.

Portugal

Setúbal: Produced mainly from the Moscatel grape and bottled after several years' cask ageing these wines are noted for their intense amber colour and delicious raisiny fruit. *Fonseca* (Mitchell) is a famous producer of this style. *J. P. Vinhos* (Reynolds) produce an intense rich style with grapey tones and a long smooth finish.

BOTRYTISED DESSERT WINES

France

Sauternes is the supreme example of a luscious wine produced from grapes affected by noble rot. Examples include:
Château de la Chartreuse (Quinnsworth)
Château le Bouade (Dunnes Stores)
Château Coutet (Barsac) (Searson)
Château Filhot (Febvre)
Château Lafautie-Peyraguey (United Beverages)

Australia

Brown Brothers Noble Riesling (Molloy's) is intensely rich with superb balance between honeyed fruit and citrus acidity; *d'Arenberg Noble Riesling* (Taserra) is deep golden, rich and ripe with honey and raisin fruit and a delicious bite of limey acidity.

SWEET WINES

Greece

Mavrodaphne of Patras (Superquinn): this famous dessert wine has intense port-like flavours.. *Samos* (Superquinn) produced from the Muscat grape is rich and round with concentrated raisin fruit flavours.

Italy

Peruini Primitivo di Manduria Dolce Naturale (Findlater) is produced mainly from the Primitivo grape. It is very rich and smooth with a wonderful spicy baked red berry fruit finish. *MezzaCorona Moscato Giallo* (Mitchell) is extremely elegant with rich aromatics and flavours. Delicate, yet rich, it has a long unctuous finish.

Directory of Wine Importers

Listed below are the importers whose wines are included in The Best of Wine in Ireland 1997. *Those marked * are also the sole retailers of the wines they import.*

Adam, James, 1 Charleston Road, Dublin 6 Tel (01) 496 3143 Fax (01) 496 0186

Allied Drinks Ltd, Merchants' Yard, East Wall Road, Dublin 1 Tel (01) 836 6898 Fax (01) 874 3998 Windsor Hill House, Glounthane, Co Cork Tel (021) 353 438 Fax (021) 354 362

Bacchus Wine and Spirit Merchants, T.28 Stillorgan Industrial Park, Stillorgan, Co Dublin Tel (01) 294 1466 Fax (01) 295 7375

Barry & Fitzwilliam, Glanmire, Cork Tel (021) 821 555 Fax (021) 821 604 50 Dartmouth Sq, Dublin 6 Tel (01) 660 6984/66 Fax (01) 660 0479

*Best Cellars, Coill Bhuí, 4 Knocklyon Road, Dublin 16, Tel (01) 494 6508/088 598 516 Fax (01) 494 6508

Brangan and Co Ltd, 7 Deerpark Avenue, Dublin 15 Tel/Fax (01) 821 4052

*Burgundy Direct, 8 Monaloe Way, Blackrock, Co Dublin Tel (01) 289 6615/288 6239 Fax (01) 289 8470

Callaghan Wines, 19 Maywood Lawn, Raheny, Dublin 5 Tel (01) 831 1369

Cassidy Wines Ltd, Unit 1B, Stillorgan Industrial Park, Co Dublin Tel (01) 295 4157

Dalton, Peter A., Food and Wine, Loch Grein, Ballybetagh, Kilternan, Co Dublin Tel (01) 295 4945 Fax (01) 295 4945

Dillon, Edward, & Co Ltd, 25 Mountjoy Sq, Dublin 1 Tel (01) 836 4399 Fax (01) 878 6502

*Dunnes Stores, Head Office, 67 Upper Stephen St, Dublin 8 Tel (01) 475 1111 Fax (01) 475 1441

Ecock Wine & Spirit Merchants, Unit 3 Newpark Centre, Newtownpark Ave, Blackrock, Co Dublin Tel (01) 283 1664

Febvre & Co. Ltd, 60 Stillorgan Industrial Park, Blackrock, Co Dublin Tel (01) 295 9030 Fax (01) 295 9036

Findlater (Wine Merchants) Ltd, The Harcourt Street Vaults, 10

Upper Hatch Street, Dublin 2 Tel (01) 475 1699 Fax (01) 475 2530

Fine Wines, 48 Roches Street, Co Limerick, Tel (061) 417 784 Fax (061) 417 276

Fitzgerald and Co, 11–12 Bow St, Dublin 7, Tel (01) 872 5911 Fax (01) 872 2809

Foley Fine Wines, 33 Johnstown Road, Dublin 18 Tel (01) 285 0026 Fax (01) 284 0671

Gilbeys of Ireland, Gilbey House, Belgard Rd, Dublin 24 Tel (01) 459 7444 Fax 459 0188

Grants of Ireland, St Lawrence Rd, Chapelizod, Dublin 20 Tel (01) 626 4455 Fax (01) 626 4680

Greenhills Wines, Aisling House, Shannon Road, Santry, Dublin 9 Tel (01) 842 2188

Hugan Wines, 21 Idrone Drive, Knocklyon, Dublin 16 Tel (01) 494 5871

Italfood, Unit 46, Coolmine Ind. Estate, Clonsilla, Dublin 15 Tel (01) 820 9192 Fax (01) 820 9151

Jenkinson Wines, 4 Sylvan Lawns, Kilcoole, Co Dublin Tel (01) 287 3533

Karwig Wines, Kilnagleary, Carrigaline, Co Cork, Tel/Fax (021) 372 864

Kelly and Co (Dublin), 89 Gardiner St Dublin 1, Tel (01) 873 2100 Fax (01) 874 2245

Koala Wines, 2 East Street, Warrenpoint, Co Down BT 343 JE, Tel (08) 016937 52804 Fax (08) 016937 52943

Mackenway Distributors, 27 Farmleigh Close, Stillorgan, Co Dublin Tel (01) 288 9010 Fax (01) 288 3830

*****McCabes**, Mount Merrion Avenue, Blackrock, Co Dublin Tel (01)288 2037 Fax (01) 288 3447

*****Mitchell & Son, Wine Merchants**, 21 Kildare Street, Dublin 2, Tel (01) 676 0766 Fax (01) 661 1509

Molloy's Liquor Stores, Head Office, Block 2, Village Green, Tallaght, Dublin 24 Tel (01) 451 5544 Fax (01) 451 5658

Moore's Wines, 26 South Hill, Dartry, Dublin 6, Tel (01) 496 7617 Fax (01) 497 8142

Parsons, Kevin, Wines Ltd, 21 Liosbourne, Carrigaline, Co Cork, Tel/Fax (021) 373 237

*****Quinnsworth**, Head Office, Gresham House, Marine Road, Dun Laoghaire, Co Dublin Tel (01) 280 8441

Remy Ireland Ltd, 101 Monkstown Rd, Monkstown, Co Dublin, Tel (01) 280 4341

Reynolds, T. P. & Co, 50 Pembroke Rd, Dublin 4, Tel (01) 660

0246

Searsons Wine Merchants, 6a The Crescent, Monkstown, Co Dublin, Tel (01) 280 0405 Fax (01) 280 4771

*Superquinn, Superquinn Support Office, Sutton, Dublin 13, (01) 832 5700

Taserra Wine Merchants, Hogan House, Grand Canal St, Dublin 2, Tel (01) 490 0537 Fax (01) 490 4052

TDL, 47-48 Pearse Street, Dublin 2, Tel (01) 677 4381 Fax (01) 677 4775

*Terroirs, 103 Morehampton Road, Donnybrook, Dublin 4, Tel (01) 667 1311 Fax (01) 667 1312

United Beverages, Finches Industrial Park, Long Mile Road, Dublin 12 , Tel (01) 450 2000 Fax (01) 450 9004

*Verlings Wines and Spirits, 360 Clontarf Road, Dublin 3 Tel (01) 833 1653 Fax (01) 833 3954

Wine Barrel, The, Johnstons Court, Sligo, Tel (071) 71730 Fax (071) 70483

Wine Vault, The, High Street, Waterford, Tel/Fax (051) 53444

*Wines Direct, Lisamate, Irishtown, Mullingar, Co Westmeath, Tel 1800 579 579 Fax (044) 40015

Woodford Bourne, 79 Broomhill Road Tallaght, Dublin 24, Tel (01) 459 9000 Fax (01) 459 9342

Index